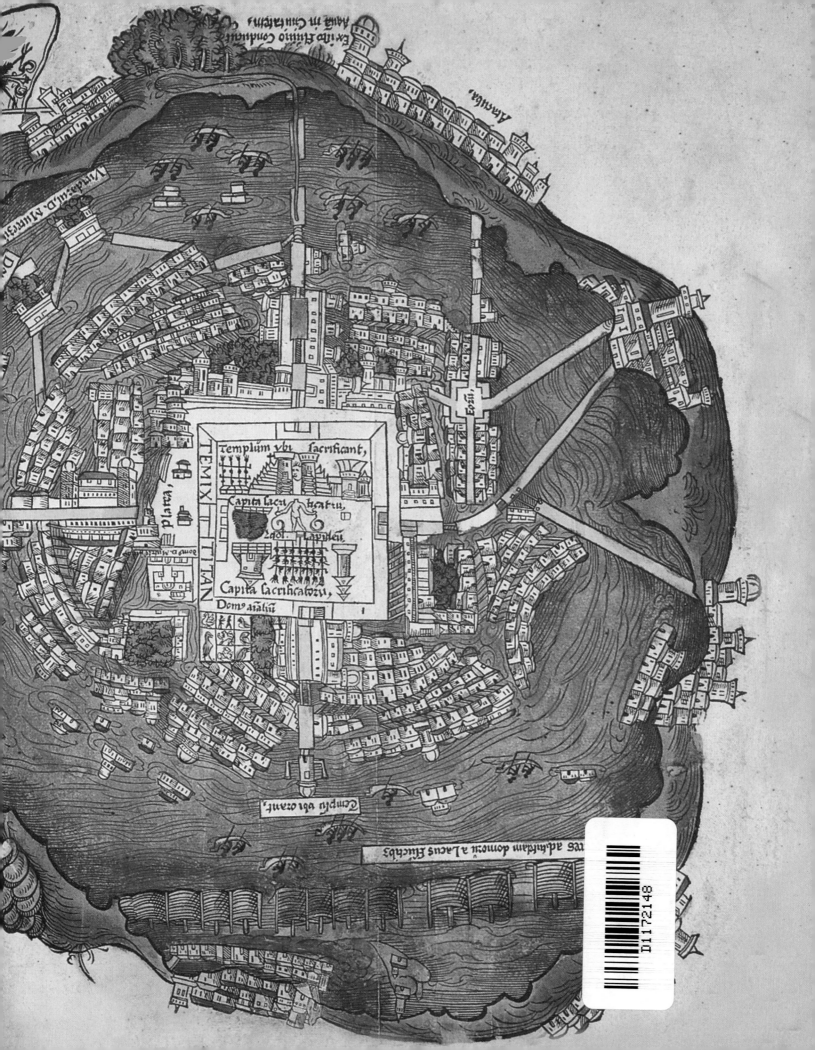

IDEAL CITIES

Utopianism and the (Un)Built Environment

RUTH EATON

IDEAL CITIES

Utopianism and the (Un)Built Environment

With 300 illustrations, 250 in colour

Thames & Hudson

To the memory of my father,

Peter Eaton

First published in the United Kingdom in 2002 by
Thames & Hudson Ltd, 181A High Holborn, London WC1V 7QX

First published in hardcover in the United States of America in 2002
by Thames & Hudson Inc., 500 Fifth Avenue, New York, New York 10110

British Library Cataloguing-in-Publication Data
A catalogue record for this book is available from the British Library

Library of Congress Card Catalog Number: 2001098727

ISBN 0-500-34186-9

Printed and bound in Italy

Frontispiece: SITE, *Highrise of Homes*, 1972.
SITE, *New York*

Contents

Acknowledgements

This book results from discussions about ideal cities with Jean Dethier, architectural advisor at the Centre Georges Pompidou in Paris, in connection with his 1997 proposals for the creation of an open-air museum on this theme in the grounds of Claude-Nicolas Ledoux's Saltworks at Arc-et-Senans in France, and from those about utopia with Roland Schaer, curator of 'Utopia. The Search for the Ideal Society in the Western World', an exhibition about the history of utopian thought, presented at the Bibliothèque Nationale de France in Paris and the New York Public Library in 2000–01. While these two people were the source of stimulating debate and, hence, of my interest in the subject, neither holds any responsibility for the book's precise content nor, above all, for its errors and omissions for which I alone am accountable. I am grateful to them both for setting me on the ideal-city path, and particularly to Jean Dethier for his continual encouragement and enthusiasm. I would also like to thank Gérard Bauer, Margaret Eaton, Ben Gibson, Professor Antoine Grumbach, Professor Harry Keen, Anne Moreau and Dr. Lindsay Sharp for their kind support and suggestions. This book is written in memory of my father, Peter Eaton, who dreamt of and fought for a better world, but it is also dedicated to a friend of his, Professor Charles Mann, Chief Librarian at the Pattee Library at Pennsylvania State University, whose curiosity and knowledge seemed fathomless and who was responsible for building up, for his university's library, a special collection on the subject of utopia.

Humankind has tried again and again to operate on a lofty plane, close to the divine, in attempts to imagine the ideal arrangement of the city and society. We have sought to establish the superiority of the human intellect, often in proclaimed harmony with absolute laws that govern the universe, upon the natural world. In so doing, we have been ignorant of context, intolerant of difference. The projection of ideal cities is a perilous exercise whose arrogance and aspiration for realization can be destructive. Yet when it remains in the virtual domain of the spirit or its application in the real world is restrained, together they can enjoy a strong and beneficial relationship.

This book aims to present a survey of ideal-city planning spanning more than two millennia. It does not intend to be exhaustive but hopes to be thought-provoking and to inspire the reader further to explore a field of design which is exciting on account of its very precariousness and of the fine line that it treads between dream and nightmare. Despite all its reservations, this book shares Lewis Mumford's recommendation on the title page of his work, *The Story of Utopias*, that 'A Map of the World that does not include Utopia is not worth even glancing at'.

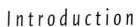

Introduction

The history of ideal-city design is, to a great extent, a story of architects and others who dream of mastering the world. It is that of so many blueprints, invented by the human intellect, for the best possible city and society. In many cases, it is a tale of immodesty, of the belief that something as complex as the city can be projected in the mind's eye; the belief that it can ignore natural contextual conditions, often in the name of conformity to universal laws to whose secret solution only an élite holds the key.

DEFINITIONS

Pages 8–10
Ambrogio Lorenzetti, *The Effects of Good Government*, 1337–39. Palazzo Pubblico, Siena, Sala della Pace

Ideal cities. In order to determine the scope of our subject, let us clarify our understanding here of some key words. The English 'idea' and the French *idée*, whose origins lie in the almost synonymous Greek words *idea* or *eidos* and the Latin *idea*, define an intellectual conception or representation. *Murray's Dictionary* gives the wider use of 'idea' as 'Any product of mental apprehension or activity, existing in the mind as an object of knowledge or thought; an item of knowledge or belief; a thought, conception, notion; a way of thinking.'[1] Such broader applications of the word became common by the end of the sixteenth century, but prior to this the Platonic sense prevailed.

In Platonic philosophy, *idea* – which is often translated as 'idea', 'form' or 'configuration' and is analogous in derivation and original sense to *species* (from *specere*, 'to behold') – describes what is seen not by the physical but by the mental eye. It designates a general or ideal form, an absolute pattern, the eternally existing and purely intelligible essence of the sensible things in the ordinary world we inhabit, while the latter derive their existence from these archetypical *ideas* and are but imperfect copies of them. This Platonic use of the word 'idea' forms the premise to many of the ideal cities we shall encounter: their designers invented them in the conviction that they belonged to an élite capable of understanding the nature of these original patterns and hence of attuning the city as closely as possible to their perfect harmony. Hence, the *noun* 'ideal' describes that which is presented as the absolute model, a standard of perfection, whereas the *adjective* 'ideal', whose source is the Latin *idealis*, defines that which is conceived and represented in the spirit, the implied meaning being: that which achieves all the perfection that can be imagined or hoped for, that which cannot be improved upon. What we are concerned with here is, above all, those cities which exist in this virtual domain of the mind, in other words cities whose life begins (and usually ends) in the form of ideas and which are often presented as being as close to perfection as possible. Our subject area does not include – not directly, that is – those cities that have grown up in an organic fashion, the ever-changing product of so many layers of individual contribution.

The source of the English word 'city' and the French *cité* is the Latin *civitas*, which described a federation of tribes grouped under common political and religious institutions. In Antiquity, both the Greek *polis* (from which derives our 'politics', the science of governing states) and the Latin *civitas* defined the city-state, an urban as well as a political organization. (The existence of the City of Westminster and the 'square mile' City of London within the larger city known as London, still reflects this earlier use of the word, although the term has become extended in the English language to designate any large centre of population such as, indeed, the English capital.) This dual significance of the word 'city' – encompassing both the physical place and the body politic – is of importance in the context of this book for, in the majority of cases we shall consider, the spatial models that are projected are indissociable from the social and political arrangements to which they are believed to correspond. Their production is guided by a long-standing conviction that the physical form of a city can both reflect and condition the workings of a society and the behaviour of its citizens. Although such a belief in architectural determinism may be partially (or even completely) misguided, it is the premise to most of the schemes we shall explore. This notion is suggested in the famous allegorical frescos painted by Ambrogio Lorenzetti on the walls of the Palazzo Pubblico in the Italian town of Siena in the fourteenth century, where good and bad government are represented by two townscapes: on the one hand a handsome, well-maintained city set within a landscape of tilled agricultural land and peopled with finely dressed citizens in a seemingly happy, festive mood, and on the other a dilapidated one in which buildings are falling into ruin and the inhabitants appear to be fleeing from invading soldiers.

'Utopia' has provided a source of inspiration and heated debate for scholars for almost half a millennium, ever since Thomas More's provocative and masterly combination of the ancient Greek words *topos* ('place') and the prefix 'u' – a contraction of *ou* and/or *eu* ('no' and/or 'well') – signifying 'no place' and/or 'place of well-being', was launched into the world with the publication in 1516 of *Libellus vere aureus nec minus salutaris quam festivus de optimo reipublicae statu, deque nova insula Utopia*, better known simply as *Utopia*. In the prefatory poem to his text, we are told that 'The Ancients called me Utopia or Nowhere because of my isolation.... Deservedly ought I to be called by the name of Eutopia or Happy Land.' Utopia was a common word by the eighteenth century, and the '*Dictionnaire de Trévoux*' spoke of a 'region which exists nowhere'.[2] It is often employed to mean 'chimeric, impossible', which fails to do justice to the seriousness and the desire for realization behind many a utopian project. The word is applied to the literary genre of which More's work is the foundation text, and it could be argued that this literary form of utopia, strictly conforming to the model set by More, is the only true one. However, utopianism is also extended to embrace a more general mode of which the literary genre is one of many manifestations. Here, the word is employed in its wider sense to include urban projects. We shall also consider a number of communities (such as the withdrawn monastic orders or the socialist projects of the nineteenth century) that have actually been created parallel to, but as a substitute for, a predominant existing situation, and which are considered utopian even though they have thus moved from the ideal to the real domain.

The sociologist Karl Mannheim, in the early twentieth century, drew a distinction between ideology – signifying those political ideas which are sustained by the system in power – and utopia – those which are in opposition to it. He thus introduced the notion that the former is static and reactionary while the latter is dynamic and progressive.[3] Such boundaries are blurred in some of the ideal-city designs we shall encounter, not least because the motivation and ambition of the designer are not always clear. In some instances, the projected built environments are novel but only seek to reinforce an established power structure (socially 'ideological'). This is the case with Italian Quattrocento schemes, which proposed a framework for the Renaissance power structure in contrast to the existing medieval city. In other cases, novel physical conditions are designed to bring about social change (socially 'utopian'), as is the case with Ebenezer Howard's idea of the garden city. The word 'ideal' is sometimes used to cover those city plans that accept the political status quo, while 'utopian' is employed for those that are designed to induce a radically new political situation. We will call these different types of ideal city socially reactive in the former case (where the city is 'adjusted' to reflect an established social order) and proactive in the latter (where a new urban design is intended to provoke and accommodate a society which is either as yet unconceived, in gestation or even in the pangs of birth, still rich with the dynamism and enthusiasm of the revolutionary momentum, young enough to be utopian). As the panoply of schemes unfolds, however, we shall refrain from any pedantic attempt to label every individual case according to these criteria.

The projects discussed here are thus considered by their initiators to offer the best possible urban framework, mirroring and/or inducing the best possible social arrangement. They are the product not only of architects but also of people from a variety of professional backgrounds. While the majority of the people we shall encounter employ the architectural medium, producing drawings, models or computer graphics to convey an impression of their ideal city environment, for many others – such as writers, philosophers, or social reformers – this is not their primary field of expression and action. The latter none the less place a great deal of importance upon the physical aspect of their project. That the ambition of the former category extends beyond spatial concerns to embrace wider issues is expressed in the words of the seventeenth-century French architect Claude-Nicolas Ledoux

The Island of Utopia, in Thomas More, *Libellus vere aureus nec minus salutaris quam festivus de optimo reipublicae statu, deque nova insula Utopia*, Louvain, 1516. Sir Paul Getty KBE – Wormsley Library, Oxford

VTOPIAE INSVLAE FIGVRA

(to take just one example): 'Everything is within their realm – politics, morality, legislation, worship, government.'[4] For the latter group, the significance of the built environment is made evident by the fact that the name of Thomas More's ideal island, Utopia, is concocted from the ancient Greek *topos*, meaning place, and that its geography, its rivers, its towns, its peoples, its traditions, its customs and its laws are presented to the reader in that order.

STEPPING STONES

As this book sets out to present a survey of ideal cities, it may be instructive to recapitulate some of the major stepping stones that have punctuated the path of ideal-city design. Ideal cities are imagined by the human intellect as being the fruits of human endeavour, but they have much in common with the dreams of better worlds provided by the divine. Some of these will be discussed in our opening chapter on the sources of this field of design. The most important influence of Antiquity is surely that of Plato, whose great significance should be emphasized here in a few words. Plato idealized a city-state of the past which he contrasted to the degenerate (in his opinion) Athens of his day, tempted by democracy and defeated during the Peloponnesian wars. This ancient city represented an ideal, and any digression from this ideal could only represent a negative dilution of its original perfection. The *stasis* that Plato extolled would be a feature of most future ideal cities. Plato's ideal city corresponded to his *idea* of the city, the essence of which could only be apprehended by an élite whose self-proclaimed members are to appear throughout the history of ideal-city planning. For Plato it implied those philosophers – such as himself – who were in a position to bring society into tune with the universal laws and thus to introduce harmony into a chaotic world. 'Until the race of philosophers become masters of a city,' he argued, 'there will be no

cessation of evils for city or citizens,'[5] and a city 'will never know happiness unless its draughtsmen are artists who have the divine as their pattern.'[6] The famous words, 'Nobody untrained in geometry may enter my house', that dominated the entrance to Plato's Academy, reflected the importance of mathematics for an apprehension of the nature of the laws that governed his universe; it was to find echoes right up to the twentieth century, when Le Corbusier wrote that 'Geometry is the basis ... the whole contemporary era is geometrical – eminently so.'[7] During the Italian Renaissance, the vocabulary of the ancients was reinstated and the mathematical laws that had been so important to the Greek philosopher were explored and developed. Although the philosophers' claim to be suitable candidates for the post of ruling the world was still reinforced in the early seventeenth century by Tommaso Campanella, in whose City of Sun the sovereign was none other than a Metaphysician reminiscent of Plato, it would seem fair to say that during the Renaissance the architects sought to steal the mantle from the philosophers (even though the partitions between fields were of course far less hermetic then than they are today). In *Momus (The Prince)*, the satire written by Leon Battista Alberti, the protagonist Momus, the capricious son of Night who has been expelled from the heavens, is wreaking havoc on the earth. In order to remedy the consequent chaos, Jupiter sets out to install a new order and seeks the advice of the philosophers. However, they fail to provide a satisfactory solution to the problem. It is then that he perceives the vision that will resolve his difficulties: a magnificent Colosseum-style theatre whose harmonious design symbolizes the rational system according to which the world should be organized. Thanks in part to the development of techniques of surveying and delineation, the Quattrocento architects' claim to possess an understanding of the dialectics of the universe measuring up to that of the philosophers coincides with their move away from the specific context of a given site to the abstract one of the drawing board. The natural workings of the real world are henceforth to be subjected to an

Anonymous, Central Italy, *Ideal City*, late 15th century. The Walters Art Gallery, Baltimore

uncompromising intellectual exercise, supposedly aligned with the mechanics of the universe, in a string of ideal-city designs.

In the mid-fifteenth century, Filarete designed Sforzinda, generally recognized as being the first ideal city of the Renaissance on the Italian peninsula. Shortly afterwards, Thomas More published his famous *Utopia*, claiming that his imaginary island was the realization of Plato's dreams in the *Republic*. This famous work is composed of two books: firstly, a critique of an existing situation (that of More's contemporary England) and, secondly, the projection of a contrasting one that is considered superior in the mind of its inventor (the imaginary island of Utopia). More's territory is punctuated by an isotropic arrangement of 54 almost identical cities. Their close similarity suggests not only equality but also a Platonic notion that any digression from the ideal model could only be detrimental. It announces the dangerous tendency of future generations of utopians and ideal-city designers towards global uniformity: 54 cloned cities on an island will generate, before long, thousands across the surface of a planet, as the very term 'International Style' was later to betray in the twentieth century.

Later utopian texts rarely provided an explicit critique of the status quo such as that contained in More's first book but only proposed a supposedly superior alternative to the real world. More had presented his imaginary land as though it was contemporary to his own but existed elsewhere in space. During the eighteenth century, when scientific discovery appeared able to solve all manner of problems, the future took on an increasingly rosy appearance. Sébastien Mercier, in *L'An 2440. Rêve s'il en fut jamais* (1770), placed his contrasting environment elsewhere not in space but in time, and indeed in the future. Despite some earlier examples of this,[8] his work is generally considered to have introduced a new 'uchronic' precedent for the utopian literary genre. As the ideal moved into the future, it appeared increasingly realizable. The following years witnessed revolutions such as those in France in 1789 and during the nineteenth century or those in Russia and Germany during and after the First World War. They also saw a series of small-scale and often short-lived experiments such as the communities set up by those whom Marx and Engels labelled 'utopian socialists', in contrast to their own more 'scientific' method. Marx's historicist belief in a revolution that

would radically transform the whole of society is of course, arguably, no less utopian or idealistic than the approach of figures like Robert Owen. With increasingly large-scale attempts at realization, however, the desirability not only of the means of achieving an ideal world but also of the very ends themselves began to be questioned by writers, filmmakers and others who produced anti-utopian works. They portrayed visions of a 'dystopia', a utopia-gone-wrong, where the dream has turned to nightmare and the dark, totalitarian side of the coin predominates. Their observations are not related from the spatial or temporal outside this time, but from the inside in a manner which recalls – although the reality on this occasion is exaggerated and distorted fictionally – the first book of More's *Utopia*. It is rare to find counter-utopian works within the architectural field, a domain whose aim is usually realization. Exceptions to this rule appeared during the second half of the twentieth century.

CHARACTERISTICS OF UTOPIAN WORLDS

Finally, let us summarize some of the characteristics that typify the many expressions of the utopian

tradition, for most of the ideal cities we shall consider display some if not all of these. Utopian environments are intended to be realized through human effort without supernatural assistance. While they have much in common with a number of related places such as Arcadia, the Golden Age and Paradise – which will be mentioned briefly – they are quite distinct from them. Often produced during times of profound social unrest by people frustrated by their lack of room for manoeuvre and power to change an actual scene, they are the intellectual dreams of would-be reformers. Their realization is often desired (although such longings may remain covert) and their inventor, impotent alone, often seeks a sort of marriage contract with a ruler who might implement the proposed plan – hence the numerous dedications of these projects to people in power.[9]

Utopias are presented as alternatives to established situations which are perceived as chaotic and may be criticized, with varying degrees of explicitness, as such. Their ambition is the greatest collective happiness and harmony achieved through efficient social restructuring and/or scientific progress. They are most usually urban (or suburban) and laid out upon geometrical lines, suggesting humankind's rational domination of the chaotic forces of nature. They are presented as absolute solutions, panaceae

Attributed to Piero di Cosimo, The Building of a Double Palace, c.1515–20. The John and Mable Ringling Museum of Art, Sarasota

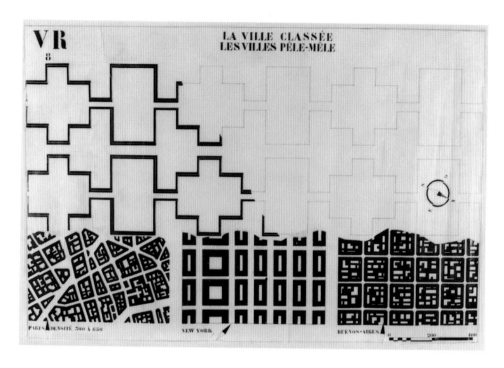

LA VILLE CLASSÉE
LES VILLES PÊLE-MÊLE

VR
8

PARIS DENSITÉ 500 À 650   NEW YORK   BUENOS-AIRES

La Ville classée, les villes pêle-mêle,
in Le Corbusier, La Ville radieuse: éléments
d'une doctrine d'urbanisme pour l'équipe-
ment de la civilisation machiniste,
Boulogne-sur-Seine, 1935

applicable worldwide and indifferent to factors of local context whether historical, geographical, cultural or other. Utopias are usually implanted upon virgin or razed soil: it was Plato who quoted Socrates saying that the artists 'will not start work on a city nor on an individual (nor will they draw up laws) unless they are given a clean canvas, or have cleaned it themselves'.[10] Divorced from the influences of time, their break with the past is emphasized by the currency of new costumes, calendar or language, and they are but rarely programmed to undergo future change. Insular and, indeed, often xenophobic, they are protected symbolically and physically from pernicious outside influences either by natural barriers, such as stretches of water or mountain ranges, or by man-made fortifications or greenbelts. The means are of little interest to designers of utopian cities, who would dismiss their relevance with the nonchalance of Lenin ('you can't make an omelette without breaking eggs') in their uncompromising drive to achieve their ideal. Being as close to perfection as possible, they are not intended to undergo future

development but merely to be emulated in the fashion of clones, as in More's disposition of 54 almost identical towns across his insular territory. Both the uniformity of the urban plan, extended to embrace many aspects of life in its drive to rule out differences between individuals, and the industrial process considerably aided this dream of standardization. The rigidly hierarchical social structure in utopian societies may be reflected in strict codes of dress, while deviant behaviour – deemed potentially anti-social – is often discouraged through the employment of materials like glass or of plans which facilitate surveyance, such as the panopticon. For creators of utopia favour the collective and work on the presumption that the interest and will of the individual are in perfect harmony with those of the group, and can be programmed with the precision of a bee in a hive. It is a sad truth that diversity, pluralism and tolerance, the essence of democracy, are frequently sacrificed in utopian societies, an almost inevitable result of the painful, eternal conflict between the collective and the individual, between equality and fraternity on the one hand, liberty on the other.

Such, then, are some of the features of ideal or utopian projects, curious and fascinating Janus-like beasts, driving forces that are capable of improving the real world or bringing further disaster upon it.

2

Sources of the Ideal City
from High Antiquity to the Middle Ages

Since time immemorial, people have sought to
alleviate the hardship of their everyday existence by
dreaming of other, better environments. Such realms
– be they the imaginary products of divine or of
human intervention or even linked to actual places –
have offered the image of a happier way of life than
that experienced in the real world.

This longstanding tradition was later to contribute
to the design of ideal cities and utopian societies
that flourished during and after the Renaissance.
Urban patterns practised from high antiquity –
particularly geometrical forms such as the circle or
the square – were also to influence those employed
for ideal cities in later centuries.

Pieter Bruegel the Elder, *The Land of Cokaigne*, 1566. Alte Pinakothek, Munich

Pages 18–20
Lucas Cranach the Elder, *The Golden Age*, c. 1530. Alte Pinakothek, Munich

On heavenly and earthly paradises

Throughout history and in many cultures, the existing world has been contrasted with pictures of idyllic alternative environments, created thanks to the intervention of some divinity or other force. The freedom they enjoy from the burdens of pain, hunger, insecurity, conflict or, indeed, death itself provide powerful visions, capable of alleviating the drudgery and sufferings of reality. Not being the product of human effort, they are often envisaged in pastoral settings, although urban environments are not altogether uncommon. As they are necessarily situated elsewhere, be it in space or time, conditions of access vary but are usually reserved for an elected few. Those located in a dim past, perhaps retrievable for people with a cyclical notion of time, remain hopelessly lost to those with a linear view: for these a compensatory source of hope might be found upon some shimmering future horizon.

The epic of Gilgamesh, the Babylonian tales

Sources of the Ideal City from High Antiquity to the Middle Ages **21**

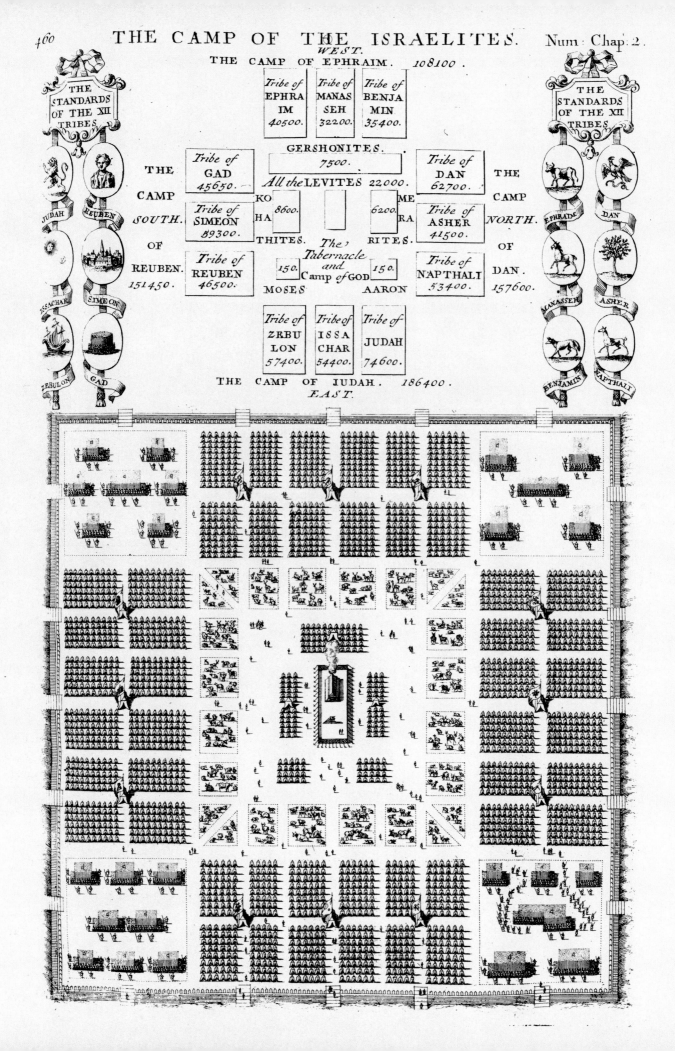

THE STANDARDS OF THE XII TRIBES

JUDAH · REUBEN · ISSACHAR · SIMEON · ZEBULON · GAD

THE STANDARDS OF THE XII TRIBES

EPHRAIM · DAN · MANASSEH · ASHER · BENJAMIN · NAPTHALI

WEST.
THE CAMP OF EPHRAIM. 108100.

| Tribe of EPHRAIM 40500. | Tribe of MANASSEH 32200. | Tribe of BENJAMIN 35400. |

GERSHONITES. 7500.

THE CAMP SOUTH. OF REUBEN. 151450.

Tribe of GAD 45650.		Tribe of DAN 62700.	THE CAMP NORTH. OF DAN. 157600.
Tribe of SIMEON 59300.	All the LEVITES 22000. KOHATHITES 8600. / MERARITES 6200.	Tribe of ASHER 41500.
Tribe of REUBEN 46500.	The Tabernacle and Camp of GOD 150. / 150. MOSES · AARON	Tribe of NAPTHALI 53400.

| Tribe of ZEBULON 57400. | Tribe of ISSACHAR 54400. | Tribe of JUDAH 74600. |

THE CAMP OF JUDAH. 186400.
EAST.

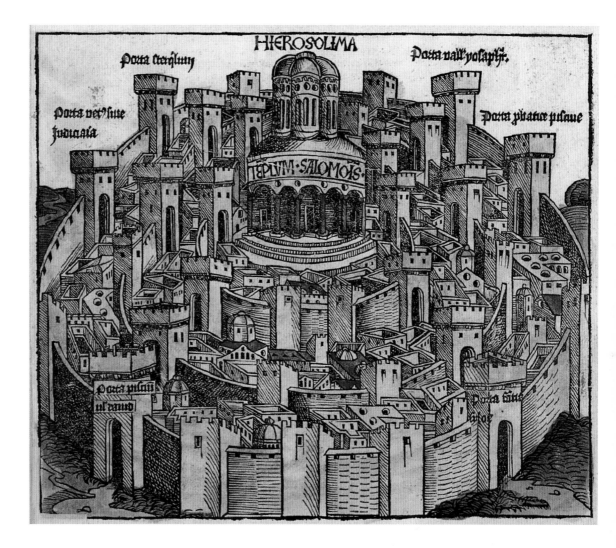

The Camp of the Israelites, in
A. Bedford, *The Scripture Chronology
demonstrated by Astronomical
Calculations*, London, 1730. British
Library, London, Printed Books

View of Jerusalem, in Hartmann
Schedel, *Liber chronicarum*, fol. xvii,
Nuremberg, 1493. Bibliothèque Royale
de Belgique, Brussels, Réserve
précieuse

recounting the wanderings of Gilgamesh, believed
to date from 2000 BC and handed down to us upon
stone tablets in the royal collection in the palace of
Nineveh, is the earliest recorded example of a
journey in quest of an earthly paradise.
The legendary king of the city of Uruk in ancient
Sumeria makes a journey to the idyllic land of
Dilmun in search of Ut-Napishtim, the survivor of
the Babylonian flood, in order to discover the secret
of eternal life, but learns that this is the privilege of
the gods' favourites alone, and that the sad,
shadowy existence of the dead is the inevitable
destiny of most mortals.
In the classical world, the Greek poet Hesiod was the

first to write, in *Works and Days* in the eighth
century BC, of the Golden Age before history when
men lived like gods. Its appeal also seduced Ovid,
who described it as follows:

> *The golden age was first; when Man yet new,*
> *No rule but uncorrupted reason knew:*
> *And, with a native bent, did good pursue.*
> *Unforc'd by punishment, un-aw'd by fear,*
> *...*
> *No walls were yet; nor fence, nor mote, nor mound,*
> *Nor drum was heard, nor trumpet's angry sound:*
> *Nor swords were forg'd; but void of care and crime,*
> *The soft creation slept away their time.*
> *...*

The flow'rs unsown, in fields and meadows reign'd:
And Western winds immortal spring maintain'd.[1]
The Roman poet Virgil likewise expressed a longing
for a new era of world peace and happiness in the
fourth poem of the *Eclogues* (a hope kindled by the
treaty of Brundisium between Octavian and Mark
Anthony at the time of his writing in the first century
BC), revealing the influence of the Greek myth of the
Golden Age. The memory of Lucian's entertaining
True History can be traced in Swift's *Gulliver's Travels*,
Rabelais's *Voyage of Pantagruel* and Cyrano de
Bergerac's *Journey to the Moon*. According to
Erasmus, Thomas More particularly appreciated the
work of this Greek satirist who warned the reader

that his tale contained nothing but lies from
beginning to end in a protective foil similar to that
employed later by More himself and by Shakespeare's 'all-licens'd fool' in *King Lear*. During an
ocean voyage, Lucian, his fifty companions and their
ship are all wafted up into the skies where the 'man
in the moon' engages them as Moonites in his war
against the inhabitants of the sun. On returning
safely to sea and after numerous amusing adven-
tures in the belly of a giant sea serpent, they finally
sail out between the monster's teeth to discover the
'Fortunate Islands', resting-place of the heroes and
philosophers of antiquity. The resident spirits of this
insular idyll spend their time making love, drinking

Flemish School, *Panorama of
Jerusalem, c.*1510. Museu Nacional
do Azulejo, Mosteiro da Madre de
Deus, Lisbon

from the springs of laughter and pleasure and reclining upon beds of flowers while nightingales shower them with petals. Here amid beautiful landscapes lies a city built of gold and jewels and paved in ivory; the Elysian Fields are meadows in the heart of a wood. Another powerful image, that of the Land of Cockaigne, reserved for an élite of industrious poor, has also continued to underpin popular thinking since ancient Greek times.

Paradise, that supernatural locality reserved for God and for chosen men, occurs in the Septuagint (the Greek version of the Hebrew Bible) and is clearly designed to express the original godlikeness of human nature and the hope of a future rapprochement between God and man. It encompasses both the heavenly garden where true Israelites after death see the face of God and the earthly Garden of Eden.[2] People were still trying to locate the earthly Eden in Thomas More's day, and indeed exploration of the New World led some to believe it had been found there at last. The promised land, a real place or an imaginary goal at the end of a long road of spiritual quest, was originally the land of Canaan, offered by Jehovah (Yahweh) to Abraham in Genesis and then to Isaac, Jacob and Moses. The Tabernacle, the ideal portable sanctuary erected by Moses as the place of worship described in the Pentateuch, was placed at the heart of the tents of the Hebrew tribes. The gradation of the parts and the building materials of the Tabernacle and the arrangement of the camp – court, holy place and 'holy of holies' containing the ark of the law – were in accordance with strict instructions, as they were meant to express an ascending degree of sanctity. All these features reinforce the idealized concept of a sanctuary whose historicity is unlikely. It was the expression of a religious ideal, reflecting the harmony and perfection of the deity whose glory filled the dwelling, a holy God in the midst of a holy people: 'Let them make me a sanctuary, that I may dwell among them.'[3] The layout and measurements of the camp and particularly the Tabernacle have exercised a profound and enduring influence over ideal urban design. The Temple, symbolizing the idea of redemption and fulfilment[4] and replicating the pattern of the Tabernacle on a larger scale, was supposedly located in Jerusalem. The city of Jerusalem offered another lasting – and now urban – source, the early, terrestrial city becoming mingled with the

heavenly vision. According to Tacitus it was a circular city, and it is frequently depicted as such, but the form of the Holy City is described as square in Ezekiel, as indeed it is in the powerful image of the city's descent from heaven in the accounts of the Apocalypse. In Revelations, John the Divine describes the opening of the seven seals, the blowing of the seven trumpets and the horrendous punishments which lead to the destruction of the earth. Thereafter the devil is to be bound and the righteous are to rule for a thousand years. After this period, the devil, released, goes into the world and creates chaos before God finally intervenes by

throwing him into a lake of fire and brimstone. All the dead then rise up, are judged and the wicked condemned to join the devil. The rest can then live in a new heaven and a new earth with a New Jerusalem, the Holy City, as John recounts: 'Then I saw a new heaven and a new earth; for the first heaven and the first earth had passed away and the sea was no more. And I saw the holy city, new Jerusalem, coming down out of heaven from God, prepared as a bride adorned for her husband; and I heard a great voice from the throne saying, "Behold, the dwelling of God is with men. He will dwell with them, and they shall be his people, and God himself will be with them; He will wipe away every tear from their eyes, and death shall be no more, neither shall there be mourning nor crying nor pain any more, for the former things have passed away."'[5] New Jerusalem is built out of precious metals and jewels: 'And the

building of the wall of it was of jasper: and the city
was pure gold, like unto clear glass.'[6]
Jerusalem had its counterpart in Babylon. Tyconius
expressed the notion, derived from Revelation, of
Jerusalem and Babylon as the epitome of saintly and
sinful cities in the Middle Ages: 'Here are the two
cities, that of God and that of the Devil … it is evident
that they are two cities, two kingdoms, two kings,
Christ and the Devil; each of them lives in the one or
the other … these are the two cities, the one of the
world and the other which wishes to serve Christ.'
Saint Augustine continued this idea in *De cate-
chizandis rudibus* ('Instruction of Beginners'), saying:
'Jerusalem signifies the city and the society of saints
and Babylon signifies the city and the society of the
godless'. In *De civitate Dei* ('City of God'), written
after the sack of Rome by the Goths in 410,
Augustine opposed two symbolic cities: the celestial
Civitas Dei, the city of saints which gathered all the
nations together, a city without boundaries, created
by the love of God, and the earthly *Civitas terrena*,
that of the impious, born of self-love.

THE FRUITS OF HUMAN ORGANIZATION

Certain early examples of cities created, or imagined
to be so, by humankind were to influence future
ideal-city planning from a complex intertwining of
formal and social viewpoints. Throughout the
history of utopian design, geometrical patterns
appear and reappear and the legacy of the two basic
forms – the circle and the square – will become
evident in the places now under consideration.
We have already encountered them in spatial
arrangements mentioned above, such as the city of
Jerusalem. Their employment often appears as an
expression of sacred order. The ancient Egyptian
hieroglyph for a 'city' takes the form of a circle
enclosing a cross. The circular city (including concentric and polygonal variants), although seldom
actually built, is a persistent feature in Western
culture and reflects the deep and ancient symbolism
of the circle, on both the conscious and the unconscious levels, and its associations with the self, with

Symbolic representation of Babylon,
in Athanasius Kircher, *Turris Babel*,
Amsterdam, 1679. Bibliothèque Royale de
Belgique, Brussels, Département des
Imprimés

Master François, *The Celestial and
Terrestrial Cities*, 1473. Miniature in Saint
Augustine (translated by Raoul de Presles),
La Cité de Dieu, 1473. Bibliothèque
Nationale de France, Paris, Ms. fr. 18,
fol. 3v

eternity and with the divine. The earliest known example of its materialization is in the Hittite city of Zincirli, built at the beginning of the first millennium and boasting a circular wall with a hundred rectangular towers and three equidistant gateways. Although its historicity has been doubted, Herodotus was to provide an impressive description of the city of Ecbatana, site of Hamadan in present-day Iran, founded in 715 BC by the Medes after their overthrow of the Assyrians.[7] Situated upon a hill, Ecbatana reputedly contained seven concentric walls increasing in height towards the centre, each containing a distinct rank in an ascending order in the social hierarchy and painted in a different colour to represent the planets: white (Jupiter), black (Mercury), purple (Saturn), blue (Venus), orange (Mars), silver (the moon) and gold (the sun). The grid, the orthogonal plan with parallel streets and right angles, used frequently in ancient planning, appears to be the ideal-city form *par excellence*. It represents the most common and universal pattern in urban history, a reflection of order, and has been heralded as the spatial mirror of all sorts of political systems. The study of pre-Hellenic antiquity has revealed numerous early examples of its employment in, for instance, the Indus Valley, Mesopotamia and Assyria. Herodotus[8] and Ctesias recorded that the great city of Babylon, one of the wonders of the ancient world under the rule of Nebuchadnezzar in the sixth century BC, boasted a square form enclosed within lofty clay walls and parallel streets spanning the river Euphrates. In fact its regular layout may have already existed as early as 2000 BC during the time of Hammurabi. The square but not the circle was used in urban design in the Far East as Norman J. Johnston explains: 'Whereas in the West the circle was a characteristic theoretical device and was occasionally realized, for the East a different application of the mandala concept was employed. The Eastern mandala combines two sacred elements within its context, the circle and the square, with each assigned a different symbolic task. The circle is a representation of the heavens while the square is that of the earth.

This is established with most clarity in Chinese practice and is rigorously reflective of their interpretation of the universe. For the ancient Chinese, as for the Western world, the heavens were round and celestially ordered. The earth, however, was conceived by the Chinese as a square, an artificial human world, whereas in the ancient West it was always circular.... It follows then that the Chinese with their ancient ritualistic observances attending the building of cities would acknowledge their earthbound nature and human roots by decisions affecting urban design. From as early as the fifth century BC the evidence suggests that the Chinese did identify city design with their view of the earth as square or rectangular in shape and ritualistically oriented to the four cardinal compass points.'[9]

During the classical period the grid had religious origins: the augurs, when observing the flights of birds for divinatory purposes, proceeded by first hypothetically dividing up both the air and the land along ideal perpendicular straight lines. The word 'geometry' derives from the Greek *geometria* which means 'earth measurement' and indicates the most practical way of measuring and dividing up land, either urban or rural, into plots, in accordance with the level of the surveyors' expertise at that time. While cities that developed organically such as Athens were not actually laid out upon a grid plan, it was used frequently by the Greeks for newly created settlements, whether military bases or new towns created to accommodate the overflow once a population exceeded the optimal figure of about 6000. In these early colonies it assured the establishment and duration of a hereditary territorial aristocracy owning land both within and beyond the city walls. The belligerent Alexander the Great, whose education had been directed by Aristotle, transported the grid across the ancient world and Deinocrates laid out Alexandria for him as a series of parallel streets within a protective enclosure. The Greek model dominated Mediterranean city planning for over a thousand years, stretching as far as Syria and central Asia.

The invention of the grid was famously, and erroneously, attributed to the somewhat mysterious Greek architect, mathematician and *meteorologos* (specialist in celestial phenomena), Hippodamus, whose renown is largely attributable to the words of the great philosopher Aristotle: 'Hippodamus, son of Euryphon, came from Miletus. It was he who invented the division of cities into precincts, and he also laid out the street-plan of Piraeus ... and he was the first person not actually taking part in the workings of a constitution to attempt some description of the ideal one.

'Hippodamus planned a state with a population of 10,000, divided into three parts, one of skilled workers, one of farmers, and a third of armed defenders of the state. He also divided the territory into three parts, a sacred, a public and a private: the worship of the Gods was to be maintained out of the produce of the *sacred* land, the defenders out of the *common* land, and the *private* land would belong to the farmers.'[10]

The arrangement of three major urban creations of the fifth century BC have all been attributed to Hippodamus – Athens' neighbouring harbour-town of Piraeus, the Athenian colony of Thurii in Italy and the new city of Rhodes – as indeed has the reconstruction of his home town, Miletus, on occasion. Yet these appear to be exaggerated hypotheses and his role on site may have been limited to the design of the *agora* in Piraeus. Aristotle expressed some reservations about the 'Hippodamean' grid despite his general approbation. He recommended a combination of straight axes and clusters of houses and narrow lanes: 'In the matter of defensive positions, what is advantageous for one constitution is not so good for another. A lofty central citadel suits both oligarchy and monarchy, a level plain democracy; neither suits an aristocracy, which prefers a series of strongly held points. As for the layout of private dwelling-houses, the modern or Hippodamean scheme of regularity is more attractive and more useful for all activities except ensuring safety in war, for which the old-fashioned layout was better, being hard for foreign forces to get into and to penetrate in their attack. It follows that both methods should be used, and this is quite possible: arrange the buildings in the same pattern as is used in fields for planting vines, in what some people call clusters, and do not lay out the whole city with geometric regularity but only certain parts and localities. This will meet the needs both of safety and of good appearance.'[11] This rational approach to city planning provided a source of amusement to the comic dramatist and poet of Athens, Aristophanes, who is generally recognized as being the precursor of the

Nicholas Polani, Saint Augustine and the City of God. Miniature in Saint Augustine, La Cité de Dieu, 1459. Bibliothèque Sainte-Geneviève, Paris, Cabinet des Manuscrits, Ms. 218

counter-utopian tradition. In *The Birds* (414 BC), the enterprising Athenian Peisthetaerus and his accomplice Euelpides persuade the birds to build 'cloud-cuckoo land', a 'woolly' city floating high in the sky between the realms of gods and humans, a state free of geometrical order, where everything is considered beautiful that is shameful or forbidden by law in Athens. Hippodamus himself is caricatured by Aristophanes in his portrayal of the pedantic astronomer and land surveyor who wants to measure the air and divide it into arpents; his methods are described as follows:

> With a straight rod I measure out, that so
> The circle may be squared; and in the centre
> A market-place; and streets be leading to it
> Straight to the very centre; just as from
> A star, though circular, straight rays flash out
> In all directions...

The importance of Hippodamus lies less in his reputation regarding the grid than in his quest to establish guidelines for creating an ideal city, achieving perfect concordance between its urban fabric, its constitutional organization and the harmony of the cosmos. These were surely matters of great concern among philosophers in classical Greece of the fifth and fourth centuries BC, with its myriad of city-states scattered around the fertile Mediterranean basin. The heritage of the word *polis* is worth recalling here: it signified both the urban space and the constitutional organization. Although the political system differed from one city-state to another, Athens provided the model that posterity has retained. Power was shared between three institutions. Of these the popular assembly, the *Ecclesia*, was open to all citizens and was held on the Pnyx, a hill to the west of the Acropolis which could accommodate some 6000 people. The city represented a territorial space divided into zones, a group of men *and* a political structure. The population of the Greek city was relatively modest and citizenship laws were frequently tightened or relaxed in response to demographic growth. When the population of Athens, at the height of the city's splendour, reached a figure now estimated at 40,000, this was

considered exceptionally large; in the eyes of some, indeed, excessively so.

Among the ideal environments which are imagined to have been the result of social organization in the face of – but not free of – the real hardships of existence, the ideal cities projected by Plato are of great importance to the utopian tradition. Plato addressed the subject of the ideal city in a number of his writings. The *Laws* is a legislative projection,

Joos van Gent, *The Greek Philosopher Plato*, 1473–75. Musée du Louvre, Paris

while the more fabulous works, the *Republic* and also the *Timaeus* and the *Critias*, in which he introduced the famous tale of Atlantis, anticipated the utopian literary genre. Thomas More made his debt to the Greek philosopher clear in his prefatory poem to *Utopia*, suggesting that the island of Utopia was the realization of the place imagined in the *Republic*. To the Greek mind, the social environment was paramount and Plato, having defined the just, ideal life, sought to identify the ideal commonwealth without which mankind could not attain its highest possible development. In the *Republic*, written after the end of the Peloponnesian War of 431–404 BC, when Athens and the league of democratic cities were defeated by the confederation of oligarchies grouped around Sparta, he outlined the organization of the perfect state. Plato believed that the unrest, suffering and unsatisfactory government of his own contemporary Athens was a result of its having digressed from the social organization of an ideal ancient city; his interpretation of this latter was based upon his reconstruction of the earliest forms of Greek social life, predating, but similar to, the ancient aristocracies of Sparta and Crete, which he believed most closely approximated the original idea of the state. Having distinguished three parts of the soul, the sensual appetite, courage and reason, he divides his ideal society into three corresponding classes, the productive farmers and craftsmen, the guardians and the philosophers who govern the state. Priests are not part of this social hierarchy in which the city alone intermediates between humankind and the Invisible. Many aspects of the community Plato envisaged in the *Republic* were to resurface in the utopian schemes of later generations. These include, for example, the general consideration that the state is a higher and more abstract unity than the family, the eugenic practice of abandoning the infirm offspring of legitimate unions, the public education system available to both sexes, the limitations on the ownership of property and government by the wisest citizens professionally trained for the task.

Some thirty years after the *Republic*, Plato wrote the

Laws in which an aged Athenian is imagined as discoursing on legislation with the Spartan Megillus and the Cretan Cleinias, who were considering the foundation of a new colony. Actual Greek methods of colonization, such as the foundation of Thurii

(Thurioi), may have influenced the philosopher here, and he aims at moderating between and refining Dorian and Ionian law. He opts for the Spartan custom, later also to be appreciated by Macchiavelli, of not protecting the city with ramparts behind which the population might seek refuge rather than relying on its own vigilance and courage. Instead he proposes: 'But if men must have walls, the private houses ought to be so arranged from the first that the whole city may be one wall, having all the houses capable of defence by reason of their uniformity and equality towards the streets. The form of the city being that of a single dwelling will have an agreeable aspect, and being easily guarded will be infinitely better for security.'[12] A later-to-be-repeated notion of uniform, anonymous housing is thus introduced. The population is set at 5040 citizens, which implies a total of about 20,000 people; the land is equitably divided into 5040 lots, each split into two to provide the inhabitants with parcels close to the city and on the outskirts – on account of the variations in fertility – and each citizen has two houses.[13] The Acropolis with its circular wall occupies the centre of Plato's town and from there radiate twelve segments, housing the twelve population groups and ordering the organization of society. His suggested circular plan is unusual in fifth-century Greece, where actual circular cities were virtually unknown; the rough oval walls of Mantinea, rebuilt in 371 BC, offer a rare but not so convincing example. Once more, in the *Laws*, Plato sets the precedent for many aspects of utopian thought, although, in this case, he does include a cautious provision for change in his projected constitution. In producing this prescription for government, this code of laws in later life, Plato betrayed his undiminished hope that some Hellenic state might sanction the creation of such an ideal city. Indeed, it was almost realized in the third century by Plotinus, an important representative of Neoplatonism who was teaching in Rome and wished to found a Platonic Commonwealth, as Porphyry recounted: 'The Emperor Gallienus and the Empress Salonina, his wife, held Plotinus in high regard. Counting on their good will, he besought them to have a ruined town in Campania rebuilt, to give it with all its territory to him, that its inhabitants might be ruled by the laws of Plato. Plotinus intended to have it named Platonopolis, and to go and reside there with his disciples. This request would easily have been granted, but some of the Emperor's courtiers opposed this project, either from spite, jealousy or other unworthy motives.'[14]

The fictional narratives, the *Timaeus* and the unfinished *Critias*, were written before the *Laws*, probably around 355 BC. Here Plato contrasts his vision of an ideal, modestly sized Athens of some 9000 years earlier (in a way which recalls the retrospective idealization of the visions of the Golden Age) with the giant empire of Atlantis. The most glorious and powerful city of its day, in the philosopher's imagination, the former Athens boasted a population of limited size with strict class divisions and a lifestyle that was neither overly abundant nor spartiate. Before the columns of Hercules, however, there existed a great island which had been attributed to Poseidon who had surrounded it by two circular enclosures of earth and three of water.

Henceforth, the ten offspring of the god and his mortal lover, Clito, had become the rulers of the majestic empire of Atlantis and had undertaken major works of construction upon it. The physical aspect of Atlantis owes much to the philosopher's probable reading of Herodotus' extravagant descriptions of the oriental cities of Ecbatana and Babylon and the theocratic kingdom of Egypt.[15] In the midst of a vast rectangular plain of 60,000 orthogonal plots lies a grandiose central complex and the concentric walls surrounding the sacred inner mount, each painted a different planetary colour, obviously recall Ecbatana. Both the grid and the circle are present upon Plato's island, causing later speculation about the philosopher's personal opinion of these forms and his position as critic or champion of Hippodamean practice. The question of scale is clearly of concern to him. His island has some of the trappings of many an ideal plan but these are exaggerated to a massive, decadent degree: a grid system of thirty canals, huge metal-covered walls bristling with defensive towers, and so forth. It does not correspond to the limited dimensions of a city such as that in the *Laws* with a compact series of buildings and spaces whose arrangement reflects a rational political structure. Instead it provides a picture of sprawl with its continual repetition of basic elements including the ten royal cities across the territory. Plato clearly prefers the modest city-state to the immodest empire. It is the realm of reason and restraint rather than that which produced such excesses that comes to triumph in his imagination: when the empire attempts to subjugate Greece, the city of Athens rises to the occasion and triumphs against the monstrous island which finally plunges to the bottom of the oceans amid thundering earthquakes.[16] In these remarkable works, Plato's Atlantis – the antithesis of his idealized model of an Athens of the past – represents not only the menace of the Orient but above all the decadence of imperial Athens of his own day with its apparent ambition to resemble a new Persia. For posterity it is a universal, negative vision of a land which may bear certain physical features shared by

Vitruvius de Architectura prologus liber incipit feliciter

um diuina tua mens
et numen imperator cesar
imperio potiretur orbis
terrarum: Inuictaq́
uirtute cunctis hostib́
fratis triumpho uictoriaq́ tua ciues gloria
rentur et gentes omnes subacte tuum etiam
spectarent nutum: ppl̃sq́ q́ romanus et
senatus liberatus timore: amplissimis tuis
cogitacionibus consilius q́ gubniaretur: No
audebam tantis occupacionibus de archi
tectura scripta: et magnis cogitacionibus
explicata edere: metuens ne non apto tpr̃e
interpellans subirem tui animi offensione

Cum uero attenderem te non solum de
uita comuni omnium cura publice q́ rei
constitucione habere sed etiam de opertuita
te publicorum edificiorum: ut ciuitas p te
non solum prouincus esset aucta uer̃i et
maiestas imperii publicorum edificiorum
egregias haberet auctoritates no putaui
pmittendum quin pmo q́uoq́ tempore
de his rebus ea tibi ederem Ideo q́d
primum parenti tuo de eo fueram notus et

eius uirtutis studiosus Cum autem eo
silium celestium in sedibus immortalitatis:
cum dedicauisset et in ertium parentis in
tua potestatem transtulisset: deū studium
meum in eius memoria permanens: inte
contulit fauorem Itaq́ cum an aurelio
et pd minidio et tu cornelio: Ad appari
cionem balistarum et scorpionum: Reliquor̃
tormentorū refectionem sui priesto: et cum
eis comoda accepi: que cum pmo mihi
tribuisti: recontinuacionem per sororis comē
dacionem seruasti Cum igitur eo bñ
essem obligatus: ut ad exitium mte no haberem
inopie timorem: h́ tibi scribere cepi: quod
animaduerti: multa te edificauisse et nunc
edificare: religuo q́ tempore et publicor̃
priuatorumq́ edificiorum pro amplitudie
rerum gestarum ut posteris memorie tradēē
rentur curam habituum: conscripsi pre
scripciones terminatas: ut eas attendens: et
ante facta et futura qualia sint opa per te
posses nota habere Namq́ hus uolu
minibus aperui omnes disciplie raciones:

De architectura prosequendo

utopia but whose excess is clearly condemned by its inventor as dysfunctional, a true dystopia, worthy of the greatest to be invented in the twentieth century. The first-century historian Plutarch depicted a society whose values he considered superior to those of his contemporary environment: the early Sparta he described in his *Life of Lycurgus*. Plutarch recounted that Lycurgus, who had reputedly founded, or re-established the city-state of Sparta, had banished money, replacing gold and silver by iron bars, and equitably redistributed rural land in a way that enabled each citizen to enjoy an austere lifestyle, thus eliminating the source of social caste distinctions and the need to enforce laws. In fact, Sparta was run on a permanent war footing with citizens devoting almost all their time to military exercise and tactics. Men slept in dormitories, marriage was virtually eliminated, and children, murdered at birth if they appeared infirm, were considered state property, grouped into companies at the age of seven and by that of twelve suffered an inhuman regime with strict punishments, deprivation and war games, such as the massacre of slaves. Utopia? Dystopia? The similarities speak for themselves. In *Germania*, Tacitus similarly lauded, at this time, the life in German communities free of exploitation and usury, in contrast to his perception of the decadence of the Roman Empire.

The Roman army constructed fortified encampments laid out in geometrical order, as the Greek historian Polybius informs us in his forty-volume history which endeavoured to explain how and why 'all the known regions of the civilized world had fallen under the sway of Rome' within the half-century from 220 to 168 BC. They were arranged within a rectangular enclosure around two main axes, the north–south *cardo maximus* and the east–west *decumanus maximus*, which intersected in front of the headquarters (*praetorium*). The layout was said to have been adopted from King Pyrrhos of Epirus (he of the famous 'Pyrrhic victory') against whom they did battle in 280–75 BC. The grid and its axial partition had been employed by the Etruscans and had not only spiritual significance as the repre-

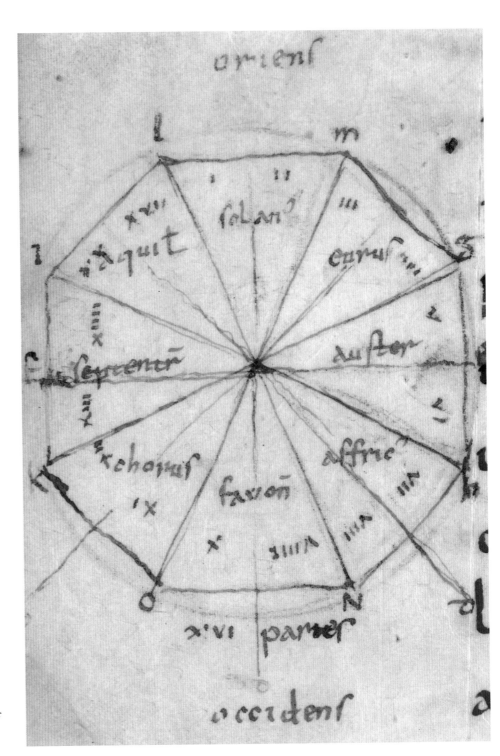

Vitruvian diagram of winds. British Library, London, Manuscripts Department, Ms. Harley 2767, fol. 16v

sentation of the order of the heavens, but also practical advantages, as the outer boundaries of new cities were traced by plough and oxen during the foundation rituals. The Romans used the grid not only in their military camps but also in new colonies, capitals of provinces and *civitates*, a clear representation of the order imposed by the imperial power. Thamugadi, now Timgad in Algeria, built in the early second century, provides a very fine example of the use of the grid (in this case, chequerboard) in Roman colonies. In fact, it was so vital an element of the Roman colonizing process that municipalities did not hesitate to demolish areas of existing towns when they became subjugated to the empire (the Greek city at Marseilles was thus razed to the ground). Plutarch's reference to Rome has caused speculation about its possible original circular form, but is too vague to permit serious conjecture that this was the case. By the third century, in contrast to the limited populations of the Greek city-states, that of the capital of the Roman Empire approached the million mark, with the majority of its inhabitants housed in apartment buildings, often earthen, reaching up to six storeys in height. Yet the memory bequeathed by this great city focused almost exclusively on its famous monuments which came to represent a long-lasting architectural ideal. Apart from the fact that these monuments better resisted the passage of time, Marcus Vitruvius Pollio, the author of *De Architectura Libri Decem*, also had a regrettable tendency to neglect humbler dwellings in his influential work. Dedicated to Augustus, Vitruvius' text is the only extant treatise by a practising architect of the Roman period, although many others no doubt existed. The ten books deal with the science of architecture generally, with materials, styles, symmetry, proportion and orders, public buildings, sites and planning, methods of decoration, hydraulic engineering and astronomy. Vitruvius combines theoretical and historical conjecture, and here he makes frequent reference to ancient Greek authors, with a mass of practical knowledge acquired as a result of his own professional experience. While mainly preoccupied by specific buildings, he also proposes guidelines about urban design. In addition to such practical recommendations as the use of a polygonal protective wall reinforced by towers, he suggests that the site be divided by eight (or sixteen) radial streets.

This pragmatic suggestion of a circular scheme, counter to common Roman orthogonal practice, may be considered representative of a practical – if not spiritual – ideal, one whose inheritance will prove particularly rich from the Renaissance onwards.

The Middle Ages were to fascinate many architects and artists in later centuries as a period in which humankind experienced a harmonious relationship with the production process and society as a whole. In particular, the monastic tradition offered an appealing example of an ideal way of life of which many aspects – such as the sharing of tasks, meals and prayer or the suppression of property – were to exercise a lasting influence on utopian thinking. The confines of the monastery resembled a complete, independent town in which the various buildings were distributed according to function and certain symbolic obligations. The plan of a Carolingian monastery probably dating from the ninth century and preserved in the library of St Gall in Switzerland is of significance in this context; it is a blueprint for an ideal monastery rather than a precise place known to have existed. The design is believed to be attributable to Haito, Abbot of Reichenau from 806 to 823, Bishop of Basle from 802 to 823 and an important figure at Charlemagne's court. Haito addressed 'this modest example of the disposition of a monastery' – which is most probably a copy of an original document, since lost, in Reichenau – to Gozbert, Abbot of St Gall, so that he might 'dwell upon it in spirit'.[17] The monastery is clearly divided into four main areas around the church: the isolated world of the monastic enclosure where the Rule was strictly followed around the cloister; a further open area to the north of the church with the school for laity, the accommodation for guests and the abbot's house; the domestic zone; and, lastly, that reserved for the sick and noviciate (neither of which groups, though attached to the monastery, was bound to observe the strict life of the Rule). This plan may be considered a spatial representation of monastic life in accordance with the resolutions of the 817 Synod of Aachen and indicated by a number of details. Features such as the presence of an internal workspace for craftsmen to produce clothes and shoes indicate a desire to enhance the autonomy of the monastic community. The elements of this very

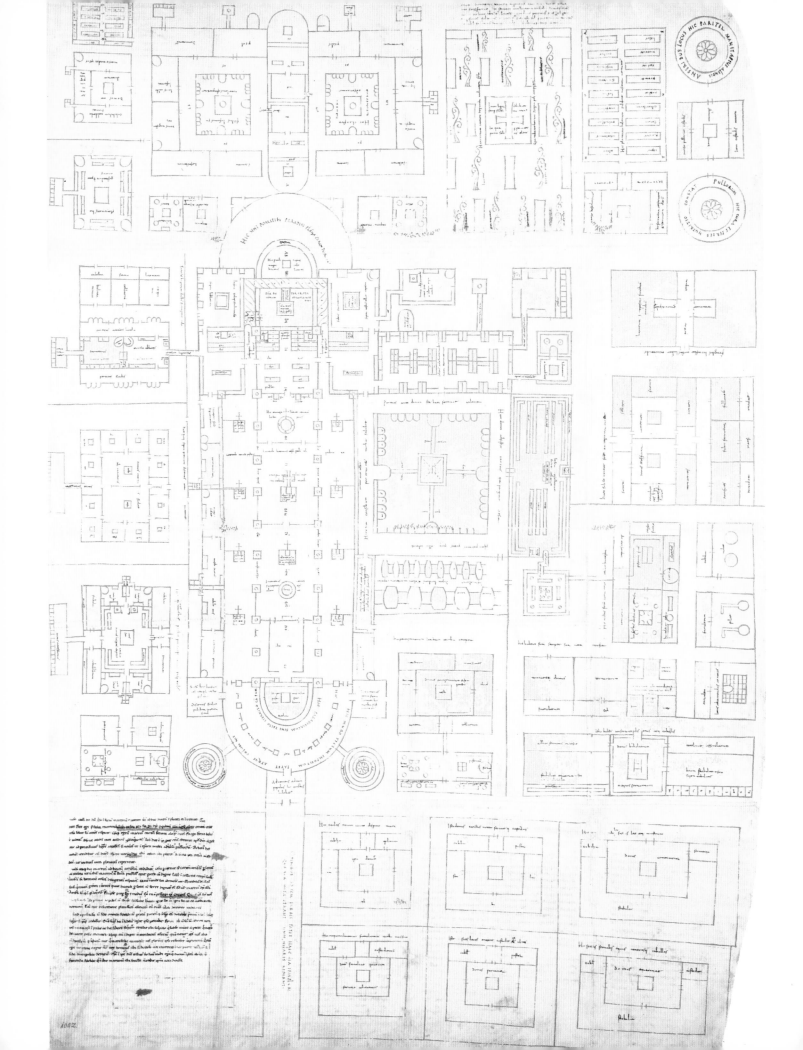

detailed plan were thus determined by function, but the internal regimentation was also reflected in the regular and symmetrical positioning of architectural elements and monastic spirituality was further expressed in inscriptions and the use of proportions such as the application of the triple ratio, the so-called Golden Rule, in the design of the church. The design for the St Gall monastery, with its diverse cluster of buildings reflecting the workings of the community, may seem formally a distant cry from the uniform façades of Plato, where one imagines internal functions to be frequently hidden, subjugated to the external appearance of the city as a whole, but both reflect the social organization through the zoned arrangement of the urban fabric. Shortly before this, the foundation of Baghdad by the Caliph al-Mansur in 762 provided a powerful vision of a city of circular form. Its official name, Madinat-al-Salam, city of peace, with its Koranic reference to Paradise, suggests its religious significance. From the caliph's focal Golden Gate Palace with its massive green dome, four great avenues radiated, oriented according to the points of the compass, to reach four gates in the two external walls. The perfect order of the plan soon gave way to more chaotic development, due to rapid demographic growth and the banishment of certain urban functions beyond the town walls. The caliph's laying out of the city must have been spectacular and indicates that he had an ideal design in mind, which he verified *in situ* prior to its realization: 'The overall plan of the Round City seems to have been al-Mansur's personal creation, although the actual task of tracing the city plan was entrusted [to others]. In order to see the form of the city plan, the Caliph ordered that the lines be traced with ashes.... When this was accomplished, the Caliph gave the site his personal inspection, walking about and looking at the outline of the *fasils*, gates, arcades, courtyards, and the city moat. He then ordered for cotton seeds which were subsequently placed along the ash marks. The seeds were doused with naphtha and set on fire. After viewing the flaming outline, he commanded that the foundations be laid on exactly these lines ...'[18]

The geometrical layouts and the communal lifestyles of the settlements we have encountered here will haunt ideal-city planning throughout future centuries. However, the city-founding rituals of the Etruscans and the Romans as well as the Caliph al-Mansur's magnificent on-site way of determining his perfect town will soon be replaced by increasingly detached methods of urban design in the Western world.

'In the Middle Ages both sides of consciousness –
that which was turned within as that which turned
without – lay dreaming or half awake beneath a
common veil,' wrote the historian Jacob Burckhardt.
'Man was conscious of himself only as a member of
a race, people, party, family, or corporation – only
through some general category. In Italy this veil
first melted into air; an *objective* treatment and
consideration of the State and of all the things
of this world became possible. The *subjective* at
the same time asserted itself with corresponding
emphasis; man became a spiritual individual,
and recognized himself as such.'[1] An increasingly
objective appreciation of the existing city
contributed to the birth of ideal-city design during
the Renaissance as the humanists freed themselves
from the constraints of real context and instead
invented cities which existed almost exclusively
in the ideal domain of the human intellect.

Circle of Piero della Francesca, *Ideal City with circular temple*, late 15th century. Palazzo Ducale, Urbino

Pages 38–40
Raphael, *The School of Athens*, c. 1509. Musei Vaticani, Rome, Stanza della Segnatura

THE CITY: AN OBJECT, AN IDEA

Among the developments to occur during the Renaissance that contributed to the birth of ideal-city design, both the progressive objectivation of the city and the detached and intellectual approach adopted by the planner were essential. As early as the outset of the fifteenth century one finds indications that the city was increasingly being considered an object that could be described. Works by artists such as Ambrogio Lorenzetti already provided examples of the visual representation of the city. The contribution of the Florentine Leonardo Bruni, though not an ideal-city planner, provides a stepping-stone in this context. Chancellor, expert on constitutional matters and historian of Florence, Bruni was one of the first humanist translators of Plato and Aristotle and wrote a *Laudatio Florentinae urbis*, a panegyric inspired by Aristides' *Panathenaïca*, in 1403.[2] Taking the relationship between the institutions of the *res publica* and the built environment for granted, he viewed Florence as the perfect city since it represented the city-state which was, in his eyes, the ideal form of government. Brimming with praise for his town – which he considered surpassed all others in splendour, ornament and cleanliness – Bruni's laudatory text was the first methodically to describe a city as an objective space.

This shift in perception went hand in hand with the development of the role and status of the architect. Master builders of the Middle Ages had been practical, pragmatic men, acting directly on the spot. In the fifteenth century, while the word architect itself (derived from the ancient Greek) became current in Italy, the role of the architect changed. Social esteem for what was becoming an increasingly intellectual profession developed considerably during this period, as indeed it did for artists in general. An indication of the respect with which artists were now treated is provided by the fact that, despite a ruling forbidding burial within the walls of the cathedral of Florence, Brunelleschi was none the less interred there and a monument was also erected in his honour in the *duomo*. Advances in drawing methods – such as the invention of perspective by Brunelleschi in or before 1413 and the development of the ichnographic plan first used by Leonardo da Vinci in his depiction of Imola – improved the architect's powers of representation. The increasing sophistication and employment of surveying and drawing instruments contributed further to the distancing between the architect and the city, while the increasing availability of paper and the introduction of printing rendered his delineations easily distributable in quantity. These developments all contributed to the depiction and objective consideration of the existing city. However, the great step was not yet made from the city as a place experienced to the city as invention, capable of breaking with urban tradition. This required the realization of the fact that the existing city could indeed be other than it was, an understanding aided by comparison with other realities.

Observing Other Worlds

The opening up of horizons and the confrontation with other worlds, removed in time and space, greatly contributed to putting the city and society into perspective. A cultural shock of this nature occurred during the early part of the fifteenth century with the arrival in Italy of scholars from the East, after the Council of Florence and the fall of Constantinople, and the discovery of hundreds of Greek and Byzantine texts. The close of the century provided another when the encounter with the New World in 1492 further reinforced the now established awareness of other possibilities. News and descriptions of the travellers' discoveries provided much to

excite the imagination of their contemporaries in Europe. The voyagers claimed to exercise a scientific method in their reports: as early as 1503, Amerigo Vespucci expressed his desire to describe this new world as accurately as possible in his famous 'Mundus Novus' letter to Lorenzo di Pier Francesco de' Medici. Europeans were soon to be confronted not only by numerous descriptions of submissive, noble savages living in simple settlements but also, in striking contrast, by those of the vast, absolutist empire that extended over Mexico and the Aztec capital of Tenochtitlán or Termistitan missico. Here was a sophisticated society where the tributes paid by the vassal states served not only for the maintenance of the ruling nobility's luxurious lifestyle and the construction of architectural and urban master-

Plan of Rome, in Georg Braun and Frans Hogenberg, Civitates orbis terrarum, Cologne, 1597. Bibliothèque Royale de Belgique, Brussels, Réserve précieuse

pieces, but also as sacrificial fodder during the conduct of religious festivities in a frenetic race to nourish insatiable gods, regenerate the cosmos and delay the disappearance of the world. Though contributing to a broadening of the intellectual horizon of the Europeans, the New World was to offer less a source of inspiration to the old one than a clean slate upon which the latter might project its own ideals. Throughout this period, ancient Rome naturally formed a most important point of comparison, an inexhaustible source of fascination. Awareness of its legacy was far from new – how could it be in Italy? – but what changed in the fifteenth century was the intensification of interest and the inductive approach adopted in the study of that universe. Knowledge and myths which had been handed down through the centuries were verified as philologists and architects literally scoured the buildings and texts (often mere fragments) inherited from their ancestors. Moss and bramble were overcome by intrepid architects and antiquarians venturing on

site to take the measurements of ruins and transcribe their inscriptions. The results of the humanists' investigations were recorded and vulgarized in publications such as Alberti's *Descriptio urbis Romae* or Palladio's *Antichità di Roma*. In 1430, Poggio Bracciolini produced the first systematic inventory of the ruins of Rome, contrasting the former beauty of the city, since robbed of its adornments over the centuries, to its present state which he evocatively compared to that of a corpse, rotting and mutilated. In 1515 Pope Leo x instigated an ambitious programme to produce an exhaustive survey of ancient Rome, unfortunately not completed, under the general direction of Raphael, and in the sixteenth-century plans of the ancient city included those by Ligorio, Bufalini and Tempesta. Numerous manuscript copies of Vitruvius' *De Architectura Libri Decem* existed during the Middle Ages, and it was first printed by Giovanni Sulpicio in Rome in around 1486.[3] The inclusion of illustrations and the use of the vernacular in later editions rendered Vitruvius'

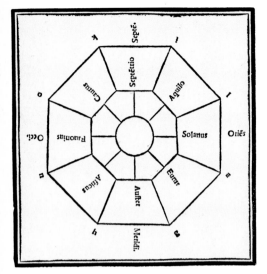

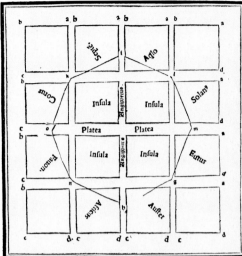

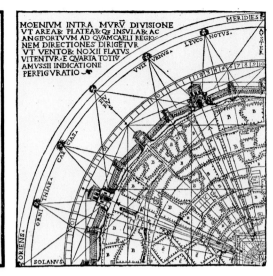

text, describing current Roman architectural practice, more accessible.

In fact, despite the apparently systematic methods employed, a degree of fanciful speculation was inevitable as antiquarians and architects found themselves confronted with virtually no buildings as complete as the Pantheon. They were therefore obliged to reassemble, in their imagination, the pieces of a gigantic three-dimensional puzzle. Owing to limited historical understanding, distinctions were not clearly drawn between the various types of production emerging from different periods of ancient Rome's past. And further confusion resulted from the fact that the text of Vitruvius did not always correspond to the actual architecture of the Augustan period in which he was writing. Above all, the study of the past concentrated primarily on the splendour of the monuments and showed little concern for the far less magnificent realities of the ancient urban environment. Plans of ancient Rome depicted an accumulation of important prestigious structures but failed to consider the buildings and spaces between them in any depth, often simply adopting medieval notions of the layout of the city or even just presenting monuments within a grid. The contradiction between the scientific ambition to examine the past and the imprecision of such study,

still in its embryonic phase, contributed to the humanists' idealization of the magnificent civilization of their forebears and was to encourage them in their establishment of the rules whereby modern architecture could achieve similar standards as it threw off its Gothic mantle. The humanist architects did not seek to duplicate the past but, from an understanding of the canons which governed it, to draw precise inspiration from it and aspire to equalling – or improving on – its built achievement.

ESTABLISHING AN IDEAL VOCABULARY

Objectivized and placed in perspective, the city was now to be imagined. The rather enigmatic painting, *The Building of a Double Palace*, attributed to Piero di Cosimo and dated to about 1515–20, might be interpreted as a metaphor for the relationship between the two newly separated but interdependent aspects crucial to successful architectural achievement: conception and realization. The virtually finished palace, embodying the architect's intellectual projection of his ideal creation, appears to indicate the way in which Renaissance architects imagined their

Vitruvian town plans attributed to Fra Giocondo, in Vitruvius, De Architectura Libri Decem, Venice, 1511. Bibliothèque Royale de Belgique, Brussels, Réserve précieuse

Vitruvian town plan, in Marcus Vitruvius Pollio, De Architectura Libri Decem, Como, 1521. Ecole Nationale Supérieure des Beaux-Arts, Paris

Giorgio Vasari, The Architects Show Cosimo I the Project of the Fortress-City of Portoferraio on the Island of Elba, third quarter 16th century. Palazzo Vecchio, Florence, Sala di Cosimo I

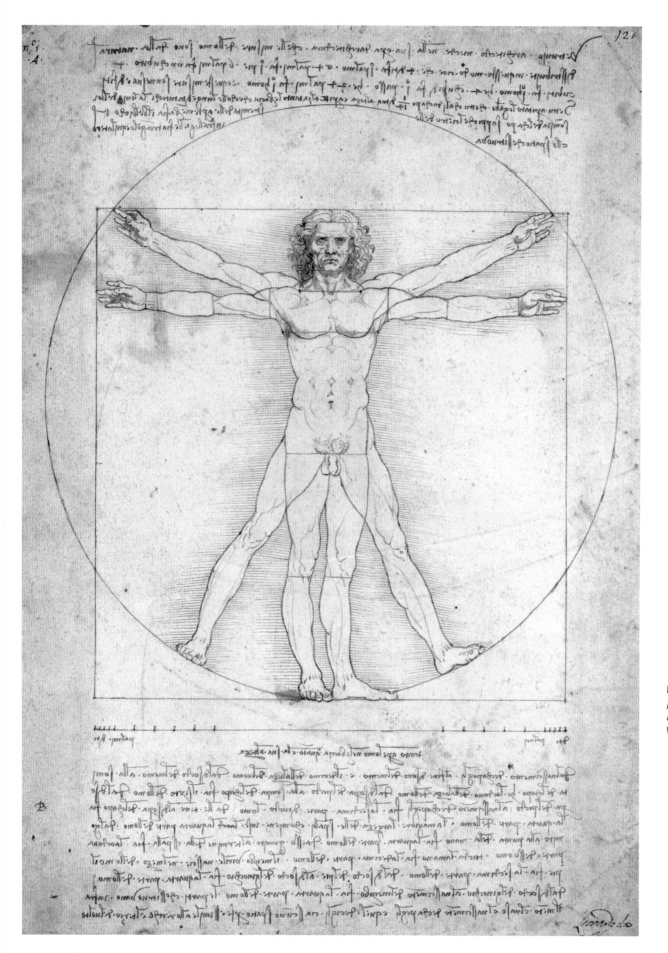

Leonardo da Vinci, *Study of the proportions of the human body,* c.1490. Galleria dell'Accademia, Venice

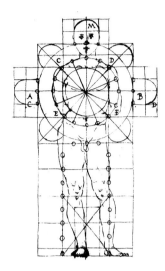

Francesco di Giorgio Martini, *Study of the proportions of the human body*, late 15th century. Biblioteca Nazionale Centrale, Florence, BNCF II.I, 141e, fol. 42v

Jacopo de' Barbari, *Fra Luca Pacioli with a Young Man*, 1495. Museo e Gallerie Nazionali di Capodimonte, Naples

designs in completed form before their execution and then produced technical drawings and models to convince their clients and facilitate the manual interventions of skilled craftsmen such as those depicted in the foreground. In the case of a busy humanist like Alberti, the direction of the construction work was indeed often left in the hands of specialists such as Matteo de' Pasti in Rimini, Bernardo Rossellino in Florence or Luca Fancelli in Mantua. This painting appears to demonstrate that the architect had acquired the ability to invent freely, i.e. liberated from the 'constraints' of context. The humanists' understanding and appreciation of the classical world provided the foundations of their own ideal vocabulary. In the eyes of the ancients, there existed a divine universal order whose nature was mathematical. In ancient Greek, the word *kosmos* meant arrangement and it was believed that

the scheme of the macrocosm, the heavens, like that of the microcosm, humankind, conformed to a series of forms and proportions, the relationships between dimensions. Plato had regarded the five regular bodies (tetrahedron, hexahedron or cube, octahedron, dodecahedron and icosahedron; polyhedrons with four, six, eight, twelve and twenty faces, respectively) as the archetypal forms of the elements, the quintessential building blocks of the cosmos. The figure of the human being, centre of the world, embodied the perfect measurements and the universal principles of natural order. This was expressed in the ancient philosopher Protagoras' statement that 'man is the mean and measure of all things',[4] and depicted by Leonardo da Vinci – and several others – in his famous drawing of Vitruvian man. Thus by fathoming the mathematical rules which the human body obeyed, the sense and order

of the universe could be mastered. Figures of the
stature of Piero della Francesca, Leon Battista
Alberti, Albrecht Dürer and Luca Pacioli, who allied
the cosmological geometry established by Plato with
the 'divine' harmony of the golden section,[5]
explored these rules in depth, employing the ruler,
the square and the compass. Echoing the words of
Cicero, 'There cannot be art without science', the
arts were considered veritable sciences. Aesthetic
perfection was a function of mathematical perfection since, as Plato had asserted, essential, not
relative, beauty was to be found in the strict respect

of ideal measurements, in straight or circular lines.
The cosmos was thus perceived as being rationally
arranged, the physical representation of divine
order and right. The ideal city, by conforming to the
same rules, sought to achieve the harmony of the
cosmos. Humanist architects thus came to apply
these mathematical principles to city design.
Moreover, they drew analogies between the city's
layout and, on the one hand, the microcosm (the
head signifying the centre of direction, the arteries,
the streets, and so forth) and, on the other hand, the
macrocosm (the central *piazza* representing the sun,

Anonymous, Central Italy, *Architectural perspective*, late 15th century. Staatliche Museen zu Berlin, Preussischer Kulturbesitz, Gemäldegalerie, Berlin

appearance of a ray of sunshine directly on the site just when the priest was posing the first stone. Since the city (as well as the society it reflected) was considered as something that could be invented in the human mind, its design reliant upon mathematical formulae that were believed to represent the divine universal order, the complexity of the ideal city became a function of the extent of the mathematical knowledge of the time.

Alberti's treatise *De re aedificatoria*, written in 1452 and published in 1485, was the first major architectural treatise of the Italian Renaissance. Taking Vitruvius' work as its point of departure but elaborating greatly upon it, a set of theoretical utilitarian and aesthetic principles were established, which formed the basis of the ideal order. Although Alberti mingled medieval and Renaissance ideas about civic design, as shown, for example, in his inclusion of both winding and straight streets,[6] he offered detailed advice and guidelines on how to achieve fine building in keeping with the canons of his period, explaining that 'The principal ornament to any city lies in the siting, layout, composition and arrangement of its roads, squares and individual works; each must be properly planned and distributed according to use, importance and convenience. For without order there can be nothing commodious, graceful and noble.'[7] He explained the types of buildings that suited various functions within society, as well as their positioning and visual ploys that expressed social hierarchies.

The three magnificent Ideal City *spalliere* painted by an anonymous central Italian artist (speculation has included Alberti and Piero della Francesca as possible authors) at the close of the fifteenth century epitomize the humanist ideal of the perfect urban landscape. Referred to as the Baltimore, Urbino and Berlin panels on account of the collections in which they are housed, these works most probably had a rhetorical value, stressing the social function of architecture and recommending the use of the language of classicism in order to create a perfect, harmonious society. They were not necessarily designed as specific architectural projects, but

radial streets, the rays, and so on). This desire to conform to the layout of the cosmos explains the repeated use of the rather impractical radial form, whose architectural parallel was the cupola-crowned church built to a central plan, in the design of ideal cities from Filarete on throughout the Renaissance. It should be recalled that Copernicus formulated his theory of heliocentrism in the first decades of the sixteenth century. Astrolatry was rife at that time to such an extent that the small fortified town of Terra di Sole, founded by Cosimo I in 1565, was named the City of the Sun on account of the

rather as imaginary visions of a superior world, intended to capture the imagination of potential patrons. The architectural ideal is portrayed in the classical detail of the various individual buildings in the townscape, while the urban ideal is also conveyed through the functions of these components and the relationship between them. The noble palaces, administrative buildings, triumphal arch, central *templum* and so forth in the heart of the city are positioned in accordance with the humanist vocabulary and reflect the social structure of the ideal society. More modest streets of houses can be glimpsed beyond these central *piazze*, as can the adjoining port and the surrounding countryside. The fact that the buildings themselves have become the main actors in these scenes (only one contains some human figures) bears testimony to the fact that the city is considered in an increasingly objective manner. Above all, space – no longer just an environment to which the individual is subjugated – has become rationalized, the human mind has expressed its superiority over natural circumstances, and matters of context have become irrelevant.

Ideal cities are imagined according to absolute standards. They aim to provide the best possible accommodation, according to their inventors' criteria, for the society to which they aspire. Let us then consider the ambitions of the humanists in these respects. The period of transition from the Middle Ages to the Renaissance witnessed major political and social changes in the Italian peninsula including the decline of the communal government and the concentration of power in the hands of seigneurial families or individuals. Architects, dependent upon the patronage of the emerging leaders, sought not an alternative society to that arising in the Quattrocento but a new urban environment, an alternative spatial setting to the medieval city whose spontaneous development they perceived as chaotic. The new rulers required a suitable aesthetic and formal framework to set the emerging society in stone and convey a subliminal message: if the divine order of the cosmos could be applied to the city's design – given that the latter reflected its social, economic and political organization – the urban government must equally share the rational harmony of the universe.

QUATTROCENTO APPLICATIONS OF THE IDEAL

Alberti had set out guidelines for the attainment of an ideal urban order. Antonio Averlino, known as Filarete, proposed the first complete ideal city to be produced in the Renaissance in his treatise written during the period 1457–64. Moreover, he set it upon a virgin site, thus condemning the exigencies of context to an oblivion that was to characterize future ideal-city design. It was dedicated to his patron Francesco Sforza, who was responsible to a great degree for the influence of the Florentine school in Milan and dominated the political scene there from 1450, after the eviction of the Visconti, to 1499, when Louis XII of France took possession of the city. Among the manuscripts of his treatise, which was not published until the nineteenth century, the *Codex Magliabecchianus* in the Biblioteca Nazionale in Florence contains many illustrations of the projected town. In this lengthy work, Filarete described an entire city – which was to be called Sforzinda in the duke's honour – in great detail and reputedly he even made a model of his scheme. Its radial layout was created by the superimposition of two squares within a circle and sixteen radial routes. This is the first known example of the use of the radial plan at this time, and the cluster of squares at the heart of the design is not very satisfactory from a visual point of view. A single building would have worked better and, in fact, Filarete had announced his intention to place a tower in this spot originally (which reminds us of that occupying the central position in certain illuminations of Saint Augustine's cities). Central observation towers were later to be projected in a number of military schemes during the sixteenth century (for example, by Maggi and Castriotti) and

Leon Battista Alberti, *De re aedificatoria*, title page, 15th century. Biblioteca Estense Universitaria, Modena, Ms. Lat. 419

LEONIS BAPTISTE ALBER
TI DE RE AEDIFICATORIA
INCIPIT LEGE FELICITER:

VLTAS ET VARI
AS ARTES QVE AD
VITAM BENE
BEATEQVE AGE
DAM FACIANT
SVMMA INDV
STRIA ET DILIGE
TIA CONQVISI
TAS NOBIS MA
IORES NOSTRI
TRADIDERE.

Quæ omnes et si ferant præ se: quasi certatū huc
tendere ut plurimum generi hominū possint:
tamen habere innatum atq; insitum eas intelligi
mus quippiā: quo sigulæ sigulof præterens diuersosque
polliceri fructus uideantur: Nanq; artes quidem
alias necessitate sectamur: alias probamus utilitat.
Aliæ uero quod tantum circa res cognitu gratissi
mas uescentur in precio sunt: qualef autē hæ sunt
artes nō est ut prosequar: īpromptu enim sunt:
uerum si repetas ex omi maximarum artium numero t
nullam penitus inuenies: quæ nō spretis reliquis
suos quosdā et proprios fines petat et contemple
tur. Aut si tandem comperias ullam: quæ cū hu
iusmodi sit: ut ea carere nullo pacto possis: tum

iquali sidebbono adoperare & ancora ache tempo sidebbono tagliare p̃ch̃
siano piu durabili & buoni & cosi daltre pietre uiue chesanno adoper̃a
re nelledificio & quelle chesono dafare calcina & cosi daltre cose oppor
tune lequali sono hutili tutte alledificare :mmmm

A me par pure douere cominciare imprima abedifichare questa citta m̃a
inanzi come to detto faro prima eldisegnio poi secondo miparra &
secondo neuerra ilbisogno dituite quelle cose lequali faranno mestiero:
allora dichiareremo tutte lesopradette cose ouero to dapoi nefaro uno tr̃a
ctato diperse sommario dituite generalmente come appresso intenderai :~

Il disegno della citta
chiamato Auerliana

Siche io intendo adesso diprincipiare ildisegno della sopradetta citta ilqua
le disegnio appellero Auerliana & lacita appelleremo sforzinda laqua
le bedificheremo inquesta forma & eleggero ilsito ilquale io o gia ue
duto & examinato piu uolte & accio chetu ancora lo intenda telodiscriu
ero permodo chetu lopotrai intendere & uedere chiaramente mmmmm

Ilsito chio o uisto sie che ame pare chequesta citta sia ben posta illuogho
salubre cioe sano & anche fertile & almeno aluiuere humano sie questo:
ilquale alpresente tidiscriuerro . Elle una ualle circundata damonti & dalla
parte meridiana emonti sono piu alti ĩmodo chequello uento ilquale sidi
ma austro ne affricho ne notto nogliupossono offendere . Euro subsolano Vul
turno ancora e assai difesa perispetto demonti orientali leparti occidenta
li sono alquanto piu basse . Zephiro & Circio & Fauonio assai temperata
mente cispirano . Maisi chelaparte settantrionale Borea con Aquilone &
eurus pure alquanto acerti tempi compiu ardire lauictano chenessimo:
deglialtri . Quando lafonderemo allora tidiro sotto che clima & pianeto
& punto . & hora & tutto quello chesara mestiere intendere tutte le
proprieta . Io tinarrero tutto questo sito come egli sta dipinto & quello
chenoi trouamo inquesta ualle auisandoti chetutta lacerchai & acca
demi una uentura che io trouai ungentile huõ ilquale era propinquo
acquella ualle & piu chelui andaua auncerto suo luogho chelui aueua
quasi alentrata desso rileuato su uno monticello chetutta quella ualle si
uedeua Ilquale mise molte acchoglenze & menomi acquella sua staza
& uolle chio desinassi collui & desinato chenoi auemo conmolti & uarij
ragionamenti uedendo egli chio aueuo piacere diuedere questa ualle
come gentile huomo disse montiamo acauallo cheuoglio uenire conuoi
& mostrarui questo luogho . Io desideroso disapere tutte lebonta & lutu
lita didetta ualle domandai come sichiamaua quello fiume chedorreua
perlomezzo didetta ualle & lui disse chesichiamaua sforzindo & lanalle
sidnamaua inda ilperche molto mipiacque & accettai laproferta chedett̃o
gentile huomo maueua fatta & cosi insua compagnia andai uedendo qũe
sto sito & questa ualle mella quale non era gia terre grosse mamolte mille

Il fiume sforzindo
La ualle inda :~

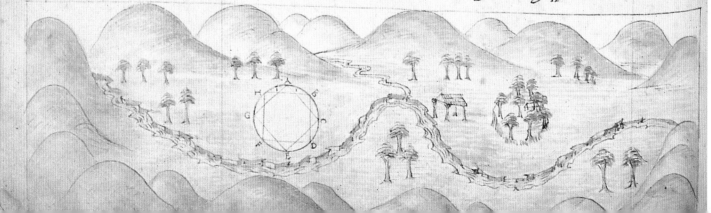

Antonio di Pietro Averlino, known as
Filarete, Sforzinda in a landscape and the
House of Vice and Virtue in Sforzinda,
in *Trattato di architettura,* second half
15th century. Biblioteca Nazionale
Centrale, Florence, Ms. II.I (*Codex
Magliabecchianus*), fol. 140c, 11v and 145

we find their echo in the design for the Panopticon at
the end of the eighteenth century. For Filarete, this
would have resolved the aesthetic issue but would
not have represented the power structure – and the
ambitions of his patron – in a suitable manner,
which may be the reason for its abandonment.
He thus placed three important squares in the
centre of his city: one contained the cathedral and
the prince's palace, representing religious and
secular power, while the other two were devoted to
the market and the merchants. Filarete was also
concerned by the provision of water and replaced
every second road by a waterway in this thorough
programme which included a mint, a bank, baths,
schools, prisons, a ten-storey house of 'Vice and
Virtue' complete with lecture rooms and brothel,
a hospital and cottages for artisans. While very
practical in many ways, his design becomes more
fanciful at times: his suggestion of a labyrinth to
surround the entire city definitely borders on the
dystopian! His work was treated with ridicule by the
next generation and prompted Vasari to mock it

in the 1550s, proclaiming that not everything it
contained was bad but that the treatise in its entirety
was ridiculous and that it must surely be the most
stupid book ever written!
Alberti and Filarete had approached the problem of
fortification in the orthodox manner of the Middle
Ages and indeed military issues did not seem particularly pressing to architects in the Italian peninsula
until the French invasion of 1494 rendered existing
fortifications obsolete. Francesco di Giorgio Martini
(who had witnessed this at first hand in Naples)
completed his *Trattato di architettura* in 1495. The fifth
book contains his theories about the modernization
of medieval systems of fortification and a proliferation of plans for fortified cities. It opens the path for
the increasingly military approach of the ideal-city
designers during the next century. Despite its functional aspect, the Sienese author has a highly
anthropomorphic vision of his ideal: the fortress is
identified with the head, the temple with the heart,
the central square with the stomach or navel, the
defensive towers with the superior and inferior

extremities and the crescent-shaped gateway with the phallus.

Leonardo da Vinci made several proposals concerning city design in the late fifteenth and early sixteenth centuries. His concern was primarily technical and functional although at least one scheme leaves room for speculation about his social considerations. Working at a period when plagues decimated the populations of the Italian peninsula (Milan lost one third of its inhabitants in that of 1484–85), he experienced a profound disgust regarding the promiscuity and lack of sanitation in the medieval city which he perceived as anarchic and chaotic. The connection of filth with chaos and hygiene with order is a recurrent theme in utopian thinking and will be echoed over the centuries. Indeed, in *La repubblica immaginaria*, Ludovico Agostini suggested that obedient and physically, morally and intellectually superior beings are the fruit of a healthy climate.[8] Leonardo was concerned with practical issues: the decontamination of the city, the introduction of canals, sewerage and drinking water, the opening up of squares and avenues and the repositioning of the walls to let the city breathe. His ambitious scheme of 1493 for Milan included reducing numbers in the popular districts, constructing a number of aristocratic residences and accommodating the surplus population in ten new towns of 30,000 inhabitants each (surprisingly similar to those of Ebenezer Howard some four centuries later). Ludovico il Moro, despite his interest, was unable to execute such ideas as he lost political control of the city. A sketch of Milan, though drawn some fifteen years later, includes a bird's-eye view outlining the most important buildings with, to the right of the castle, the Lazzaretto enclosure built by Lazzaro Palgi in 1488 to isolate the contagious. Another of Leonardo's drawings, probably reproduced from memory after 1506, is believed to relate to Florence whose medieval structure is to receive a decagonal perimeter, a grid network of main streets and a straightened river Arno. In 1518, when working in France, the artist designed a project for a new town for the French king which was to have been built near to Romorantin. Here, Leonardo had the opportunity to adapt his ideas about circulation and so forth, which he had developed over the past thirty years, to a specific site, albeit one of limited scale. On either side of a central canal, a monumental

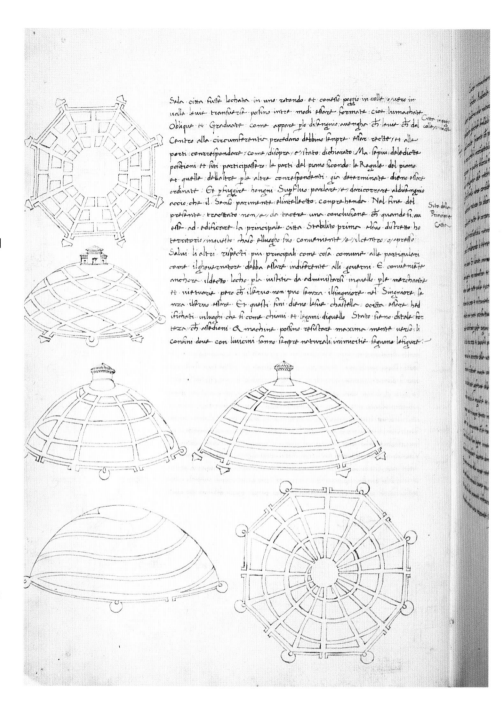

street lined with houses connects a large square to the royal château which personifies the power of the monarchy at the end of a grand urban perspective. The aforementioned plans do not conform strictly to our criteria as they are concerned with specific sites, but are worth mentioning here as the practical application of his ideas; in the case of the Florence scheme, he intended to transform the existing city so radically that it would have become almost unrec-

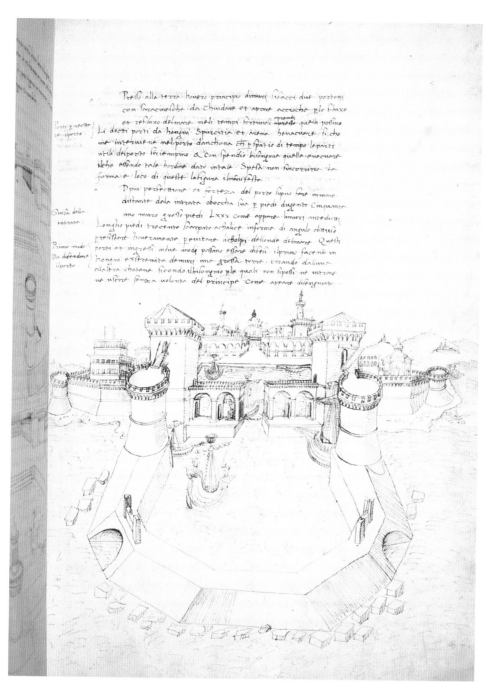

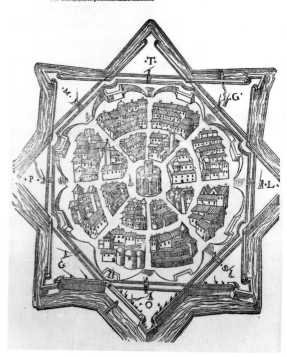

Plans and perspectives of fortified cities and
Port within the city with polygonal outport and
two water gates flanked by towers, in Francesco
di Giorgio Martini, *Trattati di architettura,
igegneria e arte militare*, late 15th century.
Biblioteca Nazionale Centrale, Florence,
Ms. II.I 140c (*Codex Magliabecchianus*),
fol. 87 and 29v

Ideal city plan, in Girolamo Maggi and Iacomo
Castriotto, *Della Fortificatione delle Città*,
Venice, 1584. Bibliothèque Royale de Belgique,
Brussels, Réserve précieuse

ognizable. Two important projects are contained in
Manuscript B in the Bibliothèque de l'Institut de
France in Paris. One is for a fluvial city (possibly for
Vigevano, where Ludovico il Moro entertained urban
ambitions, as one drawing depicts the Ticino river
nearby): it has a chequerboard network of canals
that integrates systems of cleaning, drainage and
the transport of merchandise by barge. The other
project for a city on several levels has provoked more
speculation and can be considered truly ideal. This
design introduces a system of social segregation
since the noble, upper level contains arcades and
palaces and is reserved for, as Leonardo clearly
states, 'persons of quality' on foot, whereas the
lower level is to be used for vehicles and the people.
The plan is regular with the upper network of roads
crossing the lower one at intervals of about 180
metres, and access from one level to another is
probably by spiral staircases. Canals are covered
and used now for sanitation but not for transport.[9]
In the course of the Quattrocento, the new rulers
and patrons were presented with an architectural
and urban ideal through such projects. The constructive ambitions of these oligarchies were

frustrated, however, by their limited financial and political means. Instead of building complete new towns from scratch, they almost invariably had to settle for an aesthetic reflection of their new world

resources of the principality. Aeneas Sylvius Piccolomini, who became Pope Pius II, completely transformed his native village of Corsignano – renamed Pienza in his honour – according to the aesthetic criteria of the Renaissance, although retaining some medieval features.

MILITARY APPROPRIATION OF THE IDEAL CITY IN THE SIXTEENTH CENTURY

During the course of the sixteenth century, political and military developments in the Italian peninsula precipitated a substantial shift in ideal-city design. The reins of government were held by an increasingly limited handful of individuals, ruling larger territories and greater numbers of people. Under the Medici, for example, the Grand Duchy of Tuscany was proclaimed in 1569 and Florence became the capital of an area encompassing several neighbouring cities including Arezzo, Pisa, Livorno and Siena. The new leaders had greater authority and power to build than their predecessors but the ideal cities, designed in the Quattrocento for the emerging and modest city-states, no longer matched the scale of the new political reality. In the absence of new cities, the existing ones saw surgical intervention such as, for example, the Uffizi commissioned by Cosimo I de' Medici in 1560 in Florence, which reflected the bureaucratic requirements of the concentration of power. The ideal-city concept became instead the virtual monopoly of the military. Generally, changes in methods of warfare played a major part in the urban developments of the time, not just because of the need for stronger governments to face potential enemies in this bellicose century but because the invention of the modern cannon and increased military prowess, particularly of the French, required new defensive strategies. The walls of medieval towns may have looked impressive but they offered little real resistance to modern technology. New, deep fortifications were required to stand up to the evolving situation, and the sixteenth century produced a rash of military designs which took on but compromised the notion of the ideal city not only in aesthetic terms but also in that of ambition, reducing it to a large fortress. These ideal plans were

restricted to individual buildings or small sections of the existing city. These included the creation of imposing residential palaces, the employment of certain urban scenic devices intended to accentuate the key positions of these buildings (such as creating squares in front of them, aligning streets to place them in the vanishing point of the urban perspective, setting them back from the street or indeed raising them above ground level) or cosmetically treating places *à l'antique* as in the Piazza Ducale in Vigevano (1493–94) or the *Procuratie Vecchie* erected in St Mark's square in Venice (from 1513). A more substantial programme was embarked upon in Ferrara by its prince Ercole d'Este and his architect Biagio Rossetti from 1492 but remained incomplete as its cost proved to be beyond the

Leonardo da Vinci, Plan for Florence with straightened river Arno, after 1506. The Royal Collection of Her Majesty Queen Elizabeth II, Windsor Castle, Royal Library, RL 12681

Design for a city on two levels, in Leonardo da Vinci, 'Paris Manuscript B', c. 1487–90. Bibliothèque de l'Institut de France, Paris, Ms. 2.173, fol. 16

Giorgio Vasari, *Florence under Siege by the French*, third quarter 16th century. Palazzo Vecchio, Florence, Sala di Clemente VII

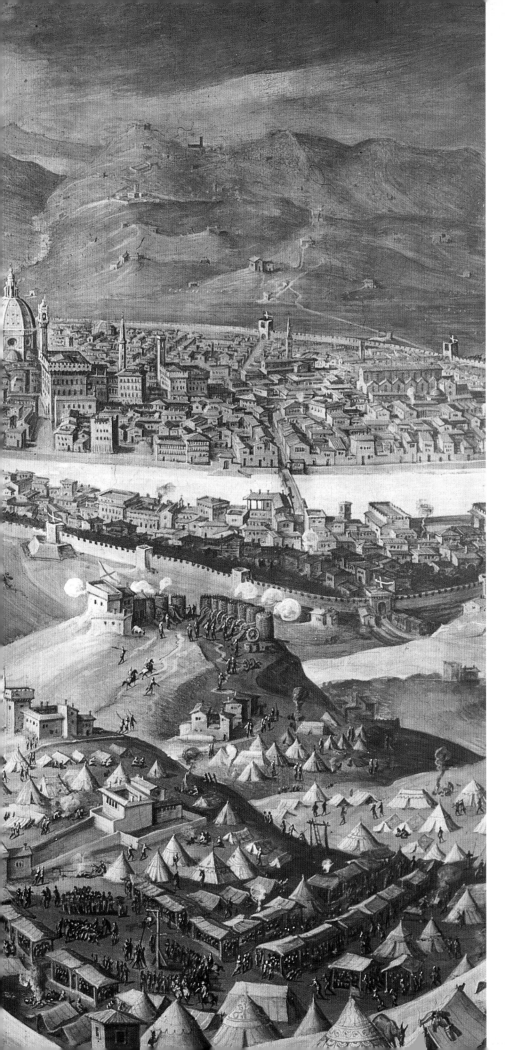

clearly suitable for execution on open plains and yet, in reluctant recognition of the unlikelihood of them being available, most Renaissance treatises (from Alberti on) devoted a section to questions of the ideal site or the adaptation of the plans to an unfavourable one. Horst de la Croix has explained the development of the radial plan which, particularly appreciated by the architect-artists as the perfect vehicle for the expression of Renaissance urban ideals in the fifteenth and early sixteenth centuries, was appropriated by the military planners – whose requirements its form suited well – from the middle of the sixteenth century.[10] This transfer, however, occasioned certain practical transformations which robbed the radial plan of much of its symbolism and its aesthetic finesse. Plans for fortifications – whether circular with a radial, a spider's web or an internal grid scheme, square or, eventually, polygonal with perpendicular streets – came to be worked and reworked to an almost monotonous degree throughout the century. Albrecht Dürer, active in Germany but in close contact with his counterparts in the Italian peninsula, proposed circular and quadrangular schemes in his *Etliche Underricht zu Befestigung der Stett, Schloss und Flecken* of 1527. The latter of the two resembles the woodcut of Tenochtitlán in Mexico published three years before. His fortress is still a small city, complete with a central castle in an open piazza and a church which is relegated to a corner, reflecting the impact of the Reformation. Numerous other treatises dealt with the matter of fortified citadels throughout the century but, with specialization into distinct fields occurring along with the growth of knowledge, civil and military architecture became increasingly divorced from one another.[11] In these later military schemes, most planners made few concessions to civilian needs, and churches, public buildings and market-places became increasingly rare. However, some continued to treat the question of the ideal city from a broader perspective than the purely military. In northern Europe, Simon Stevin developed ideas emanating from Italy and Germany to establish a system of fortification relating to the conditions of the Low Countries. Canals and roads coexist in his highly codified designs for port cities which employ standardized elements. That his ambition outstretched the purely architectural and military fields is evident in the fact that his posthumously published work was entitled *Materiae politicae* (1649), underpinning the connection between rational urban design and social organization. Jacques Perret's religious preoccupations were suggested in *Des Fortifications et Artifices* (1601), where several of Thomas de Leu's engravings of his ideal cities feature the psalms written alongside the bastions, demonstrating a belief that the word of God and a common faith are systems of defence as strong as, if not more so than, protective walls.[12] The military debate on ideal fortified planning finally moved from the pages of the numerous treatises into concrete reality in 1593 when the Venetian senate decided to protect its eastern frontier against the potential attacks of the local archduchies of Trieste and Gorizia and the Turkish enemy further afield by building the most technologically advanced fortress city of its day: Palma Nova. Designed by a military architect, probably Giulio Savorgnano, with some possible intervention by Scamozzi, it has a polygonal form with nine sides, a hexagonal central piazza (which should have contained a defensive tower surrounded by a ditch), six radial roads linking the square to the gates, other shorter radial roads leading to the gates, bastions and curtains and three concentric roads interspersed with small squares, which give the plan its spider's-web layout. This apparently complete realization of military urban theories reveals, however, a number of striking departures from both the aesthetic and the military ideals, while the actual quality of the buildings is relatively poor. The rare creation of Palma Nova in 1593 may have presented a missed opportunity, not only in aesthetic but even in military terms, yet with its thick – virtually indestructible – fortified walls, it fulfilled most successfully, by a curious twist of fate, typically utopian criteria: protection from the outside world and a certain hermetism regarding time and space. Today, it still offers a little-changed example in stone of the adoption of the ideal-city movement for defensive purposes. It bears a resemblance to Philippeville, now in Belgium, which had been constructed in the 1550s. The great military planner, Vauban, was later to have the opportunity to put many of the lessons about ideal fortification into practice in numerous constructions such as the octagonal fortified town of Neuf-Brisach, built *ex nihilo* at the end of the seventeenth century.

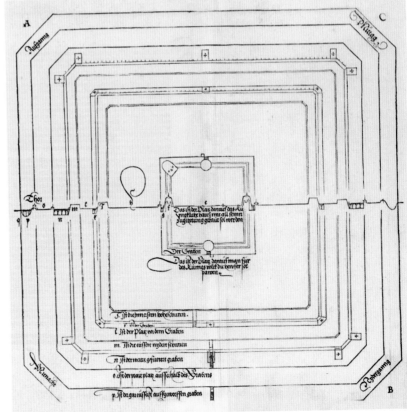

Orthogonal ideal city plans, in Albrecht
Dürer, *Etliche Underricht zu Befestigung
der Stett, Schloss und Flecken,* Nuremberg,
1527. Bibliothèque Nationale de France,
Paris, Réserve des Imprimés

Circular ideal city plan, in Albrecht Dürer,
*Etliche Underricht zu Befestigung der Stett,
Schloss und Flecken,* Nuremberg, 1527.
Bibliothèque Nationale de France, Paris,
Réserve des Imprimés

Ideal city plan, in Vincenzo Scamozzi, *L'idea
della architettura universale,* Venice, 1615.
Bibliothèque Royale de Belgique, Brussels,
Réserve précieuse

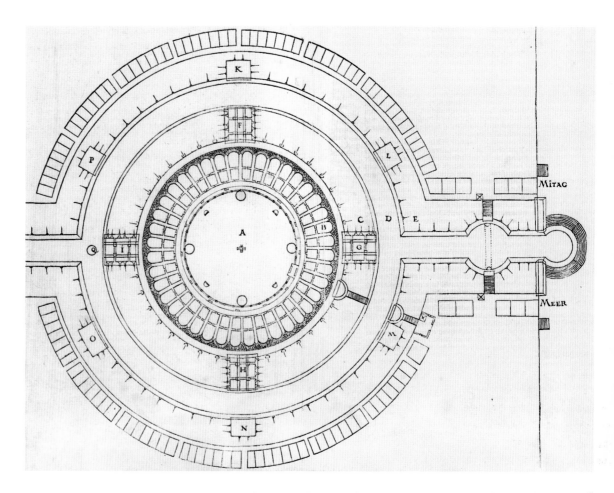

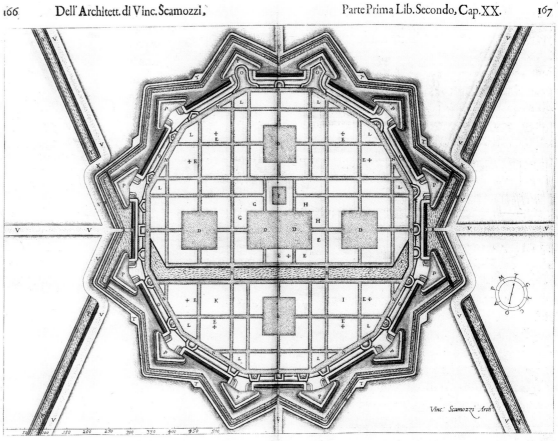

PAL MA

Outside the military field, the ideal-city aesthetic found certain other, later opportunities for realization (mainly in schemes for embellishing existing cities) in the late sixteenth and the seventeenth centuries but such examples require only brief mention here. It reappears, in an increasingly rudimentary manner, in the new feudal towns, such as Grammichele, built in Sicily. In 1599, Schickhardt was commissioned to create Freudenstadt for Protestant refugees in south-western Germany. Amid various options presented to Frederic I of Württemberg, the ruler insisted on a quadrangular scheme with a palace (unrealized) upon its central square, thus demonstrating clearly the political significance of the spatial arrangement. Schickhardt's town, which housed 2000 people by 1609, was clearly influenced by Dürer's quadrangular fortress design and the church and town hall similarly frame two of the corners of the central square which is broken by axes leading from its sides, a typical mannerist feature. In the wonderful design of Palladio's Teatro Olimpico in Vicenza, completed by Scamozzi, the stage is the ideal piazza from which the streets radiate and the audience can imagine the scheme continuing all around the spot in which they are seated. This theatrical employment

Plan of Palma Nova, in Georg Braun and Frans Hogenberg, *Civitates orbis terrarum*, Cologne, 1597. Bibliothèque Royale de Belgique, Brussels, Réserve précieuse

Ideal fortified city, in Robert Fludd, *Utriusque cosmi, majoris scilicet et minoris, metaphysica, physica atque technica historia*, 1617. Bibliothèque Royale de Belgique, Brussels, Réserve précieuse

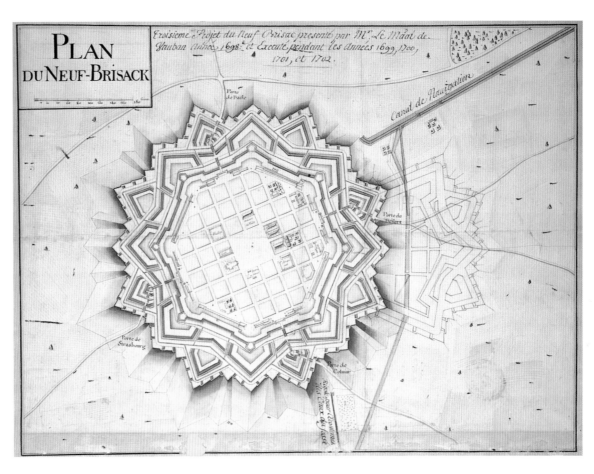

Anonymous, *Plan of Neuf-Brisach*, 1699–1702. Musée des Plans-Reliefs, Paris

may have been the closest Scamozzi was to get to producing an actual ideal city, although there has been speculation that he may have been involved in the construction of Palma Nova. Progressively, the Baroque came to dominate an urban scene appreciated in its entirety, and theatrical external spaces were created through visual ploys such as the use of perspective, diagonals converging on the most significant buildings, the uniform ordonnance of streets and the arrangement of public places. This can be seen in Sixtus v's monumental programme for a Rome worthy of being the capital of Christianity (and the stage for numerous religious processions), from 1586 to the completion of Bernini's colonnade long after the pope's death, as well as in Sir Christopher Wren's 1666 scheme for London after the fire and later around the royal châteaux in Versailles and

Karlsruhe. There the *patte d'oie* was developed to its highest degree, a realized urban reflection of absolutism and a natural progression on a grander scale from these exercises in ideal pattern-making that we have been considering.

THOMAS MORE FOUNDS THE UTOPIAN LITERARY GENRE

In 1516, *De optimo reipublicae statu deque nova insula Utopia*, the foundation text of the utopian genre written by Thomas More, the first layman to hold the office of Lord Chancellor of England, was published in Louvain by Dierck Martens. It was produced in

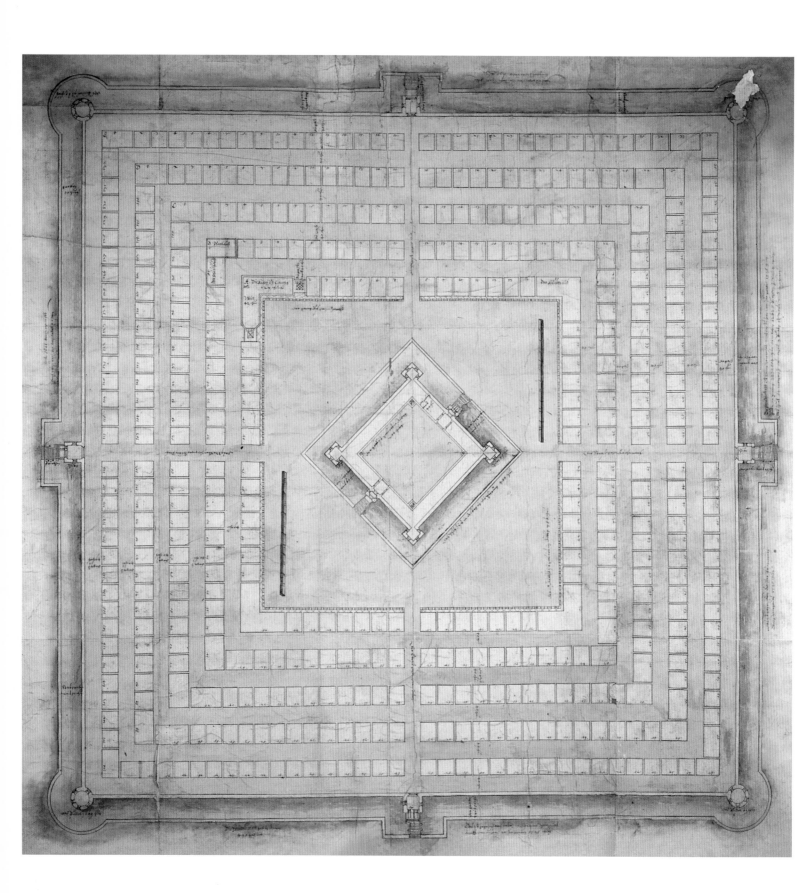

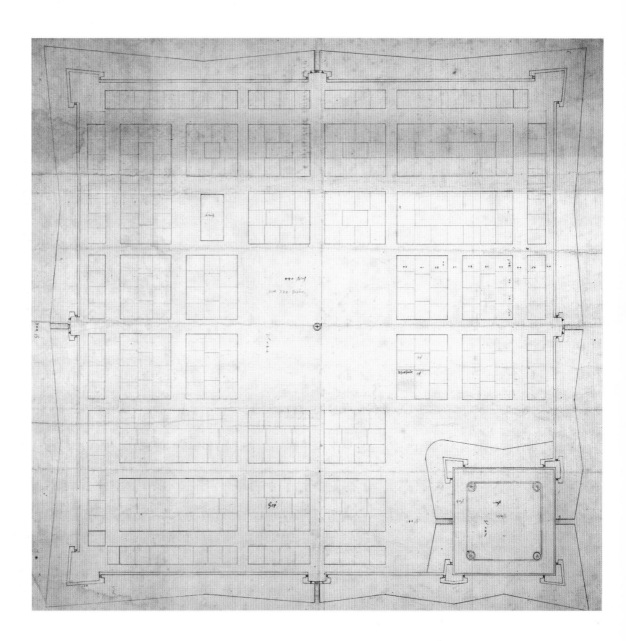

Heinrich Schickhardt, *Plan of Freudenstadt*, 1604. Hauptstaatsarchiv, Stuttgart

Heinrich Schickhardt, *Plan of Freudenstadt*, 1st project, 1599. Hauptstaatsarchiv, Stuttgart

response to profound changes in England: the decline of the feudal regime and the medieval economy, unemployment (of both soldiers, after the Wars of the Roses, and peasants, victims of a policy of enclosures due to agricultural land being converted for sheep-rearing) and a growing rift between a new wealthy merchant class and one of poor jobless vagabonds. When the Kelmscott Press published an edition of *Utopia* in 1893, William

Morris explained his predecessor's position: 'In More, then, are met together the man instinctively sympathetic with the communistic side of Mediaeval society; the protester against the ugly brutality of the earliest period of Commercialism, the enthusiast of the Renaissance, ever looking toward his idealized ancient society as the type and example of all really intelligent human life; the man tinged with the ascetism at once of the classical philosopher and of the monk: an ascetism indeed which he puts forward not so much as a duty, but rather as a kind of stern adornment of life.'[13]

Visiting his friend Pierre Gilles at Antwerp, More is introduced, in *Utopia*, to a Portuguese sailor Raphael Hythlodaeus (meaning 'Nonsense' in English), a companion of Amerigo Vespucci, who recounts his voyages and a dinner conversation at the table of the Archbishop of Canterbury, John Morton. The work contains two books: the first is a biting critique of the regime and institutions of modern England. This forms one of the elements that became essential to the utopian genre: critique of the status quo. This is coupled with the projection of an alternative model arrangement not only of society but also of space, without divine assistance, and the second book provides the latter as Hythlodaeus describes the crescent-shaped island of Utopia, its geography, its towns, its peoples and its laws. The physical place is central to the text and it is significant that the title refers to it, combining *topos* – place – and *u* – a contraction of *ou* or *eu* – to mean 'no-place' or a 'place of well-being'. The illustration for the first edition, showing a scattering of gothic-style settlements, would seem not to do More's invention justice as the regular layout and square plans he proposes are not evident in this work by a draughtsman clearly steeped in medieval architectural tradition. His words about the towns, and in particular the capital Amaurotum (from *amauros*, meaning dim, faint, shadowy and suggesting a sort of dream-town, called 'Aircastle' in the English translation from which these quotations are taken) are worth citing at length:

> Utopia was originally not an island but a peninsula. However, it was conquered by somebody called Utopos, who gave it its present name – it used to be called Sansculottia – and was also responsible for transforming a pack of ignorant savages into what is now, perhaps, the most civilized nation in the world…. There are fifty-four splendid big towns on the island, all with the same language, laws, customs, and institutions. They're all built on the same plan, and, so far as the sites will allow, they all look exactly alike. The minimum distance between towns is twenty-four miles, and the maximum, no more than a day's walk…. But I must tell you some more about the towns. Well, when you've seen one of them, you've seen them all, for they're as nearly identical as local conditions will

> permit. So I'll just give you one example – it doesn't much matter which….
> Aircastle is built on a gently sloping hill-side, and its ground-plan is practically square. It stretches from just below the top of the hill to the river Nowater, two miles away, and extends for two miles and a bit along the river-bank….
> The town is surrounded by a thick, high wall, with towers and blockhouses at frequent intervals. On three sides of it there's also a moat, which contains no water, but is very broad and deep, and obstructed by a thorn-bush entanglement. On the fourth side the river serves as a moat. The streets are well designed, both for traffic and for protection against the wind. The buildings are far from unimpressive, for they take the form of terraces, facing one another and running the whole length of the street. The fronts of the houses are separated by a twenty-foot carriageway. Behind them is a large garden, also as long as the street itself, and completely enclosed by the backs of other streets. Each house has a front door leading into the street, and a back door into the garden. In both cases they're double swing-doors, which open at a touch, and close automatically behind you. So anyone can go in and out – for there's no such thing as private property…
> By the founder I mean Utopus himself, who is said to have designed the whole layout of the town right from the start. However, he left posterity to embellish it and add the finishing touches, which he realized would take more than a single lifetime … the original houses were merely small huts or cottages, built hurriedly with the first timber that came to hand. The walls were plastered with mud, the roofs ridged and thatched. But nowadays every house is an imposing three-storey structure. The walls are faced with flint or some other hard stone, or else with bricks, and lined with roughcast. The sloping roofs have been raised to the horizontal, and covered with a special sort of concrete which costs next to nothing, but is better than lead for resisting bad weather conditions, and is also fireproof. They keep out draughts by glazing the windows – oh yes, they use a great deal of glass there….'[14]

Whereas Filarete had designed one ideal city, More invented an ideal island whose dimensions recalled his native England: the scale has changed and before long the ideal will aspire to the entire world. More's imaginary island contained 54 almost identical towns. He does leave a small window open to compromise with regard to local conditions (upon

Nicolas de Larmessin, *Tommaso Campanella*, early 17th century. Archiv für Kunst und Geschichte, Berlin

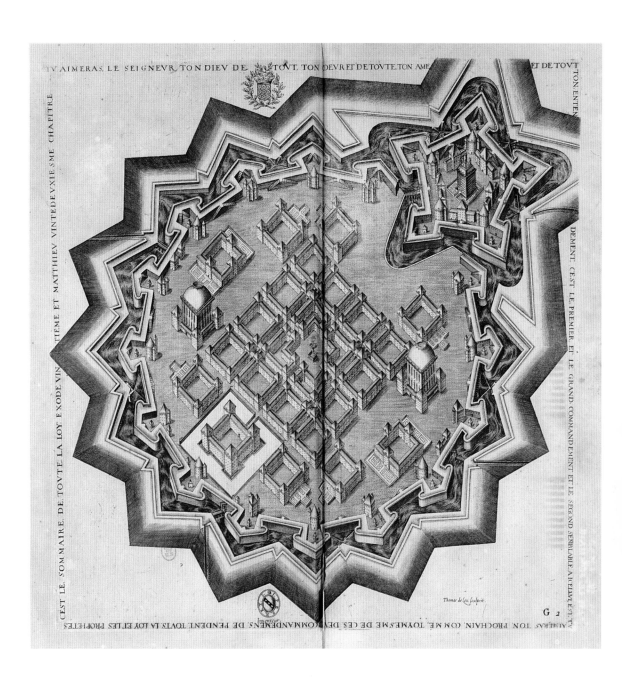

Ideal city plan by Thomas de Leu in Jacques
Perret, *Des Fortifications et artifices,
architecture et perspective*, Paris, 1601.
Bibliothèque Nationale de France, Paris,
Réserve des Livres rares

which he frustratingly fails to elaborate) and to the
passage of time which embellishes the original
design. What, one wonders, is More's intention
here? Surely, he is indicating the egalitarian nature
of his society. No doubt, he is paying homage to
Plato by presenting a city design so close to perfection that it cannot be improved upon. Perhaps, one
can speculate, he is extolling the limited, human
scale of the towns with their 6000 families in each.
Yet this series of clone-like towns is one of the most
alarming features of *Utopia* for it suggests the relent-
less domination of a single model – the brainchild,

in this case, of Utopus – across a territory. It thus
appears to vindicate the aspiration to uniform global
domination that is to characterize later utopian
schemes.

UTOPIAS BETWEEN MORE AND BACON

After More's *Utopia*, the sixteenth and early seventeenth centuries produced a myriad of utopian texts,

LE MONDÉ
SAGE.

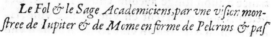

Le Fol & le Sage Academiciens, par vne vision monstree de Iupiter & de Mome en forme de Pelerins & pas

Bird's-eye view of a radioconcentric ideal city, in Anton Francesco Doni, Les mondes célestes, terrestres et infernaux, Lyons, 1578, translated by Gabriel Chappuis. Bibliothèque Royale de Belgique, Brussels, Département des Imprimés

Ideal city, in Gasparo Stiblino, Coropaedia, sive de moribus et vita virginum sacrarum, libellus ... elegans ac saluberrimis praeceptis refertu, Basle, 1555. Bibliothèque Nationale de France, Paris, Réserve des Livres rares

Hans Holbein the Younger, Sir Thomas More, 1527. The Frick Collection, New York

written from a wide variety of viewpoints. The majority shared a common feature with the architects designing ideal cities: a geometrical town plan on the scale of the city-state. Rabelais's Abbaye de Thélème described in his *Gargantua* (1534) is rather atypical in this respect for the Thelemites are housed in a large building that resembles a monastery, a castle or even a phalanstery. Indeed the whole text pokes fun at the monastic tradition. Rigid social rules have been reversed and members of the community are told to do as they desire – '*Fay que tu voudras*' – but the anti-conformism is illusory, for individual behaviour succumbs to the collective will and everyone acts in unison as in almost all utopias. The radial plan was favoured not only by architects but also by other utopian planners on account of its panoply of symbolic micro- and macrocosmic references. The idealistic rather than realistic aspect is clearly taken to its extreme in these utopian schemes: it is an understatement to note that circulation in such cities would have been severely compromised. Features such as unbroken streets without lateral passage and houses flanking the

ramparts (whose origin may well be the reading of Plato's *Critias*)[15] would have presented technical problems regarding defence and supply. In an anonymous drawing, long thought to have been by the hand of Fra Giocondo, the formal problem faced by Filarete is resolved by reserving the focal place of honour for the temple. Indeed this presented a perfect solution for the theocratic societies imagined during these times of religious persecution. This layout was taken up by Anton Francesco Doni in his *Mondi celesti, terresti ed infernali* (1555).[16] The city in Doni's work is described by the wise man who visited it during a dream as being star-like with a hundred streets connecting a hundred gates in the city walls to a central temple. A person within the temple, he explains, could perceive everything that occurred in the city by a simple turn of the head. Each street is specialized in two different crafts, one on each side of the road. In *De Eudaemonensium republica commentariolus* (1555), the Protestant Kaspar Stiblin imagined the 'happy' (hierarchical, rigorously authoritarian and ascetic!) state of Eudemone, the main city in the country of Macaria in the Indian Ocean. It too has a radial plan, protected by three brick walls, a ditch and an undeveloped stretch of land, four monumental doors oriented according to the cardinal points, a sumptuous public school building which indicates the importance attributed to education, and a governmental palace in the centre. Interestingly, the management of the other towns on the island is judged annually in function of the conditions of the buildings and the cultivation of the fields there.

The radial form, unbroken streets and house-lined walls are taken up again in the important utopian text, *Civitas Solis* (1602, published in 1623) written during imprisonment by the Dominican Tommaso Campanella, born in Calabria in 1568. His description of the city is quite detailed for a literary text:

> The greater part of the city is built upon a high hill, which rises from an extensive plain, but several of its circles extend for some distance beyond the base of the hill, which is of such size that the diameter of the city is upwards of two miles, so that its circumference becomes about seven. On account of the humped shape of the mountain, however, the diameter of the city is really more than if it were built on a plain.... It is divided into seven rings or huge circles named from the seven planets, and the way from one to the other of these is by four gates, that look towards the four points of the compass.... When I had been taken through the northern gate ... I saw a level space of seventy paces wide between the first and second walls. From hence can be seen large palaces all joined to the wall of the second circuit, in such a manner as to appear all one palace. Arches run on a level with the middle height of the palaces, and are continued round the whole ring. There are galleries for promenading upon these arches, which are supported from beneath by thick and well-shaped columns, enclosing arcades like peristyles, or cloisters of an abbey.[17]

The hill is crowned by a rather spacious plain, and in the midst of this there rises a circular temple supported by columns. Campanella's design has one particular feature which was most influential. The walls of his city are bedecked on both sides with images informing its children while they play. A wide

CHRISTIANOPOLIS

range of fields is covered, such as history or natural history, rather like an enormous open-air museum. On the inside of the second ring of buildings, for example, 'paintings of all kinds of precious and common stones, of minerals and metals are seen; and a little piece of the metal itself is also there with an apposite explanation in two small verses for each metal or stone', and on its outside 'there are also vessels built into the wall above the arches, and these are full of liquids from one to three hundred years old, which cure all diseases'.[18] This idea, that was to inspire many – including Lenin in the Soviet Union as we shall see later – is enticing but also disturbing, since it treads the borderline between education and brainwashing and seems to imply that the extent of knowledge has been fathomed definitively, fixed as it is in stone.

Like the radial plan, the similarly rational grid appealed to many a utopian author. Shortly after Schickhardt had designed Freudenstadt, another important figure on the Stuttgart scene, Johann

Bird's-eye view of Christianopolis, in Johann Valentin Andreae, Reipublicae christianopolitanae descriptio, 1619 (new edition Haarlem, 1978). Bibliothèque Royale de Belgique, Brussels, Département des Imprimés

Valentin Andreae, wrote *Reipublicae christianopolitanae descriptio* (1619). The formal similarities between the illustration of his invention, designed for 400 inhabitants, and Schickhardt's plan are clearly not fortuitous; they provide another example of the connections between the thinking of the architects and the utopists at the time, although the symbolism of the central feature has changed. Whereas the architect was working within a given set of political conditions, the Protestant writer was at liberty to place the building of his choice at the centre of his theocratic republic: the lower floor of his focal temple was reserved for religious ceremonies, the upper floors for gatherings of the community. Again we encounter a nostalgia for the Middle Ages and their communal aspects: the craft corporations form the basis of the social organization. Education once again plays an important role and the city boasts libraries, a printing house and laboratories, while its walls are decorated with pedagogical paintings relating important historical events. Andreae's design implies a somewhat menacing control, however, and parallels have been drawn between his plan and that of the labyrinths of medieval cathedrals which the faithful visited on their knees.

Before leaving this short survey of the literature after More, we should mention Sir Francis Bacon's unfinished *New Atlantis* (1627), even though it does not include a description of town planning on the island of Bensalem. For the scale of Bacon's society is larger than those mentioned above, and his work announces a new era in which knowledge and science are the driving forces. Indeed, Bacon's work precipitated the later creation of the Royal Society in London. This fact is underlined by the presence of the key institution, the House of Salomon, founded by Salomona, the king and lawgiver of Bensalem, some 1900 years earlier. It is 'the noblest foundation, as we think, that ever was upon the earth, and the lantern of this kingdom. It is dedicated to the study of the works and creatures of God.'[19] As a father of Salomon's House explains, 'the end of our foundation is the knowledge of causes, and secret motions of things; and the enlarging of the bounds of human empire, to the effecting of all things possible'.[20] In high towers, deep caves, orchards, gardens, wells and fountains, furnaces and so on, medicines are produced, animals created, light, sound, motion, smell and taste explored by the élite of Salomon's House in a rigidly segregated quest for knowledge in all fields. Emissaries known as merchants of light are sent to other lands secretly every twelve years to learn of other breakthroughs that may have escaped their expertise. Previous Bensalemites, we are told, had commercial ties with Atlantis whose population was virtually wiped out, not by an earthquake as Plato had speculated, but by a deluge which explains the 'rudeness and ignorance' of the new young peoples currently inhabiting America.[21]

As the Old World provided a frustratingly infertile terrain for the realization of ideal cities, our attention will now turn to the New. Giovanni Botero wrote in his *Relationi universali*, on the eve of the seventeenth century, that Europe was born to dominate Africa, Asia and America and indeed, confident in the conviction of their superiority, the Europeans set out to export their models to the New World.

4

When Christopher Columbus crossed the Atlantic in
1492 he 'discovered' an ancient continent and
civilizations which were soon to be described as the
'New World'. Little concerned, generally speaking,
by the realities of local conditions, the Europeans
paid scant heed to the indigenous populations with
their panoply of traditions and customs, treating
instead their lands as virgin territories upon which
their own dreams, frustrated upon the old continent,
might be enacted. The built environment played a
major role in the process of colonizing the Americas,
as it physically reflected the aspirations of the
Spanish crown and its *conquistadores*, those fleeing
from religious persecution in Europe or, indeed,
those constructing a new, democratic world.

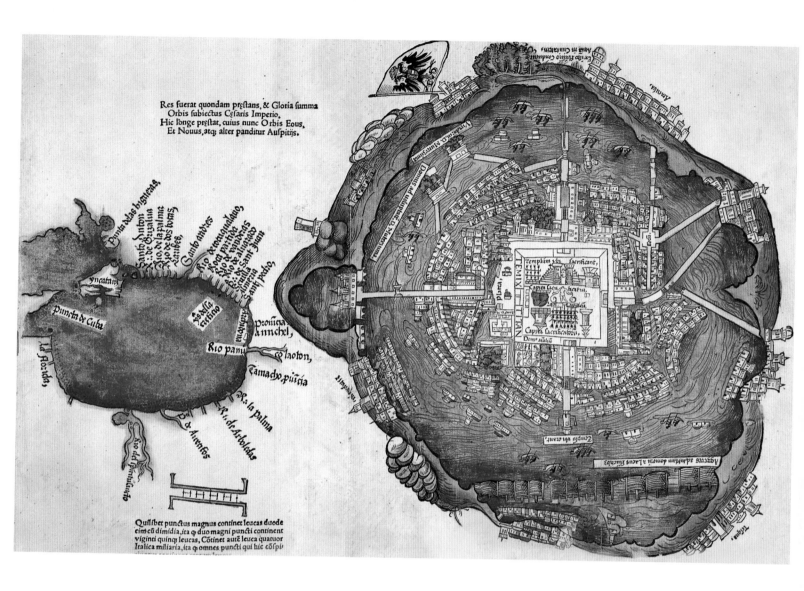

Within the map image:
> Res fuerat quondam præstans, & Gloria summa
> Orbis subiectus Cæsaris Imperio,
> Hic longe præstat, cuius nunc Orbis Eous,
> Et Nouus, atq; alter panditur Auspitijs.

> Quilibet punctus magnus continet leucas duode
> cim cu dimidia, ita q̃ duo magni puncti continent
> viginti quinq; leucas, Cötinet autë leuca quatuor
> Italica miliaria, ita q̃ omnes puncti qui hic cõspi

Tenochtitlán and the Gulf of Mexico, in Hernán Cortés, Praeclara Ferdinandi Cortesii de nova maris Oceani Hyspania narratio …, Nuremberg, 1524. Newberry Library, Chicago

Pages 72–74
Benjamin West, William Penn's Treaty with the Indians (detail), 1771–72. Pennsylvania Academy of the Fine Arts, Philadelphia, Gift of Sarah Harrison

ENCOUNTERING THE 'NEW WORLD'

'For not in vain, but with much cause and reason is this called the New World, not because it is newly found, but because in its people and in almost everything it is like as was the first and golden age.'[1] The words of Vasco de Quiroga typify the attitude of many a European on encountering the New World, 'discovered' at the end of the fifteenth century. For, despite intending to apply the scientific method to their reports, the Europeans encountered the Americas under the burden of all their own ideological baggage. Existing images, both scriptural, such as Eden or Heaven, and classical, such as the Golden Age or the Isles of the Blest, were projected onto this New World. Indeed, it would seem that this land was not discovered by chance, but that Europeans had been searching for it. After all, had not paradise on earth been speculatively located time and again, and so many mythical places been situated and resituated, ever further to the west, beyond the columns of Hercules (Gibraltar)? Christopher Columbus's belief that he had been entrusted with a transcendental mission is evident in his Book of Prophecies, which recorded many biblical, Graeco-Roman and medieval presentiments of America: 'God made me the messenger of the new heaven and the new earth, of which he spoke in the Apocalypse of Saint John after having spoken of it by the mouth of Isaiah; and he showed me the spot where to find it.'[2] Gilbert Chinard's analysis of the Jesuit reports from New France led him to identify two characters inhabiting the body of the Jesuit

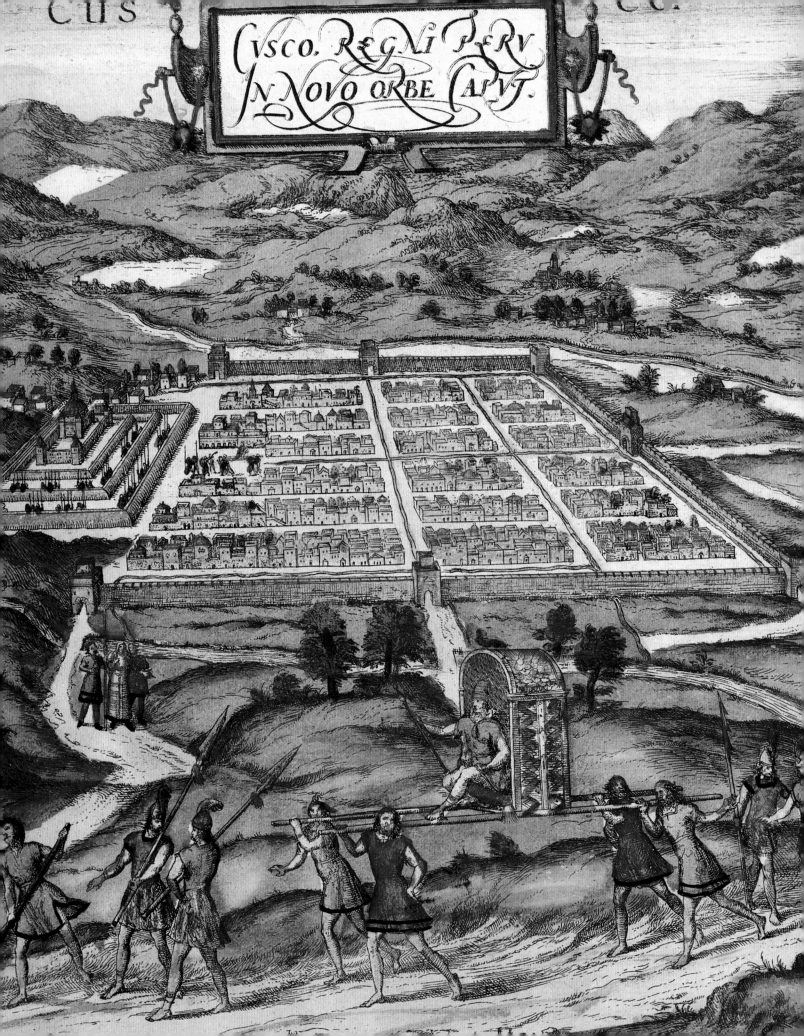

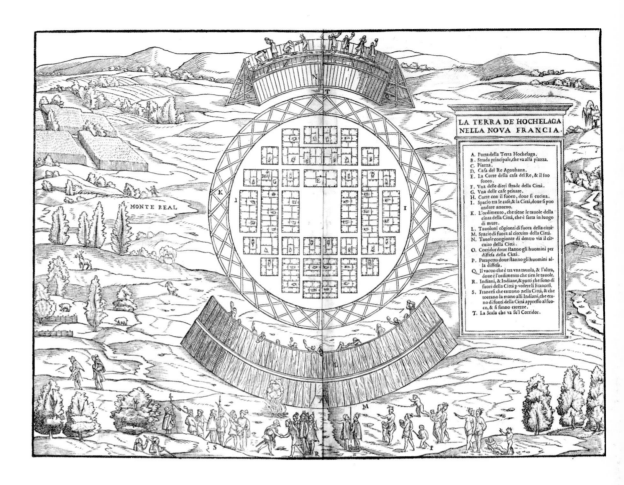

Inside the illustration:

LA TERRA DE HOCHELAGA
NELLA NOVA FRANCIA.

MONTE REAL

missionary: the priest who saw the natives as
monsters, almost demons, and the former student
of the Collège de la Flèche who could not forget the
Latin poets in the depths of the American forest.[3]
The very ability to fathom and describe the novel and
so very different realities being thus limited, the
visual repertoire concerning the New World intricately combined faithfulness to reality and the projection of European ideals. The peoples encountered
in America were often portrayed as a mixture of
feather-bedecked exoticism and the ideal classical
physique; even in as late as 1634, the Jesuit Father
Lejeune writing from New France (Canada) could
not hide his enthusiasm when he reported that he
saw 'on the shoulders of this people the heads of
Julius Caesar, Pompey, Augustus...'.[4] Depictions of
the existing settlements in which the local populations lived in the New World must be regarded
within this context. They can be broadly divided into
a majority of descriptions of small villages, usually
circular and protected by fencing and a few large-
scale agglomerations such as Termistitan missico

or Tenochtitlán, capital of the Aztec empire, and
Cusco, capital of the Inca empire. These latter
clearly impressed the *conquistadores* greatly, for they
were rapidly illustrated and reproduced in a number
of publications. A woodcut depicting Tenochtitlán
was included in the *Praeclara... de nova maris Oceani
Hyspania narratio ...* of 1524 along with Hernán
Cortés's letters relating to it. It shows the city
located within a lake and approached by four
causeways, the central enclosure with its temples
within which human sacrifices were carried out and
even the skull rack and the figure of an idol, shown
beheaded, presumably in order to convey the
Christian extermination of such idolatry. The view
bears a striking and surely not fortuitous resemblance to Albrecht Dürer's quadrangular design for a
fortified ideal city in *Etliche Underricht zu Befestigung
der Stett, Schloss und Flecken*, published three years
later. Its arrangement appears orderly and geometrical and it was published again in the 1550s in *Delle
navigationi e viaggi*, the anthology of voyages
compiled by Giovanni Battista Ramusio. The city

of Cusco in Peru was also illustrated: its size, beauty and magnificent gold-covered palace and massive protective stone walls were described by Pizarro and by Miguel de Estete, who had accompanied him during his 1533 expedition to Pachacamac. A third illustration from Ramusio's work indicates a more frequent type of settlement: Hochelaga, discovered in 1535–36 by Jacques Cartier, who named its neighbouring hill 'royal mountain', the site of today's Montreal. It shows a central square reserved for communal activities and the fire, some fifty dwellings and a circular wooden enclosure. Although the Europeans thus projected their ancient myths onto the existing Americas, the very term employed to describe it – the New World – suggested clearly that it was viewed as a place in which the passage of time could be interrupted, a *tabula rasa* upon which utopian desires might henceforth be satisfied. A paradise, created by divine forces, may have been discovered in the Americas; others, designed by the human mind, would now be implanted there. This apparently idyllic world was not considered a model worthy of emulation (in contrast, say, to the classical world from which there seemed much to learn) but a backward, natural, chaotic place that needed the rational organization which the humanist intellect could provide. The indigenous populations, whether perceived as noble and docile or as evil and wild, could, it seemed to the colonial powers, only benefit from their civilizing influence. To this land which recalled the golden age, Europe could export its ideals and above all its utopian dreams of creating the antithesis of the corrupt, decadent Old World, embedded in the iron age. The Europeans moved quickly to impose their culture, and particularly their religions, upon the New World. Spatial and social planning were to be partners in crime once more. Vernacular forms of settlement, with their panoply of deep spiritual and cultural significance for the indigenous populations, were almost invariably rejected, in favour, most often, of the planned grid layout which the Europeans had inherited from classical antiquity and beyond. By 1540, there were about 30,000

Spaniards living in America but the indigenous populations, which numbered millions, were decimated through the effects of colonization including the importation of illnesses to which the Indians were not immune and the psychological disorientation caused by enforced rehousing.

COLONIAL PRACTICE IN NEW SPAIN

Christopher Columbus set out across the Atlantic in 1492, the year in which the kingdoms of Castile and Aragon under Ferdinand and Isabella completed the Christian *reconquista* of Spain by ousting the Moors from their final foothold in Granada. The admiral's discoveries, beginning with San Salvador, Santa Maria de la Concepción, Fernandina, Isabella, Cuba or Juana and Hispaniola or Haiti, led to the Spanish and Portuguese domination of huge territories in America. The very first example of European town building in the New World was probably the fortress named La Navidad that he constructed on the island of Hispaniola out of the timber of his wrecked ship, the *Santa Maria*. By the eighteenth century, close to five hundred towns and thousands of villages had been created in the New World by the Spanish.[5] La Navidad's existence was brief as the men Columbus had left there while he went back to Spain were massacred, but in 1493 he returned with 1200 people and founded, close by, the colony of Isabella, which was replaced in 1496 by a first Santo Domingo, refounded, in turn, in 1502 by the Governor Nicolas de Ovando as capital of Hispaniola. Santo Domingo, the oldest of the long-standing American cities to be created by the Europeans, was laid out according to a rational plan with blocks of buildings arranged upon a gridiron and a great rectangular *plaza mayor* dominated by the church at its heart. This scheme was to recur throughout the history of Spanish city-founding in the Western hemisphere although it had not been explicitly outlined as a model at this initial stage.

MEXICO.

MEXICO, REGIA ET CELEBRIS HISPANIÆ NOVÆ CIVITAS.

Plan of Mexico City, in Georg Braun and Frans Hogenberg, *Civitates orbis terrarum*, Cologne, 1597. Bibliothèque Royale de Belgique, Brussels, Réserve précieuse

Before long, however, specific instructions were supplied by the Iberian authorities concerning the urban plan of new towns. In 1513, Ferdinand V of Spain had pronounced the following directives: 'let the city lots be regular from the start, so that once they are marked out the town will appear well ordered as to the place which is left for the plaza, the site for the church and the sequence of the streets; for in places newly established, proper order can be given from the start, and thus they remain ordered with no extra cost: otherwise order will never be introduced'.[6] In 1521, Charles V set out similar guidelines in a city-planning practice code issued that year. In 1573, Philip II issued a set of royal ordinances concerning the laying out of the new towns,

stipulating, for example, that 'the four corners of the plaza are to face the four points of the compass, because thus the streets diverging from the plaza will not be directly exposed to the four principal winds...', and that 'settlers are to endeavour as far as possible to make all structures uniform, for the sake of the beauty of the town'.[7] These and similar regulations were to be definitively consolidated within the *Recopilación de Leyes de los Reynos de las Indias*, known as the Laws of the Indies.

The Aztec capital of Tenochtitlán was destroyed to a great extent by the European invaders after 1521 but, despite razing the main Aztec monuments, they decided to maintain the site as Mexico City, the capital of New Spain, on account of its symbolic importance. The existing pattern was apparently a gridiron, so this was naturally preserved in many of the new causeways (which – having mostly been canals rather than streets – were often filled in using rubble from the destroyed constructions). The Inca capital of Cusco, however, after succumbing to Pizarro's forces in 1533, was not retained as the capital of Spanish Peru. Instead, the Europeans settled for leaving their mark on the face of the city by splitting the huge principal square into three smaller ones, introducing others and riddling the urban fabric with a vast collection of churches and monasteries, often strategically placed upon the sites of existing places of worship. In this form of cosmetic surgery the spiritual supremacy desired by the invaders was indicated persuasively by means of a skyline dotted with domes and spires. A new capital, Lima, was founded on another site in 1535 and Pizarro is said to have been personally responsible for tracing its plan: a central Plaza de Armas to be surrounded by 117 gridiron blocks. Just a few months after the foundation of Lima, Don Pedro de Mendoza entered the Rio de la Plata and before long selected a spot for the creation of the town he named Nuestra Señora Santa Maria del Buen Aire. However, it proved unviable and so two of his lieutenants created a new town, Asunción (later the capital of independent Paraguay), and then in the 1580s Buenos Aires (later the capital of Argentina) was

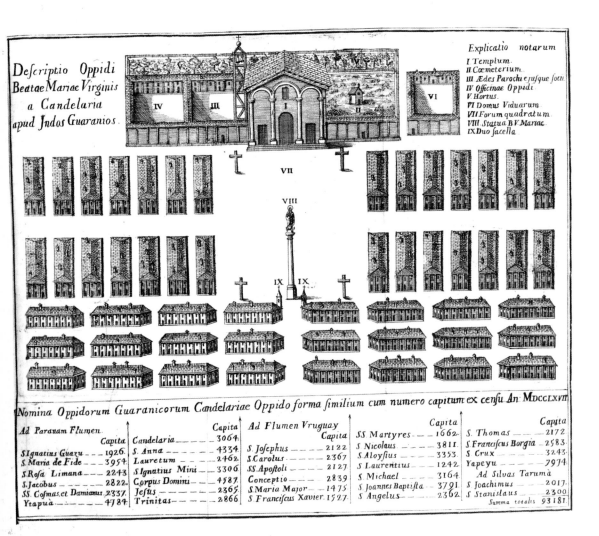

Defcriptio Oppidi
Beatae Mariae Virginis
a Candelaria
apud Indos Guaranios.

Explicatio notarum
I Templum
II Cœmeterium
III Ædes Parochi ejufque focii
IV Officinae Oppidi
V Hortus
VI Domus Viduarum
VII Forum quadratum
VIII Statua B.V.Mariae
IX Duo facella

Nomina Oppidorum Guaranicorum Candelariae Oppido forma fimilium cum numero capitum ex cenfu An. MDCCLXVIII

Ad Paranam Flumen.	Capita		Capita	Ad Flumen Vruguay	Capita		Capita		Capita
S.Ignatius Guazu	1926	Candelaria	3064	S.Josephus	2122	SS.Martyres	1662	S.Thomas	2172
S.Maria de Fide	3954	S.Anna	4334	S.Carolus	2367	S.Nicolaus	3811	S.Francifcus Borgia	2583
S.Rosa Limana	2243	Lauretum	2462	SS.Apostoli	2127	S.Aloyfius	3353	S.Crux	3243
S.Jacobus	2822	S.Ignatius Mini	3306	Conceptio	2839	S.Laurentius	1242	Yapeyu	7914
SS.Cofmas et Damianus	2337	Corpus Domini	4587	S.Maria Major	1475	S.Michael	3164	Ad Silvas Tarumā	
Ytapua	4784	Jefus	2365	S.Francifcus Xavier	1527	S.Joannes Baptifta	3791	S.Joachimus	2017
		Trinitas	2866			S.Angelus	2362	S.Stanislaus	2300
								Summa totalis	93181

refounded close to its original location. Again the gridiron dominated as the urban expression of colonization. Frequently, rapid expansion caused the initial regularity to be abandoned: this was the case at Lima in which only 67 of its blocks were completed before a less orderly development gained the upper hand.

Generally speaking, in the majority of towns created in New Spain, the grid plan was used, symbolizing the rational domination of the colonizing power and guaranteeing a means of ensuring surveillance and security without building costly walls. For, unlike the fortified ideal cities produced in Italy, these towns were not restricted by enclosures but intended to expand and designed with this in mind (a rare example of an Italian ideal-city style of design within an elliptical fortified wall was built at Trujillo in 1760). A plaza mayor took pride of place in the town centre, the seat of political, military and religious power, where armed forces could gather and numerous public celebrations could take place. The residential areas for people of European descent were usually segregated from local populations who often lived in appalling conditions. Spanish planning favoured the inclusion of open spaces and common land, a privilege lost in California when it became American territory in the nineteenth century and the law of the land speculator got the upper hand.

One of the methods used by the Europeans to 'civilize' and evangelize the populations of Latin America – and one which has inspired very heated debate – is their grouping within villages of which the Jesuit reducciones have perhaps caused the greatest amounts of ink to flow. Neither presidios (military establishments) nor religious reducciones

A Jesuit reducción in Paraguay, in José Manuel Peramás, De vita et moribus tredecim virorum paraguaycorum, Faenza, 1793. Bibliothèque Jésuite des Fontaines, Chantilly

Theodore de Bry, after John White, The Town of Pomeiock, Frankfurt, 1590. New York Public Library

were covered by the Laws of the Indies which concentrated on *pueblos* or *villas* (colonial towns). The process of gathering the natives who lived outside the cities into new villages was radical, implying the veritable uprooting of people who often still lived in a very deep spiritual relationship with their surroundings. The *conquistadores* considered it essential, however, as it proved far too difficult to convert a population that was nomadic or dispersed in hamlets of at times no more than a handful of lodgings. This process, encouraged by the Spanish Crown, in both its temporal and spiritual capacities, began early in the sixteenth century. A key figure in this context was the devout layman Vasco de Quiroga whom the Emperor Charles v had nominated member of the second *audiencia*, set up to govern the newly conquered territories in replacement of a previous one in which the successors of Cortés had committed excesses. Shortly after Vasco's arrival in Mexico in 1531, Bishop Zumarraga offered him a gift which was to have a profound influence upon his thinking: a copy of Thomas More's *Utopia*. For Vasco, Utopia existed in the New World as the three divine principles were applied there: equality, love of peace and disdain for gold and silver. There he could create the perfect Christian state. Particularly concerned by the plight of the homeless, and the sick and abandoned Indian children, Vasco, starting with a group of two dozen natives whom he had personally instructed in the Christian faith, set up, initially at his own expense, the first of his *hospitales-pueblos* (hospitality villages) close to Tenochtitlán. By the 1550s, it had accumulated a population of over 33,000. He drew up a series of regulations concerning the running of this community and it continued to function in accordance with these right up until the eighteenth century. The members of the community, who were arranged in large families, worked six hours a day both on the land and in manual crafts, were identically dressed and owned no personal property. Buildings were collective and the original village contained a school, a church, an open chapel and three hospitals, one for the young, one for the contagious and a third for the non-contagious. Vasco also went to Michoacán, 300 kilometres westwards, where Franciscans had been founding villages from 1525 on but Nuño de Guzmán, president of the first *audiencia*, had been causing havoc. He calmed the situation and created a new village. In 1535, he sent his *Información en derecho* to his king, an in-depth analysis of the colonizing process and the behaviour of both the colonial powers and the indigenous peoples. He insisted on the necessity of grouping the natives in villages or towns in order not only to 'civilize' them but also to protect them. In 1537, a papal bull made Vasco bishop of Michoacán, and he devoted a great part of the following years to the establishment of new villages and the construction of a great cathedral at Pátzcuaro which he designed himself but which remained unfinished. His intended architectural scheme is indicative of his approach in general: located upon a belvedere dominating a magnificent lacustrine landscape, his plan for a huge basilica with five aisles meeting at the central sanctuary respected both the architectural ideals of the European Renaissance and the mythical indigenous perception of the site. Similarly, he did not impose the grid scheme favoured by the Spaniards in the urban treatment of Pátzcuaro but adopted and expanded upon the existing radial use of the space, combining his social ideals with certain ingredients of vernacular culture.

Although the *reducciones* created by the Jesuits are most famous, the practice of grouping Indians into villages pre-existed the Society of Jesus, which was not founded until 1539. This was a body of highly trained, homeless and cosmopolitan religious men

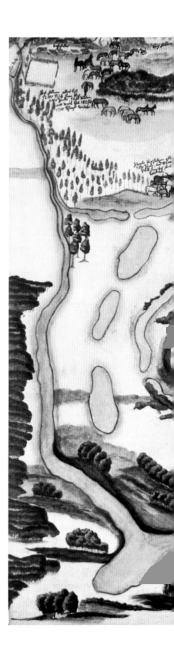

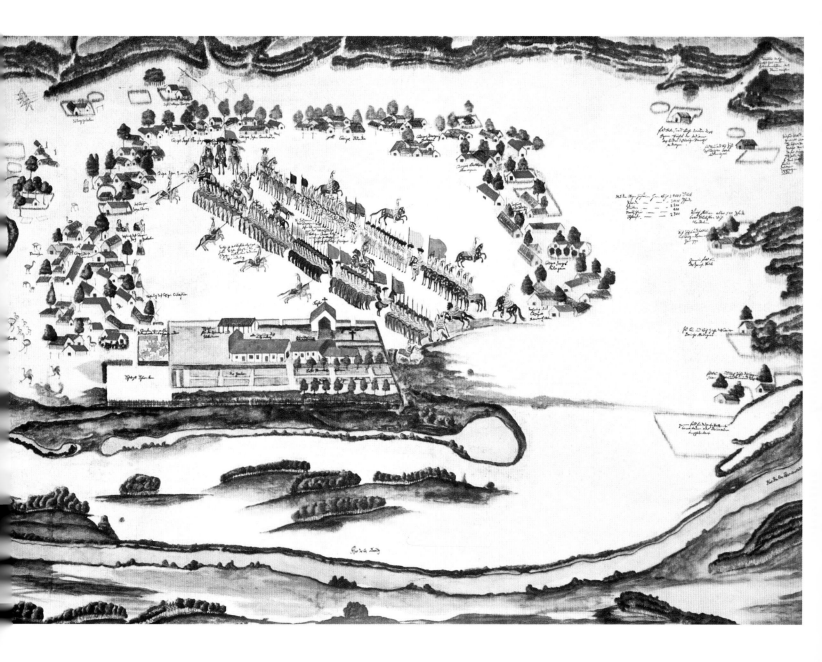

Florian Baucke, *Festivities at the reducción of San Javier de Mocobies, Paraguay.* Facsimile of a watercolour in *Hin und Her,* vol. 1, Zwettle, 1770/73–80. Stiftsbibliothek, Zwettle, Cod. Zwetl. 420

likened by its founder, Saint Ignatius of Loyola, to the light horse of the Church, in contrast to the old monastic communities that made up its infantry. Writing about the Jesuit missionaries in New France, Chinard noted that, without being 'republicans' in the modern sense of the word, or 'democrats', they were opposed to royal power, if not in France, at least on the American continent and often positioned themselves as victims or enemies of royalty. 'From the outset,' he says, 'their dream would have been to organize a Jesuit or theocratic state in New France, as they were later to do in Paraguay ...'[8] Although already active on the Latin American

continent from the mid-sixteenth century, it was not until 1609–10 that the Jesuits began, in accordance with royal instructions, to group the first Guarani Indians into villages in an area today covering the frontiers of Paraguay, Argentina and Brazil. Their positions changed during the early years, but by the middle of the seventeenth century all were located within the area measuring some 60,000 square kilometres that they still occupied at the time of the Jesuits' expulsion (1767). Thirty *reducciones* grouped a previously belligerent, polygamous, migrant people which had lived in small forest settlements surrounded by defensive fences and traps against other Indian villagers whose capture implied death and anthropophagy. The organization of the Jesuit *reducciones* was severe and their layout – which barely differed from one village to another – testifies to this rigidity. Flat sites were favoured and each village was entered via a long, straight avenue leading from a crucifix to the central square bordered by the church, the presbytery, the communal workshops, the cemetery wall and a building housing widows and unmarried women (this being interpreted as confinement or protection). Families lived in contiguous, residential constructions aligned around this pivotal place: initially these grouped numerous Guaranis together, thus ensuring a cultural transition from their traditional homes, but as the habit of polygamy died out eventually they were compartmentalized into a series of separate lodgings for each monogamous family with access provided by external passages. This typifies the symbiosis of former Guarani habits and evangelical principles practised in the *reducciones*. The built area represented about a sixth of the total *reducción*, the rest of its land being agricultural (with men now labouring in the fields, previously the task of the women alone) and the entire missionary zone was interspersed with a system of pathways dotted with chapels. The villages had populations of about 3000 each and the inhabitants were taught manual crafts, each specializing in certain domains and producing serially: their production surpluses were sent to other villages, or sold to cover the payments of tributes to the king. The Society of Jesus was suppressed in 1773 and, shortly before, the Jesuits had been expelled from the *reducciones*: the experience of the latter had been extolled as a fine model of social organization by, for example, Montesquieu, d'Alembert and Buffon, while others condemned it as enslavement. To appreciate the psychological impact of these orthogonally arranged villages upon the Indians, let us conclude by quoting the French ethnologist Claude Lévi-Strauss's words in *Tristes Tropiques* (1955) in relation to his own experiences regarding the Bororo Indians of Brazil several centuries later: 'The circular distribution of the huts around the men's house was of such great importance to the community in relation to their social life and the practice of their cult, that the missionaries in the region of Rio das Garcias soon learnt that the most sure way to convert the Bororo Indians was to make them abandon their village for another where the houses were laid out in parallel rows. Disorientated in relation to the cardinal points, deprived of the plan which underpins their knowledge, the indigenous peoples rapidly lose their sense of traditions, as though their social and religious systems were too complicated to survive if they were not expressed in the plan of the village and their contours perpetually refreshed in their daily gestures.'[9]

THE GRID ENRAPTURES NORTH AMERICA

Latin America thus witnessed a regular pattern of urban design guided by the clear regulations issued from the Old World from the early years of the sixteenth century. In the absence of any such sweeping regal instructions, the situation was different in North America (which had no cities comparable to Tenochtitlán or Cusco when the Europeans disembarked), and the newly founded towns initially enjoyed an organic development, as can still be seen today in the city of Boston. However, the grid system soon imposed its inescapable logic. When the newly independent states made claims to undeveloped land to the West, it was already in common use and represented the most straightforward method of dividing territory up for sale and distribution. The Land Ordinance of 1785 split territories into townships, each six miles square and subdivided in turn, and thus created a pre-urban, isotropic cadastre resembling those laid out by the Roman land surveyors and that projected by More for the island of Utopia, on an unprecedented scale. The first seven ranges of townships with their alternating rural areas on land north-west of the Ohio river are shown in the map of 1796: this policy

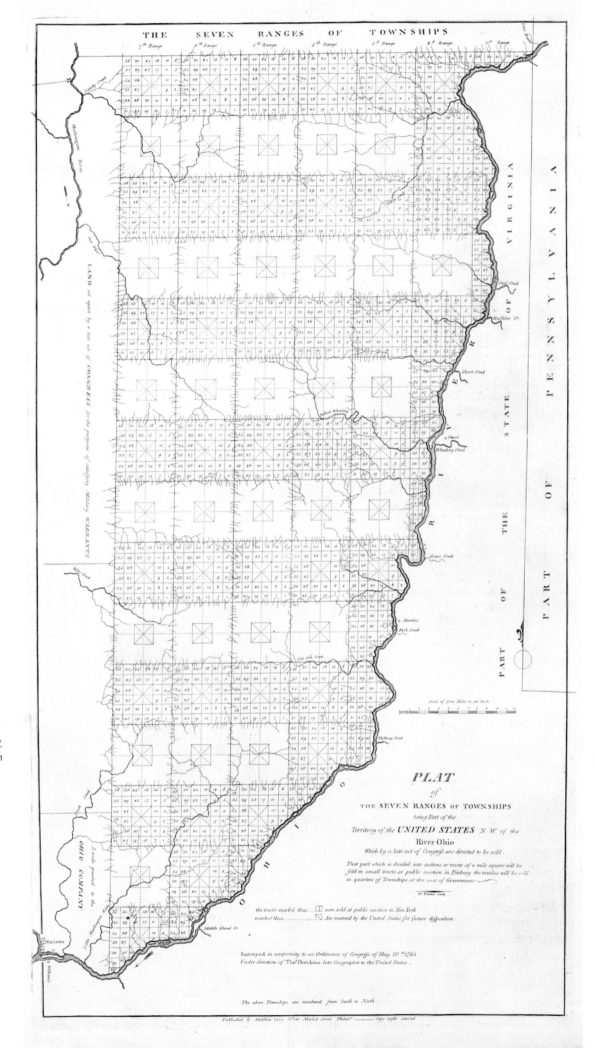

W. Barker, after surveys by Thomas Hutchins, *Plat of the Seven Ranges of Townships being Part of the Territory of the United States N.W. of the River Ohio*, Philadelphia, 1796. William L. Clements Library, University of Michigan, Ann Arbor

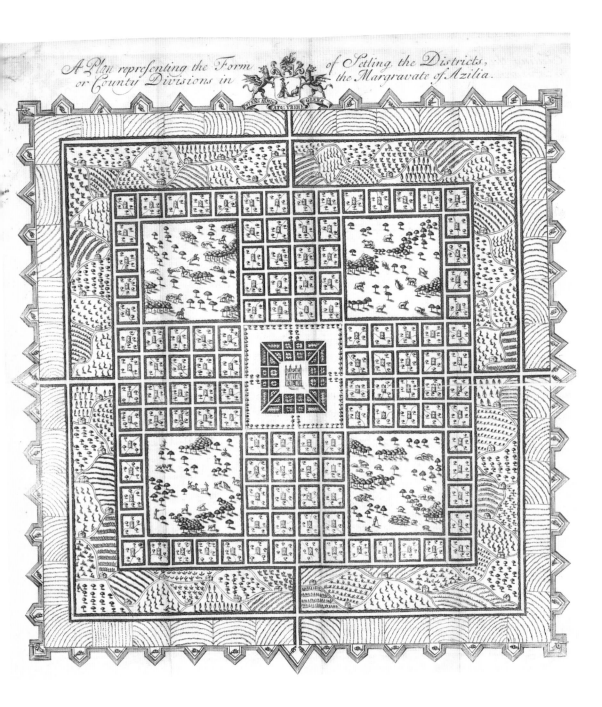

A Plan representing the Form of Setling the Districts, or County Divisions in the Margravate of Azilia.

continued until the frontiers were closed. It considerably reinforced the preference for the gridiron in cities and the pattern thus came to dominate on a national, regional and urban scale. This uniformity in plan was not matched in elevation, however, and a laissez-faire attitude determined the architectural exploitation of plots.

Frank Lloyd Wright's twentieth-century scheme for Broadacre City seems clearly rooted in this supremely American long-standing tradition of basic land division combined with individual freedom. It is important to note that Thomas Jefferson had dreamt of a country in which all white male Americans would be landowners and hence voting citizens and that the 1785 grid would consolidate this situation with a force similar to that of a Constitution. It failed, however, to ensure this ambitious ideal of land democracy.

Amidst the whole constellation of gridiron cities that developed across America, we shall recall just a

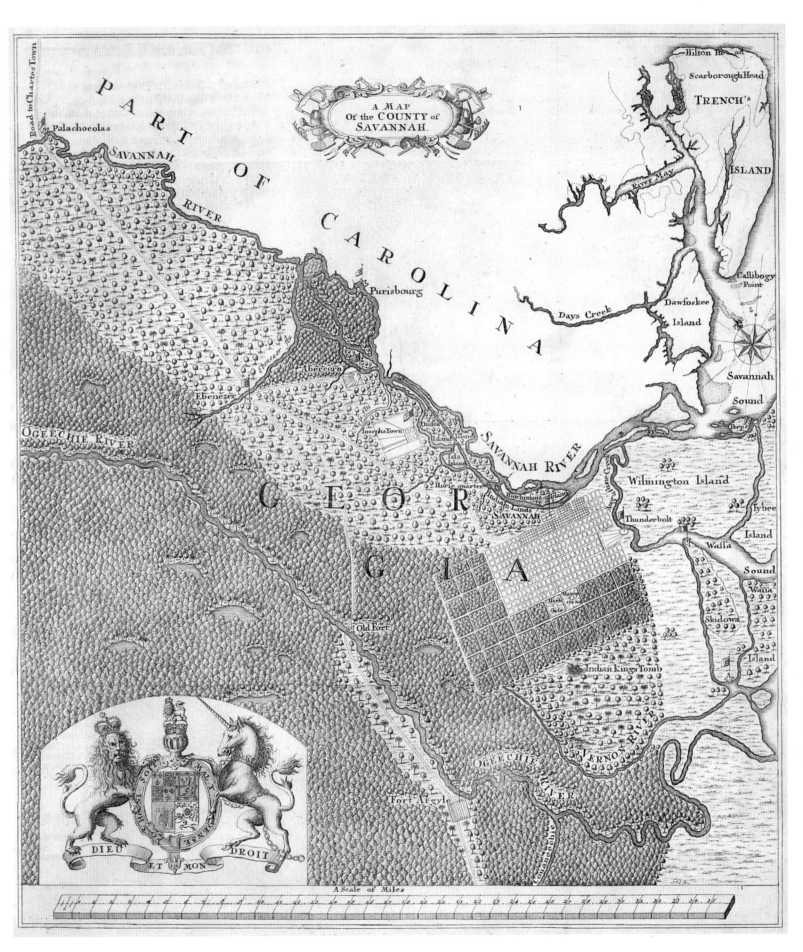

A MAP
Of the COUNTY of
SAVANNAH.

PART OF CAROLINA

PART OF

GEORGIA

handful of examples, including some of the more interesting variations on the basic theme. In 1717, Robert Montgomery had been granted permission to create a province, the Margravate of Azilia, between the Savannah and Alatamaha rivers and he published his plan of settlement in *A Discourse Concerning the Design'd Establishment of a New Colony to the South of Carolina in the Most Delightful Country of the Universe* (1717). This unusual proposal came to nothing as the land was not settled within the required period of time, but certain of its features had later influence, on James Oglethorpe among others. Four large forests, each four miles square, were surrounded by 116 one-mile-square plantation lots (this mile measure reappeared in the 1785 western land surveys). The margrave's residence was placed in the heart of the city, which was located in the centre of the plan with a sort of greenbelt separating it from the countryside, and the entire colony was protected by fortifications. When James Oglethorpe set out to colonize Georgia, he selected a site on the banks of the Savannah river to create the town of Savannah. Rather than simply dividing the land into square plots, he invented a general 'ward' unit comprised of a public square, four plots for public buildings and four clusters of ten-house plots each – an arrangement that could be reproduced in cell-like fashion. Town dwellers owned triangular plots outside the city limits and larger farm plots beyond. Oglethorpe was probably influenced by his knowledge of London's squares, the planning of Londonderry in Ulster, Newcourt's plan for the rebuilding of London in 1666, and even Renaissance ideal-city planning, although his repetition of a unit does not share the hierarchical arrangement of the towns of, say, Cataneo.[10]

Pierre-Charles L'Enfant's plan for Washington, DC, combined an unusual mixture of gridiron and diagonal elements. The latter reveal the formal and symbolic influence of Karlsruhe in Germany and childhood memories of Versailles in France (although in both these instances the radiating streets were intended to reinforce appreciation of the power of an autocratic ruler). L'Enfant's plan

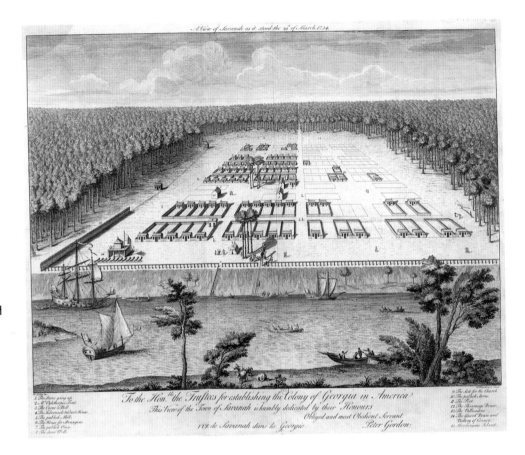

does not meet our ideal-city criteria since it was clearly and masterfully designed for one specific site, but it none the less represents an interesting contrast to another proposal for the national capital: that of Thomas Jefferson. Jefferson was a keen advocate of the gridiron, as his notes and sketches concerning the new city reveal. In a note of 1790, he suggested that the land be divided into lots and streets at right angles along the Philadelphian model and included a sketch to this purpose.[11] He then drew, on the same document, a simple grid of four by thirteen blocks for a site then occupied by Carollsburg and in a further, later, drawing for a site along Tyber Creek, he showed more attention to context. John W. Reps, the historian of American town planning, recounts that Jefferson informed Washington that he had sent plans to L'Enfant, at his request, of Frankfurt, Karlsruhe, Paris, Orléans,

Paul Fourdrinier after Peter Gordon, *A View of Savannah as it stood the 29th of March 1734*, 1734. Bibliothèque Nationale de France, Paris, Cabinet des Estampes

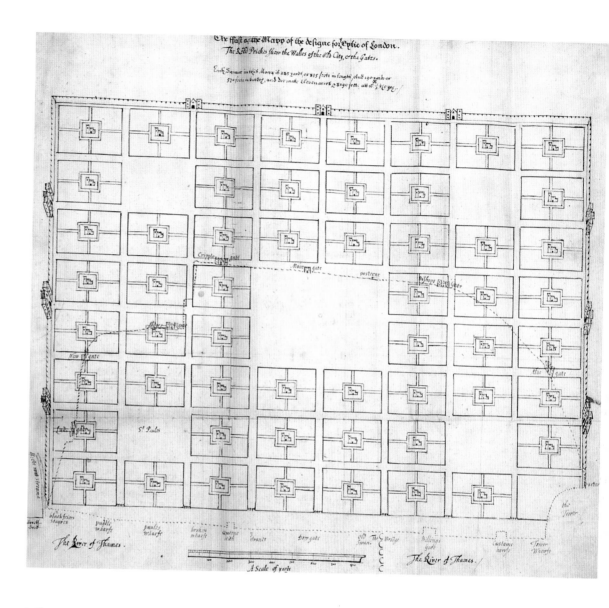

Richard Newcourt, *The First of the Mapp of the designe for Cytie of London*. Manuscript plan for rebuilding London in 1666. Guildhall Library, London

Milan, Amsterdam and other cities, commenting that 'they are none of them however comparable to the old Babylon, revived in Philadylon'.[12] While Jefferson diplomatically obliged L'Enfant, the latter, a reputedly brilliant but cantankerous character – Reps refers to him as 'L'Enfant Terrible'! – did not spare the future president's feelings. He had seen Jefferson's plans but condemned the use of the rectangular plan in no uncertain terms, which are worth quoting at length:

> ... it is not the regular assemblage of houses laid out in squares and forming streets all parallel and uniform that ... is so necessary, for such a plan could only do on a level plain and where no surrounding object being interesting, it becomes indifferent which way the opening of streets may be directed.

But on any other ground, a plan of this sort must be defective, and it never would answer for any of the spots proposed for the Federal City, and on that held here as the most eligible it would absolutely annihilate every of the advantages enumerated and ... alone injure the success of the undertaking.

Such regular plans indeed, however answerable they may appear upon paper or seducing as they may be on the first aspect to the eyes of some people, must even when applyed upon the ground the best calculated to admit of it become at last tiresome and insipid, and it never could be in its origin but a mean continuance of some cool imagination wanting a sense of the real grand and truly beautiful only to be met with where nature contributes with art and diversifies the objects.[13]

Jeffersonville, Indiana, was laid out according to a scheme which was more sophisticated than the straightforward grid. It was the product of John Gwathmey but echoed a project by Jefferson himself of 1802 (who may by then have appreciated the monotony of the simple grid). In response to the spread of yellow fever, it alternated built and unbuilt squares with the open ones devoted to parkland and

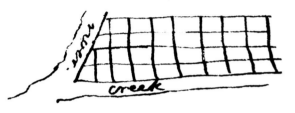

crossed by diagonal streets. Needless to say, the system – again attempted at Jackson, Mississippi – did not resist commercial pressures, and within a few years the open areas had been filled.

Although at Washington, DC, L'Enfant may have won the battle, Jefferson won the war for, thanks in great part to the 1785 Land Ordinance, the grid enveloped the nation.

In order to demonstrate the extent of the grid's tentacular grip upon North America, the later story of Circleville is too irresistible not to be recalled. When the Ohio legislature established Pickaway County in 1810, a site for the county seat was required and a location by the Scioto river was selected. It was occupied by earthworks in the form of a perfect circle with a contiguous square dating from the time of the early Indians known as the Mound Builders. Daniel Driesbach, who planned the new town, broke with tradition by producing a circular street plan. Such an initiative was doomed to failure in the long term. Circleville, as America's first radial town was called, did not conform to the needs and ideas of the real estate developers. America's first private urban redevelopment company was incorporated in 1837 to deal with Circleville and it was named ... the 'Circleville Squaring Company'! By 1856, its objectives had been reached and the circle subjugated to the square.

Shared faith ensures a strong group unity and the monastic tradition has provided successful examples of communal living for centuries. To religious groups escaping persecution in Europe, America appeared as the promised land, the terrain upon which their ideal worlds could be built. Quakers, Mennonites, Moravians, Shakers, Harmonists, Separatists, Inspirationists, Mormons and so forth: it is not the purpose of this survey to discuss the many religious communities active in America in detail, but a brief survey of some examples should indicate the manner in which certain architectural and urban formulae, often the reflection of elements of a group's ethics, were employed.

William Penn, governor and proprietor of Pennsylvania, was an exceptional character. A Quaker preacher with considerable private means, pursued and imprisoned regularly on account of his faith, and a great believer in non-violence and in freedom of thought, he expressed his ideas in some 150 works of which *No Cross, No Crown* (1669) is perhaps the most famous.

In 1681, the English King Charles II signed the Charter of Pennsylvania which made Penn the owner, but not the sovereign, of a vast territory (about 120,000 square kilometres) near to New Jersey in reimbursement of sums owed to him by the Crown. For Penn, this land was a gift of God and here he hoped to set an example for all nations, for here he would create what he called his 'Holy Experiment', a republic of kings based on the idea that the search for the king inside every individual would lead to the regeneration of humanity.

Inspired by many texts, but particularly by James Harrington's *Oceana* (1656), he drew up a Frame of Government which prefigured the *Constitution of the United States* and the *Declaration of Rights* by over a century on many points. Penn was not actually in America when the city of Philadelphia was founded in 1682, but he instructed his Surveyor-General, Captain Thomas Holme, 'to settle the

Thomas Jefferson, Sketches of a plan for a capital city on the site of Carollsburg, District of Columbia, and of a suggested land division in a city block, in a manuscript note dated 29 November 1790 and entitled 'Proceedings to be had under the Residence Act'. Library of Congress, Washington, DC, Manuscripts Division

with foot-ways of 15. feet. where a street is long & level, it might be 120. feet. I should prefer squares of at least 200. yards every way, which will be of about 8. acres each.

The Commissioners should have some taste in Architecture, because they may have to decide between different plans.

They will however be subject to the President's direction in every point.

When the President shall have made up his mind as to the spot for the town, would there be any impropriety in his saying to the neighboring landholders, "I will fix the town here if you will join & purchase & give the lands." they may well afford it from the increase of value it will give to their own circumjacent lands.

The lots to be sold out in breadth of 50. feet: their depths to extend to the diagonal of the square.

I doubt much whether the obligation to build the houses at a given distance from the street, contributes to it's beauty. it produces a disgusting monotony. all persons make this complaint against Philadelphia. the contrary practice varies the appearance, & is much more convenient to the inhabitants.

In Paris it is forbidden to build a house beyond a given height, & it is admitted to be a good restriction. it keeps down the price of ground, keeps the houses low & convenient, & the streets light & airy. fires are much more manageable where houses are low. this however is an object of legislation.

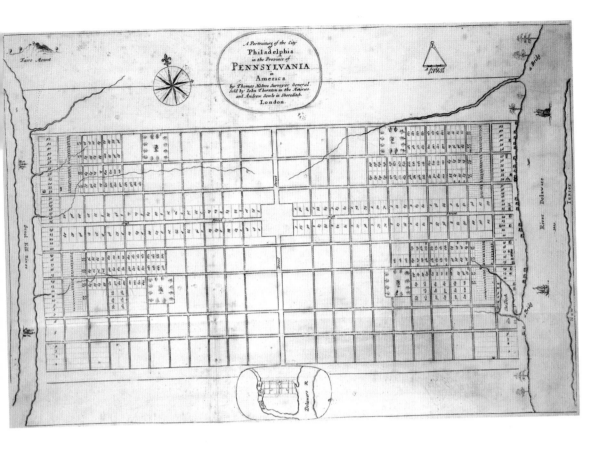

figure of the town so that the streets hereafter may be uniform down to the water from the country bounds; let the place for the storehouse be on the middle of the key, which will yet serve for markets and statehouses too. This may be ordered when I come, only let the houses be built in a line, or upon a line.'[14]

When Penn arrived, he extended Holme's original chequerboard layout across the peninsula. The Holme–Penn plan bears resemblances to that of Richard Newcourt for London; the fact that Penn had witnessed both the plague and the fire there is manifest in his own advice concerning Philadelphia, that 'every house be placed, if the person pleases, in the middle of its plot, as to the breadth way of it, so that there may be ground on each side for gardens, or orchards, or fields, that it may be a green country town, which will never be burnt, and always be wholesome'.[15] Although inhabited primarily by Quakers and Mennonites during Penn's day, the town was soon to be appreciated by people of all different faiths and walks of life.

New Ebenezer, founded in 1736, also offered a new – and orthogonally arranged – homeland for a group of Salzburgers. Similarly, when William Byrd hoped to appeal to the religious and utopian sentiments of potential immigrants from Switzerland, he depicted a place provocatively named Eden, Virginia, showing both a basic urban design (a central public square surrounded by private lots) and its possible cloned repetition across the countryside. The Moravian Church, founded in the east of Bohemia, experienced a revival which commenced in Germany after almost total annihilation during the Thirty Years' War in the early seventeenth century. A group threatened with further persecution in the early eighteenth century, led by the carpenter Christian David, fled to Saxony, where it built the town of Herrnhut in 1722–27 on a site presented by Count Zinzendorf. This provided the prototype for a number of other settlements in Germany, England, Ireland, North and South America and elsewhere during the eighteenth century. Their villages usually boasted a square ground plan with a chapel, housing, schools, shops and workshops. (It is typical of the cross-fertilization of ideas that the settlements of these German Protestants inspired much curiosity and admiration among utopians such as

A Portraiture of the City of Philadelphia in the Province of Pennsylvania in America. Engraving after a drawing by Thomas Holme (1682) in William Penn, A Further Account of the Province of Pennsylvania and Its Improvements, London, 1685. British Library, London, Prints and Photographs

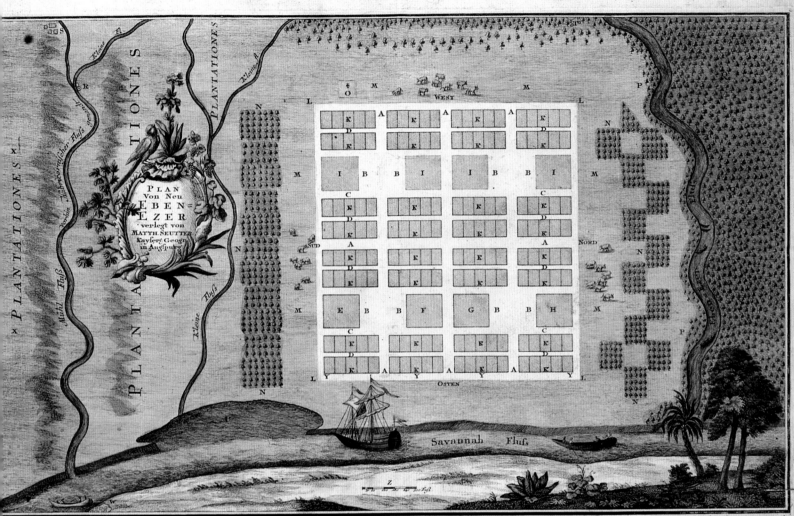

John Minter Morgan and James Silk Buckingham, who will be mentioned in the next chapter.) The Separatists, originally from Württemberg in Germany, arrived in America in 1817 under the leadership of Joseph Bimeler. In their chequerboard town of Zoar, in eastern Ohio, they planted a large garden whose plan reflected their religious inspiration: a central spruce tree symbolized Salvation, twelve surrounding trees represented the apostles and radiating routes led to Righteousness or Temptation.

The Church of Jesus Christ of Latter-Day Saints, more commonly known as the Mormons, formed large agglomerations, of which Salt Lake City, founded in 1848, was the most important. Joseph Smith, who had founded the Church in 1830, drew up guidelines for the City of Zion in 1833. Later Mormon settlements, such as Far West and Nauvoo, were all based on it. Like most ideal-city schemes, Smith's plan and doctrine was intended to achieve global domination. The grid layout of Mormon towns may not seem unusual at first sight – given the American context – but Smith's initial square model surrounded by agricultural lands was probably based directly upon biblical descriptions of the cities of the Levites[16] and Ezekiel's proposals for the construction of Jerusalem.[17]

The Shakers, previously known as the 'Shaking Quakers' on account of their frenetic religious

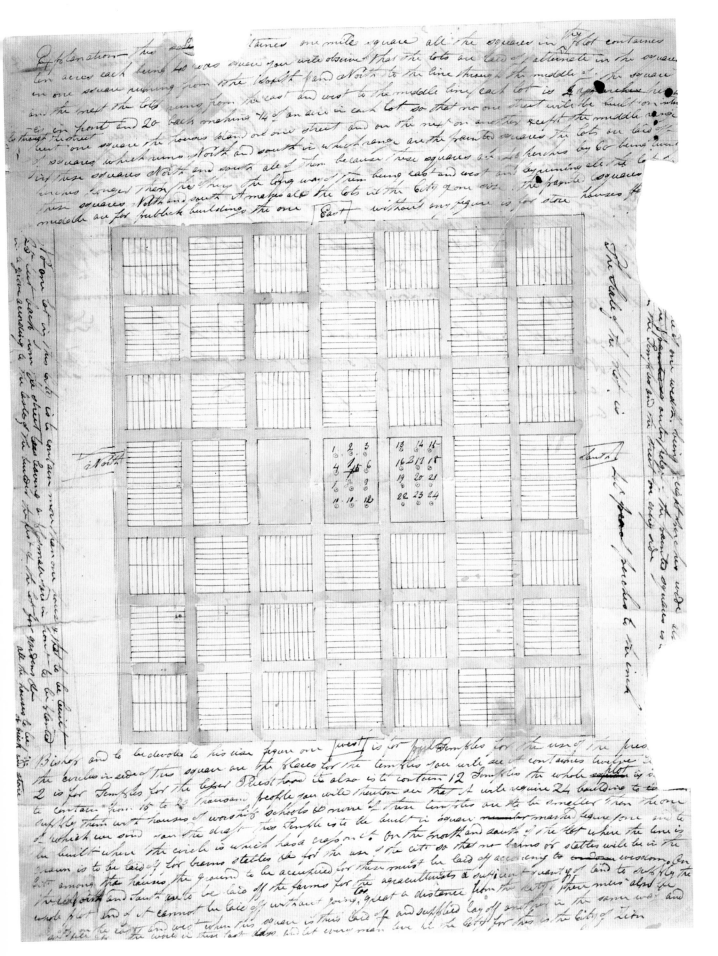

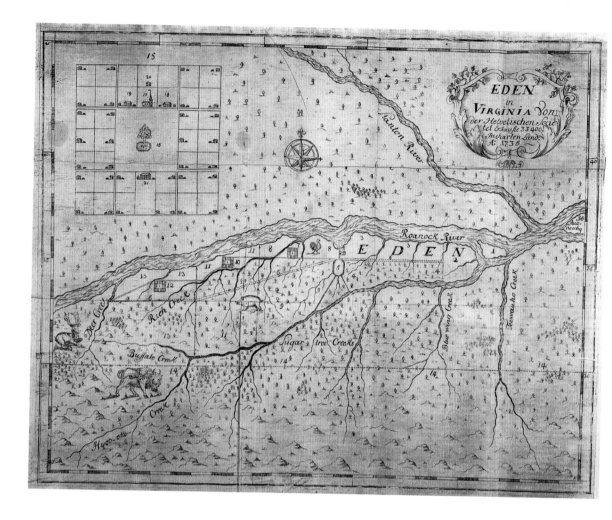

Joseph Smith, *Plat of Zion City*, 1833. Manuscript plan of the ideal Mormon city, with descriptive text. Church of Jesus Christ of Latter Day Saints, Salt Lake City, Utah, Historical Department

Map of Eden in Virginia with a plan of one of the proposed towns, 1736, in William Byrd, *Neu-gefundenes Eden. Oder: Aussfuehrlicher Bericht von Sud- und Nord-Carolina, Pensilphania, Mary Land & Virginia ...*, Helvetische Societät, 1737. John Carter Brown Library, Brown University, Providence, Rhode Island

dances, were founded by Mother Ann Lee and settled their first community in America a few miles north of Albany, New York, in 1776. They established a number of colonies dispersed across the country. By 1820 they had settled sixteen major communities – which they considered to be realizations of New Jerusalem since they believed the millennium had already begun – in nine states stretching from Maine to Kentucky. Although they usually built their villages in locations which had been partly developed, so that the basic division into roadways, fields and so forth was already fixed, their settlements bore a number of common characteristics. Shaker villages followed a linear plan with communal structures flanking a central roadway and communal land stretching back beyond the constructions. Strict instructions regarding the design of buildings and objects of everyday use had been tabulated in the 'Millennial Laws' of 1821 which prescribed the right angle as the basis of all

planning (even bread was cut into cubes or at right angles). The buildings were planned according to identified needs and arranged by function, the church near to the dwelling (where as many as a hundred people slept and ate), the laundry near to the well house and the barns near to the brethren's workshops, and they were painted in different colours, with white (the most expensive paint) usually reserved for the community's meeting house. They were placed more closely together than in traditional secular villages in order to encourage communication. The churches were built with Dutch-style gambrel roofs to avoid interior partitions and allow for freer movement during their dances. In response to their beliefs in celibacy and the equality of the sexes, the churches and communal dwellings had double doorways and flights of stairs which the brethren and sisters could use simultaneously, separately but equally. Beauty was considered a derivative of simplicity and functional-

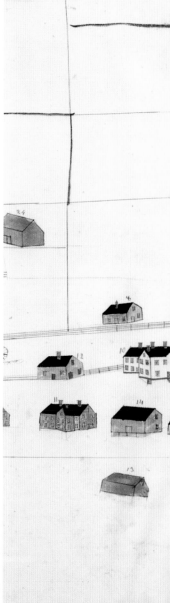

Charles F. Priest, *The Shaker Village at Harvard,* plan of the first community, 1833. Library of Congress, Washington, DC, Geography and Maps Division

ity, while superfluous, purposeless decorative elements were forbidden, as the Millennial Laws stated:

> 1. *Beadings, mouldings and cornices, which are merely for fancy may not be made by Believers.*
> 2. *Odd or fanciful styles of architecture, may not be used among Believers, neither should any deviate widely from the common styles of building among Believers, without the union of the Ministry.*[18]

It is curiously contradictory that while the naïve documentary illustrations of their villages (combining an isometric plan of the site with elevations shown from different vantage points and perspectives) suggest the gospel kindred's isolation from outside artistic influences, their buildings and objects indicate their ideological proximity to the Transcendentalists who were active in Concord, Massachusetts, near to some of the early Quaker communities. Outside of the architectural mainstream, Transcendentalism

grouped together a number of literary and architectural theorists in America from the 1830s throughout the nineteenth century and included major figures such as Ralph Waldo Emerson, Henry David Thoreau and Horatio Greenough. Their influence can be traced directly through to the Chicago School. Greenough called for a new style of architecture inspired by the laws of nature, and planned, like an organic skeleton covered with skin, from the inside out. The beauty of the style would derive from its optimization of function and, reduced to its essentials, it would be totally or partially free of ornament. Again taking God's world as his source of inspiration, Greenough also proposed standardized solutions for specific functions. The step was not so great from here, via Louis Sullivan's famous expression, 'Form follows function', to the functionalism of the twentieth century.

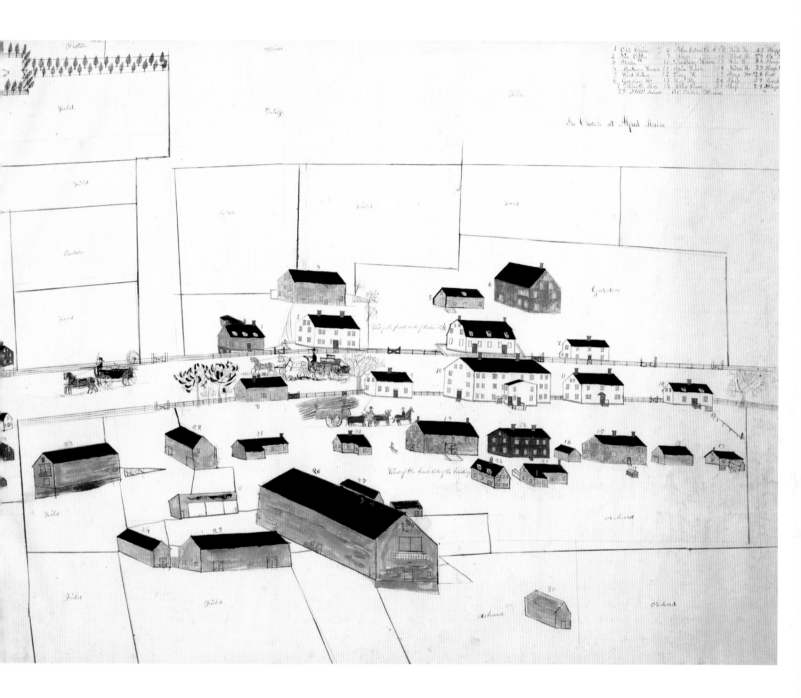

Attributed to Joshua H. Bussell, The Shaker Community at Alfred, Maine, c. 1848. Museum of Fine Arts, Boston, Gift of Dr. J. J. G. McCue

For many other groups, too, the Americas were to appear as the perfect location for the realization of a whole spectrum of ideal societies originating in Europe. Increasingly, however, the Americas, both north and south, were to generate – and export – their own ideals.

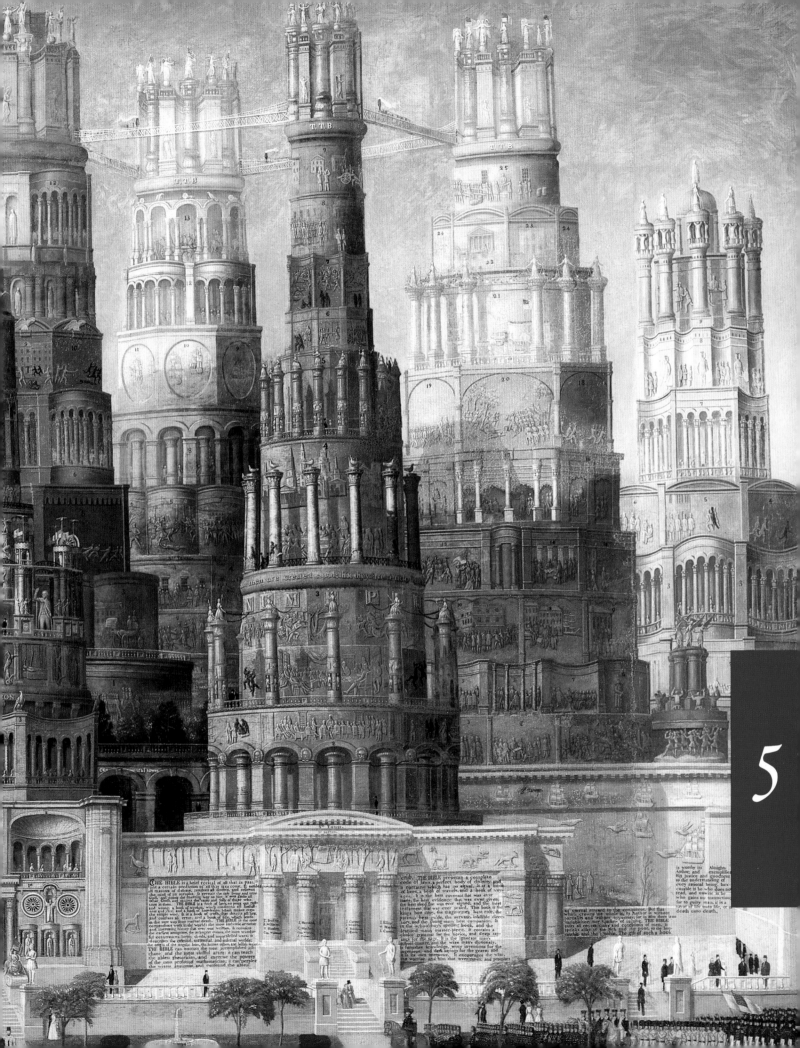

5

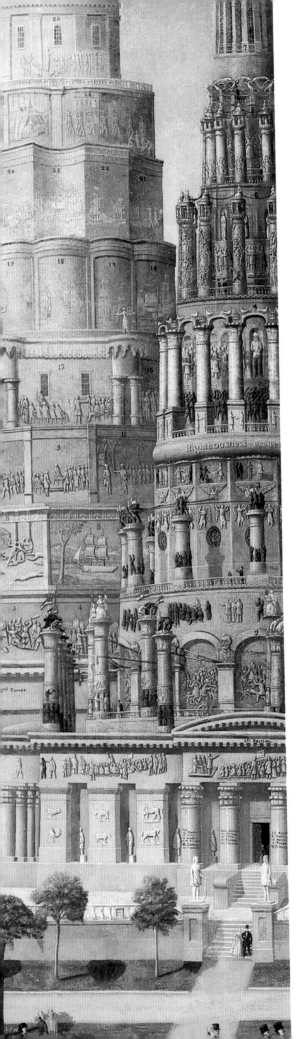

The Horizons of Knowledge

Over the centuries, shrouds of superstition and prejudice were lifted as scientific breakthroughs and a thirst for knowledge, culminating in the Enlightenment, contributed to a deeper understanding of the mysteries of the world and a belief in the promise that progress would provide the key to a better life. The eighteenth century witnessed revolutions in France and America and the increasing shift of the utopian ambition from the virtual to the real domain. In the literary field, the uchronic work of literature consolidated the utopian world's new position in a distant time – usually the future – while in the architectural domain, Ledoux sought to create the perfect setting for his ideal society in his vision of a city at Chaux.

Etienne-Louis Boullée, *Project for the extension of the Bibliothèque Nationale, c.*1780. *Bibliothèque Nationale de France, Paris, Cabinet des Estampes*

Pages 98–100
Erastus Salisbury Field, *Historical Monument of the American Republic,* 1876. *Museum of Fine Arts, Springfield, Mass., The Morgan Wesson Memorial Collection*

WORSHIP OF PROGRESS AND NATURE

In an earlier chapter, we recalled Jacob Burckhardt's description of the disintegration of a veil of faith and illusion that covered human consciousness during the transition from the Middle Ages to the Renaissance. The sixteenth and seventeenth centuries, however, were still burdened by much – albeit slowly dissipating – darkness, prejudice and superstition. Deep religious faith and belief in history as related in the Bible, along with the Renaissance idealization of the classical age, dominated the Europeans' world view. The lifting of shrouds of mystery and the broadening of intellectual horizons were ongoing processes which peaked at certain periods. The fifteenth century and the eighteenth, characterized by its supreme inquisitiveness, were such ages. Little by little, during the centuries that followed the Renaissance, the foundations of many of man's convictions regarding his place upon earth and within the universe were shaken. The geocentricity of the universe had been questioned by Copernicus from the early sixteenth century and the chronology of the Old Testament was challenged by geological discov-

eries of fossils or evidence of continental movements. The impact of some of the fruits of investigation – of which Newton's law of universal gravitation published in 1685 clearly appears as one of the most impressive – must indeed have been great. Scientific observation and experimentation slowly demystified the world; empirical knowledge waged war against obscurantism.

Sir Francis Bacon placed a great value – extraordinary by comparison to previous utopian literature – upon knowledge and science in *New Atlantis* (1627), where they are the very driving forces of society. As we have seen, Bacon's work precipitated the creation of the Royal Society in London in 1660 and ushered in a new era of utopian writing. Bacon does not tell us about the urban or rural planning in New Atlantis but only about the places designed for experimentation, for social organization has now ceded its place to discovery as the key to a better world. European and Christian beliefs were further questioned as a result of a deepening familiarity with other civilizations, considered either 'primitive' as in the Americas or 'civilized' as in China – but in any case pagan. By around the 1730s, Christianity itself began to decline in the intellectual circles in England and France. An attitude of heightened curiosity and understanding typified the Enlightenment, which reached its climax in Paris during the middle of the eighteenth century. The Enlightenment was an ideological more than a political movement and, as Norman Hampson argues, though political change of the type seen in England in 1688 may have been envisaged, the overthrow of the traditional social hierarchy was certainly not part of the plan.[1] Ideas were hotly debated in the *salons.* Information and knowledge were gathered in libraries, organized in encyclopedias[2] and made available to increasingly literate populations via newspapers and periodicals.[3] James Keir described the atmosphere in the *Dictionary of Chemistry* of 1789: 'The diffusion of a general knowledge, and of a taste for science, over all classes of men, in every nation of Europe, or of European origin, seems to be the characteristic feature of the present age.'

Etienne-Louis Boullée, *Design for the façade of the National Assembly*, c.1780. Bibliothèque Nationale de France, Paris, Cabinet des Estampes

The corollary to this boundless belief in the power of science was an optimism about the future, a new faith in the inevitable benefits of progress, which formed one of the major traits of the eighteenth century – and was still a force to be reckoned with during the twentieth. To the enlightened mind, science and reason appeared able to resolve the most difficult of enigmas, to empower humankind to ameliorate its condition and to control its destiny. The future was embraced with enthusiasm by figures who saw technological and moral improvement marching in unison, such as Chastellux, in *De la félicité publique* (1772), and Condorcet, in *Esquisse d'un tableau historique des progrès de l'esprit humain* (1795). Condorcet enthused that 'no limit has been set to the improvement of human faculties, that the perfectibility of man is really boundless.... No doubt this progress may be more or less rapid, but there will never be any retrogression.'[4] Connected to this idea of progress was a shift in the perception of time. The biblical version of history, which dated the Creation to about 4004 BC, and belief in a static providential order had been steadily undermined by the procession of scientific breakthroughs. The future came to be conceived as a state of perpetual transformation. It was within this optimistic climate that the utopian literary tradition shifted gear dramatically with the publication of Sébastien Mercier's *L'An 2440. Rêve s'il en fut jamais* (1771), generally recognized as the first 'uchronic' work, i.e. one which places the ideal society elsewhere in time, rather than in space. Mercier describes Paris in the year 2440, when Louis XXXIV, respectful of the law and modest in his lifestyle, rules as a true father to his people, while the fretful ghost of Louis XIV haunts the ruins of his palace at Versailles. The elsewheres of most subsequent utopias were to be situated no longer in space but in time, and most frequently in the future.

Alongside those who were convinced that reason and scientific progress represented the keys to a better world, others believed that this lay in achieving conformity with the universal laws of nature. Theirs was perhaps the domain less of the head than of the heart. While differing upon details, they generally agreed that man in his natural state was bestowed with a simple goodness that was corrupted by his subjection to the artificial sophistication and other nefarious effects of civilization. Such ideas appeared in a number of eighteenth-century works such as Montesquieu's *Lettres persanes* (1721), in which two virtuous troglodyte families survive after the autodestruction of a greedy people, for they alone are invested with the natural morality which assures the good of the individual as of the group, without any need for laws. Morelly's *Code de la Nature* (1755) appreciated the integrity of the American Indians and proposed an egalitarian, property-free communist society, while Diderot's *Supplément au voyage de Bougainville* (1772) lauded the primitive goodness, disrupted by the French, of the Tahitian islanders. Restif de la Bretonne imagined egalitarian communities for both urban and rural people closer to home, often run along almost monastical lines, in which each member fulfilled a specific role in the functioning of society.[5] The Physiocrats, also praising the benefits of nature, differed considerably from most in this loose group in their defence of private property. Jean-Jacques Rousseau was of course the major advocate of ideas about the natural state of humankind. He reproved the corruption of civilized societies such as that of France and sought an ideal state – resembling perhaps his idealized vision of the democratic city-state of his native Geneva – in which moral values were superior and the individual could trustingly submit his personal will to that of the majority. Rousseau, who died in 1778, was posthumously lauded as the father of the French Revolution on account of the anti-monarchic argument of his major work, *Du Contrat social* (1762), which based government on the consent of the governed. For such thinkers, the creation of an ideal society did not require that people regress to a primitive state but that they become free of the artifices of civilization, that they get back into touch with the innocent nature embedded deeply within them and live together in harmony with the virtuous natural order. Already in 1726, Jonathan Swift had expressed his profound scepticism about such notions regarding the natural goodness of a fallen humankind in his famous satire *Gulliver's Travels*.

Questions of environmental determinism debated at this time were of obvious importance to those who harboured utopian aspirations and hoped that humankind could be 'uplifted' through the influences of education, social organization and the urban setting. John Locke in his *Essay Concerning Human Understanding* (1690), partly as a result of his observations of extra-European societies, had rejected Descartes' view that ideas were innate. His refusal to accept arbitrary authority and his reverence for facts of sense opened the road to a greater appreciation of the influence of external conditions upon members of society. Montesquieu, in *De l'Esprit des lois* (1748), demonstrated the interre-lation of different factors – political, geographical, economic, etc. – and their ability to both condition and reflect a given society.[6] Kant drew a distinction between perceptions of objects as they appear via the senses and judgement, thus revealing limita-tions in the theories of materialist determinism,

while David Hume in his *Treatise of Human Nature* (1739–40) showed that experience and reason are not necessarily connected. Etienne-Louis Boullée referred in his *Architecture, Essai sur l'art* to Mon-tesquieu, and the direct influence of the latter's ideas can be seen in the *architectures parlantes*, the eloquent architecture of Boullée and others in the final decades of the century. This maelstrom of ideas circulating during the eighteenth century forms the backdrop to the architectural developments of the time and the ideal-city designs of Claude-Nicolas Ledoux in particular; its consequences will continue to be felt throughout the two ensuing centuries.

THE ASCENT OF NEOCLASSICISM

Let us now turn our attention to the architecture and urban planning of the eighteenth century. The period opened with the exuberance of the Baroque and closed with the inspired restraint of Neoclassi-cism. These developments lie parallel to many of the ideological transformations already mentioned in our brief discussion of Enlightenment attitudes. The Baroque privileged the heteronomous principle of *enchaînement* whereby an urban composition, a building and all its components are indissociably linked in a continual flowing movement destined to reinforce the dominant social hierarchy in the eye of the spectator. Its link to the ideal cities of the Renais-sance and the discovery of perspective can be seen in, for example, its visual subjugation of an entire urban plan to a building (almost invariably the church or palace) in which supreme authority is vested. In most cases it was applied to urban districts rather than complete cities. A rare exception to this piecemeal approach in Europe was Louis XIV's seventeenth-century palace at Versailles upon which the whole city and the vast park converge, a paradigmatic example of Baroque town planning. Karlsruhe, built for Karl Wilhelm, Margrave of Baden-Durlach in 1715, provides a more modest

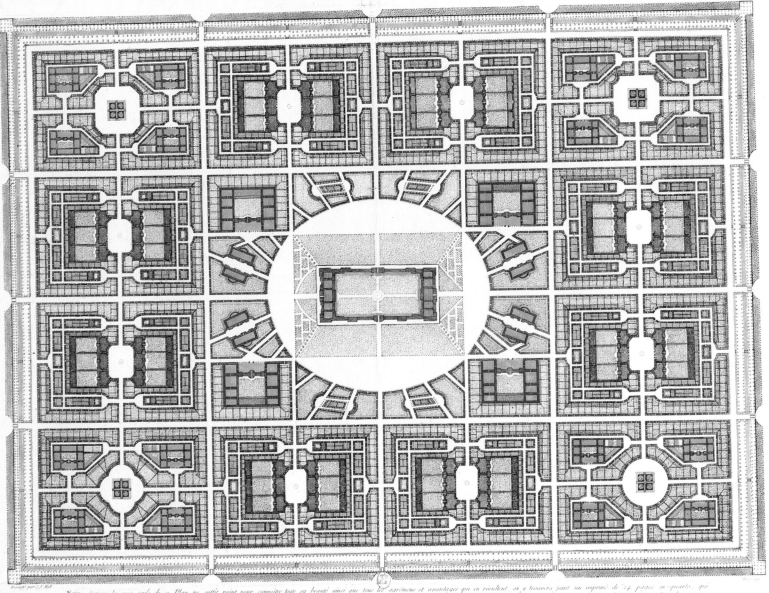

d'une Ville de cent mille ames, qui réunit tous les agrémens et avantages que l'on peut desirer.

Nota. Comme la vue seule de ce Plan ne suffit point pour connoître toute sa beauté ainsi que tous les agrémens et avantages qui en résultent, on y trouvera joint un imprimé de 27 pages in-quarto, qui non seulement donne le détail et la forme générale de chaque objet, mais encore le moyen de l'établir et exécuter en très peu de tems, avec peu de fond et aucunement à charge à l'État qui en adopte l'exécution.

instance. Pierre Patte published in *Monuments érigés en France à la gloire de Louis XV* (1765) a number of separate projects by architects such as Jacques-Ange Gabriel or Jacques-Germain Soufflot for Baroque *places royales* in honour of the king. However, he illustrated them as though they were distributed across the fabric of Paris. In so doing he indicated a dissatisfaction with the existing city which certain of his contemporaries were also expressing, suggested the need for a total rather than partial embellishment and fuelled the debate concerning such functional matters as communication. The city gradually came to be considered not just as a reflection of its prince's power but as a structure that must be distributed and organized as rationally as possible. Patte went on to set out guidelines for a city that he considered ideal from a primarily technical point of view in *Mémoires sur les objets les plus importants de l'architecture*: a hexagonal or octogonal city (for reasons of policing) with ample provision for transport, careful attention paid to water supplies and polluting activities banished to the suburbs. Again a

J.J. Moll, *Plan for a City for 100,000 Souls*, c.1809. Bibliothèque Nationale de France, Paris, Cartes et Plans

Giovanni Battista Piranesi, *Antiquities in the Via Appia*, in *Le Antichità romana*, Rome, 1756. Bibliothèque Nationale de France, Paris, Cabinet des Estampes

mix of Baroque and rational features can be distinguished in his proposal. In Britain, John Wood the Elder and his son John Wood the Younger's extension of Bath from 1728 to 1767, James Craig's Edinburgh New Town of 1766 and John Gwynn's unrealized proposals in *London and Westminster Improved* all typify this more comprehensive approach to town planning. One project of the nineteenth century deserves mention here, as it is situated within the logic of large-scale functional city embellishment of the eighteenth century. In 1802, Napoleon decided to found a new town in Brittany to be named Napoléonville but, despite even abortively starting its construction, a number of proposals for the city were rejected. J. J. Moll proposed an ideal city to the French emperor and also tried to convince the rulers of Austria and Russia to build one: a number of coloured drawings in the Bibliothèque Nationale de France illustrate Moll's plans for six model cities (of up to 100,000 citizens) and various combinations of their components. Their key characteristic appears to be their total flexibility, for they are intended to be applicable to any available site. The overall impression is of a

formalist approach to the city, which fails to convince the spectator that it would be the 'terrestrial paradise' to which its inventor openly aspired. Every field, as we have seen, came under scrutiny during this questioning age – architecture was no exception. The great authority of ancient Rome was re-examined and other sources were analysed too – Greek, Gothic, Chinese, Indian – resulting in publications such as *Antichità Romane* (1748) by Giovanni Battista Piranesi or *Gedanken über die Nachahmung der griechischen Werke* (1755) by Johann Joachim Winckelmann. In Piranesi's engravings, the archaeological concern for an accurate portrayal of actual remains is complemented by inventive and striking flights of fancy. Winckelmann professed to prefer the noble simplicity of Greek art above Roman. Classical architecture was reviewed in rational terms, whereby it was not just to be adopted arbitrarily as an unalterable absolute but only on verification of its being the best-adapted response to real building requirements. In England, Colin Campbell, author of *Vitruvius Britannicus*, was a key figure in this debate, pleading the necessity of judging 'truly of the Merit of Things by the Strength of Reason'. In Italy, the Carmelite Carlo Lodoli (whose writings were destroyed) explored a rational functionalism which reflected this return to fundamentals. In France, the Abbé de Cordemoy, in his *Nouveau traité de toute l'architecture* (1706), and the Abbé Laugier, author of an *Essai sur l'Architecture* (1752), similarly recoiled in the face of the illusionistic, plastic aspects of architecture and argued in favour of its true, functional elements. The most significant illustration of these ideas is surely that of the wooden hut of primitive man which appeared in the latter publication. Already appreciated by Vitruvius, this, the foundation of all building, appealed greatly to the Neoclassicists. Not only was it a supremely rational, functional construction, it also symbolized the powerful ideal of noble simplicity, thus satisfying two movements that characterized the century. 'Architecture ...,' proclaimed Sir Joshua Reynolds, 'applies itself, like music (and I believe we may add poetry) directly to the imagination, without the intervention of any kind of imitation.... In the hands of a man of genius, it is capable of inspiring sentiment, and of filling the mind with great and sublime ideas.'[7] Among its most inventive minds were Sir John Soane in England and Etienne-Louis Boullée and Claude-Nicolas Ledoux in France. 'The real talent of the architect,' wrote Boullée in his *Essai sur l'Art*, 'consists in presenting in his works the sublime attraction of poetry.'[8] Boullée and Ledoux were fascinated by the beauty of masses, of smooth bare surfaces free of unnecessary decoration (the 'sterile riches' of architecture in Boullée's words), the play of light and the shadows created by these simultaneously grand and simple, basic forms. In Boullée's magnificent Cenotaph for Isaac Newton, the tomb is placed at the centre of gravity of a massive sphere which represents the earth on the exterior and the universe on the interior. Light enters through the pierced surface in a manner resembling the stars in the heavens. An impressive tribute, indeed, to the great natural philosopher. At this time, a distinction was being made between the fields of architecture and engineering in France with the creation of the Ecole des Ponts et Chaussées by Turgot in 1774. This school trained engineers who applied a technical approach to the design of military construction, bridges, roads and so forth, and thus reduced considerably the domain of the architect. Indeed, architects comparing their talent to that of the poets may have coveted the exclusive right to provoke sublime emotions, but the great engineering feats of the next century were also to prove capable of inspiring such feelings.

CLAUDE-NICOLAS LEDOUX

Claude-Nicolas Ledoux is an intriguing character, embodying many of the rich complexities of the eighteenth century. He proposed two general schemes for an ideal city, although both his built and unbuilt production should be considered in its entirety in order to appreciate the ideal aspirations

Joseph Gandy, *Architectural Visions of Early Fancy in the Gay Morning of Youth and Dreams in the Evening of Life*, 1820. Sir John Soane's Museum, London

underpinning his work. Even if he did not support the French Revolution politically, and was indeed imprisoned for nurturing royalist sympathies, he shared many of the ideas of his contemporaries. His life was tumultuous and, despite the publication of a compilation of his designs accompanied by texts in 1804 under the title L'Architecture considérée sous le *rapport de l'art, des mœurs et de la législation* (referred to henceforth as *L'Architecture*), his work leaves plenty of room for speculation about his personal views and has become a source of revived interest among architects and architectural historians during the twentieth century.

Born into a relatively modest rural French family in

1736, Ledoux trained as an engraver and gleaned his knowledge of architecture from publications and from the example of his master, Jacques-François Blondel. After setting out on his architectural career with the decoration of the Godeau coffeehouse in 1762, Ledoux went on to design a number of luxurious residences for influential clients such as the Comtesse du Barry, the favourite of Louis XV, while simultaneously pursuing activities related to the rural management of water and forestry. In 1771, he was placed in charge of the saltworks of the Franche-Comté, Lorraine and Trois Evêchés areas of eastern France and commissioned, three years later, to build a complete new saltworks, the 'Saline Royale' at Arc-et-Senans, near Besançon. Ledoux broke with tradition by proposing that this be placed not at the source of the saline water, which could easily be transported by pipeline, but close to the resource required to extract the salt, the forest of Chaux. This practical breakthrough indicates the common sense and concern with efficiency that characterize his approach in the design of the manufacture in general. He presented a first proposal to the king in 1774, before the precise location had been settled upon, which combined a fairly traditional square plan with a number of innovations

such as the covered diagonal galleries intended to facilitate communications. The continuity of his layout, however, favoured not only the movement of goods and people but also the spread of fire, a risk underlined by the disastrous conflagration in Paris' Hôtel-Dieu hospital in 1772. It was therefore rejected and replaced by a second one for a now selected site, which grouped a number of autonomous buildings upon a semi-elliptical plan, resembling an antique amphitheatre. Not only was the problem of fire addressed but the optimal use of the winds would improve the movement of the smoky air. Construction began in 1775 and was completed in 1778; the buildings now figure upon Unesco's World Heritage list. The walled complex grouped together many separate but interdependent services in as organized a way as seemed possible, and announces spatially the division of labour to which Adam Smith referred in *An Inquiry into the Nature and Causes of the Wealth of Nations* (1776): 'The greatest improvement in the productive powers of labour, and the greater part of the skill, dexterity, and judgement with which it is anywhere directed, or applied, seem to have been the effects of the division of labour.' The director's apartment and offices, accounting rooms and the chapel were all

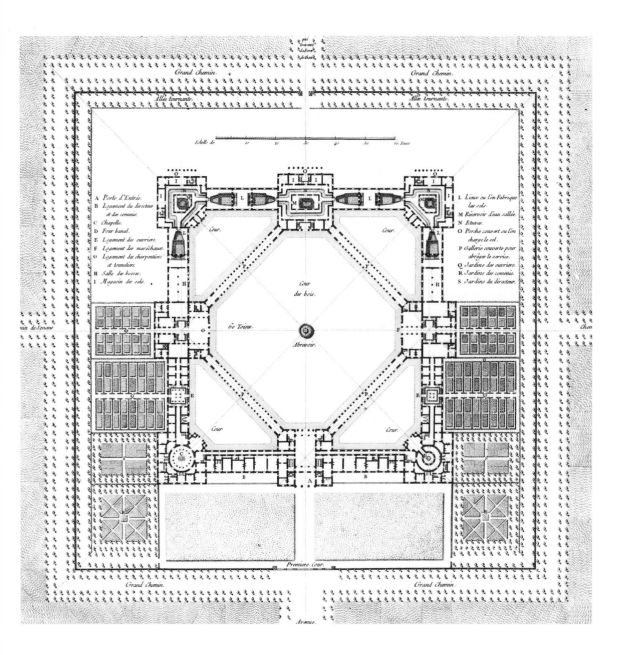

placed in the central building upon the diameter. This was flanked by two enormous buildings that housed the giant cauldrons in which the brine was heated and by two further pavilions where the controllers worked. The semi-ellipse was occupied by five similar constructions: four were home to 200 workers and their families and the central one contained the monumental entrance, guardians' quarters, a bakery, a forge, a cell, lodgings for artisans and so forth. The saltworks were run along strict hierarchical lines with workers toiling for twelve hours a day in appalling and dangerous conditions, supplementing their meagre incomes by growing vegetables in the kitchen gardens and possessing little if any property.

Ledoux's ambitions did not stop at the saltworks, however. In *L'Architecture* we find numerous other designs which indicate that they only formed the core of his intentions for the region. During the 1780s, he went on to draw up projects for a number of people and activities linked to the local economy: houses and workshops for woodcutters, for forest guards, for the directors of the Loue river and so on. Other imaginary constructions played a less immediately practical role: a 'Pacifère' and a 'Panarétéon' (these were Ledoux neologisms), a Temple of

Claude-Nicolas Ledoux, *First project for the Saltworks at Chaux*, in *L'Architecture considérée sous le rapport de l'art, des mœurs et de la législation*, Paris, 1804. Bibliothèque Royale de Belgique, Brussels, Département des Imprimés

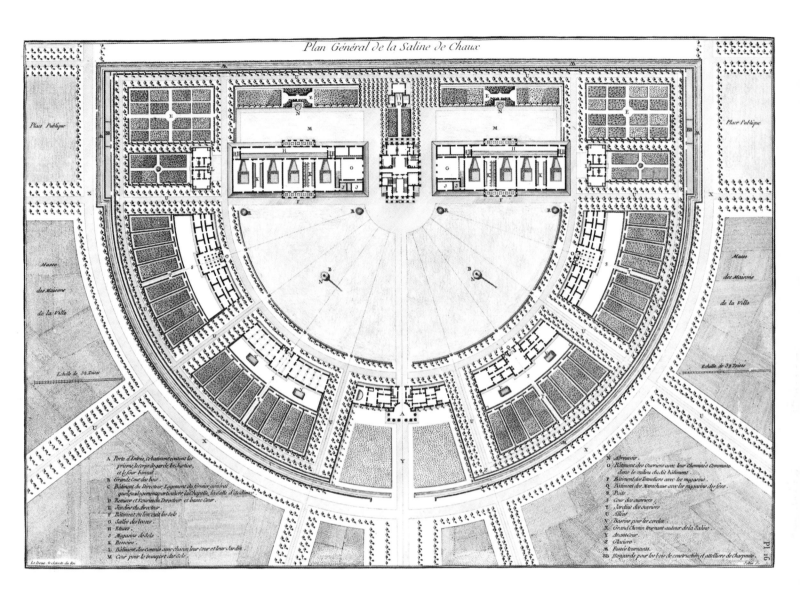

Claude-Nicolas Ledoux, *General plan of the Saltworks at Chaux*, in *L'Architecture considérée sous le rapport de l'art, des mœurs et de la législation*, Paris, 1804. Bibliothèque Royale de Belgique, Brussels, Département des Imprimés

Memory and a House of Union. Above all, he harboured the dream of building a complete city at Chaux of which the saltworks would comprise the industrial heart and into which his many designs might be integrated. Such hopes were far from unrealistic in this strategic area of France, where two other new towns, Versoix and Carouge, near Geneva, had been projected from the 1770s. Two plates in his work of 1804 provide different versions of his scheme for an ideal city at Chaux. The '*Carte des environs de la saline de Chaux*' shows the layout of the saltworks extended to complete the ellipse, contains a town hall and military barracks and is surrounded by a wall beyond which a parish church, law courts, public baths and housing are all indicated, as well as a number of constructions that actually existed in

the landscape. In the '*Vue perspective de la ville de Chaux*', probably dating from 1780–84, however, the saltworks and barracks are no longer enclosed within a wall. Ledoux appears to have given freer rein to his imagination regarding the surrounding buildings scattered across the countryside: an important church as well as some minor ones, a market, a commercial exchange, public baths, private residences. The plan has been compared to those of the garden-city movement a century later. From 1784, Ledoux saw the construction of the majority of his designs for 45 monumental tollgates (*barrières*) – of which only four survive – delimiting the French capital. These were to prove the principal, but not only, reason for the general opprobrium that surrounded the architect during the years of the Revolution.

This important programme was intended not only to control more efficiently the movement of goods into the city but also to tighten up security in several Parisian faubourgs. Over 800 workers dealing with customs were to be accommodated in the new buildings, a double wall and an avenue were to encircle the city, and Ledoux even designed seven large state taverns to replace the unruly drinking houses on the city's periphery and a House of Pleasure for legalized prostitution at Montmartre. (This latter reminds us of the Parthénions, the houses for prostitutes envisaged by Restif de la Bretonne in the *Pornographe*, 1769.) Author of these detested tollgates and former protégé of Madame du Barry, Ledoux found himself virtually without employment during the years of the Revolution and was imprisoned for over a year from December 1793. The last years of his life were devoted to the preparation of the vast compilation of his work from 1769 to 1789, *L'Architecture*, which was published in 1804, two years before his death.[9] He dedicated it to the Czar of Russia, stating that 'All the peoples of the earth will say to the Alexander of the North: You are a man! since you wish to embrace a social system which will contribute to the happiness of humankind.' Ledoux's achievements certainly have their authoritarian side. The entire scheme for Paris from the tollgates to the taverns can be interpreted as a means to control and police a section of the urban population. Surveillance is a recurrent concern in much of his work, and it is clear that in both designs for the saltworks the question of visual control was paramount. 'The supervisor, placed at the centre of the lines, can observe at a single glance all the details in his charge,' wrote Ledoux of his first scheme.[10] In the second, not only did the guardian's building at the entrance oversee the passage of every person and item, but from the window in the director's house, symbolizing the power of the

Crown, the workers could be watched in their every outdoor movement within the confines of the saltworks. The central observation tower was an old device, as we have already seen, and it was not long before Jeremy Bentham was to publish his scheme for the Panopticon. This English philosopher, jurist and author of *Principles of Morals and Legislation* (1789), sought to establish codes of law and morality whose basis was the greatest happiness for the greatest number. For many years, Bentham negotiated with the English government in the hope of seeing a Panopticon erected for convicts, a radial building working on the principle of central observation inspired by a design by his brother Samuel. Ledoux believed that architecture had the capacity to influence human behaviour. He wrote of the architect that, 'Everything is within his realm – politics, morality, legislation, worship, government',[11] and referred to him as 'rival to the Creator'.[12] Indeed the very title of his major publication indicates the extent of his ambition, for it considers architecture with respect to not only art but also morals and legislation. He sought to create the physical environment that would house an ideal society whose nature is to be surmised from a number of clues in his somewhat convoluted and verbose texts and his numerous illustrations. In his unrealized designs one can discern a desire to create an environment in accordance with the virtuous laws of natural order, a world in which Rousseau or Restif may have felt at home. In his introduction to *L'Architecture*, he wrote of the *cenobies*, his almost conventual establishments in the woodlands: 'We can become virtuous or viceful, like the rough or the smooth pebble, through the contact with those who surround us; happiness and wellbeing can thus be found in the attractive sensation of communal pleasures, hence those cenobies built within the shade of tranquil woods, where sages, living

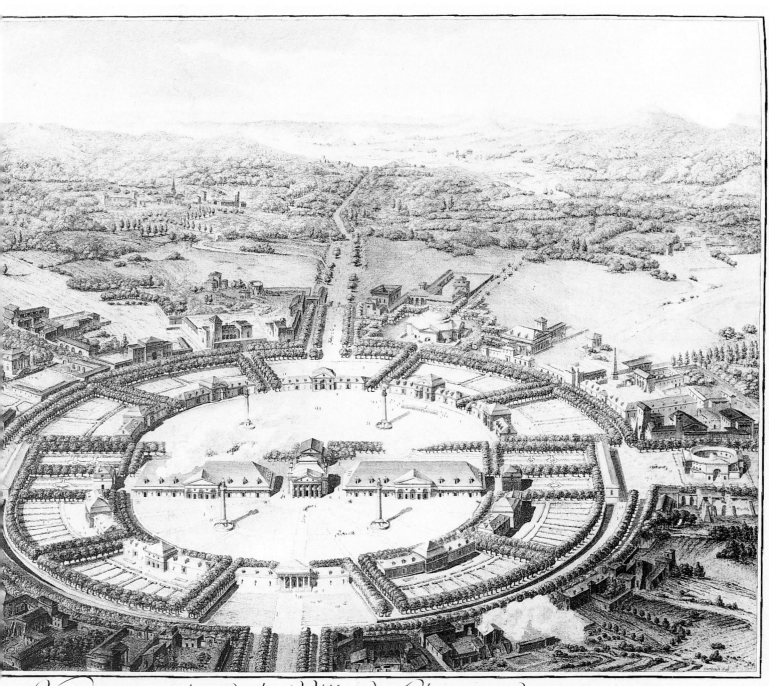

Vue perspective de la Ville de Chaux

*Perspective view of the City of Chaux.
Engraving by Berthault after Claude-Nicolas
Ledoux, in* L'Architecture considérée sous le
rapport de l'art, des mœurs et de la législation, *Paris, 1804. Bibliothèque Royale de Belgique,
Brussels, Département des Imprimés*

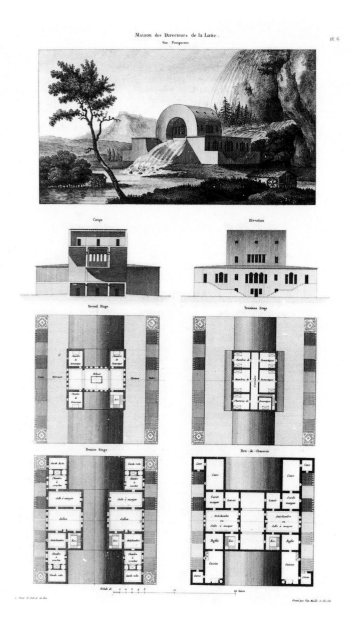

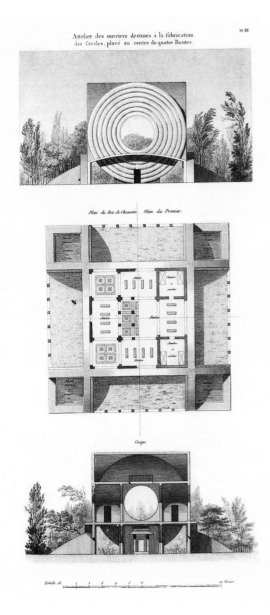

Claude-Nicolas Ledoux, *Inspectors' House at the source of the Loue* and *Cooper's workshop*, in *L'Architecture considérée sous le rapport de l'art, des mœurs et de la législation*, Paris, 1804. Bibliothèque Royale de Belgique, Brussels, Département des Imprimés

together according to the simple laws of nature, seek to realize the desirable felicity of the fabulous times of the golden age.'[13] Influences of the freemasons have also been noted in his work.[14] In a great many of Ledoux's designs, we are aware of the importance of sociable behaviour and a shared joy in living and working within a tightly knit community. Communal halls were projected in the residential areas within the saltworks but also in many of the external buildings designed for rural workers. The cubic House of Union was dedicated to virtuous and universal fraternity, for 'Union,' noted Ledoux, 'is the source of happiness', and is 'necessary for the maintenance of order'.[15] The citizens of his world would learn to behave righteously and reasonably thanks to the influence of edifices like the House of Education, the 'Panarétéon' which was dedicated to moral education and the 'Oikema', a House of Passion which was intended to lead the young onto the road of virtue via that of depravation! Misbehaviour would be judged in the 'Pacifère', a key building devoted to justice, where conciliation was preferred to punishment. His belief in determinism is clear both in his choice of the social functions of his projected buildings and in his employment of *architecture parlante*. Not only did he place inscrip-

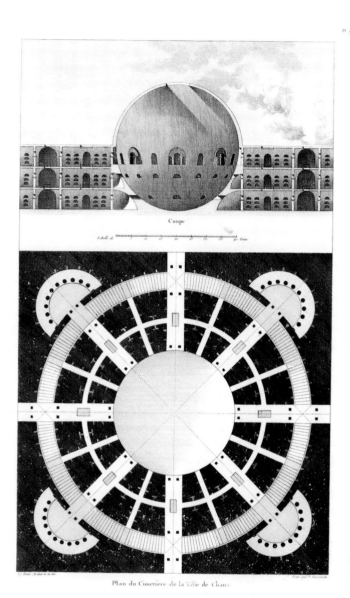

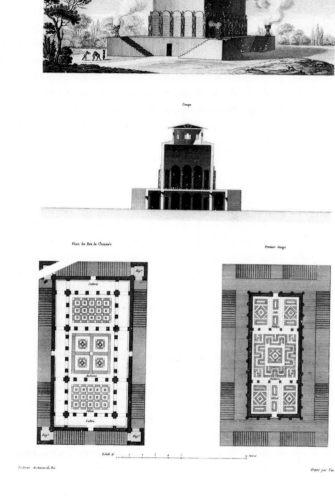

Claude-Nicolas Ledoux, *Cemetery and Palace of Concord (Pacifère)*, in *L'Architecture considérée sous le rapport de l'art, des mœurs et de la législation*, Paris, 1804. Bibliothèque Royale de Belgique, Brussels, Département des Imprimés

tions on certain of his constructions, such as the House of Union – in a tradition which we have already encountered in, for example, Campanella's *Civitas Solis*, and which will re-emerge in twentieth-century, post-revolutionary Russia – but he literally created forms which conveyed information about their function and provoked emotions. For literacy may have been on the increase at this time, but the vast majority of the French population still could not read. Thus the 'Oikema' took the form, in plan, of a phallus and the hoopmakers' workshop boasted circular designs on its façade, while in projects such as those for a prison at Aix or a cemetery at Chaux,

he revelled in the creation of an atmosphere of sublime terror.

Ledoux's ideal world certainly set a high value on fraternity and morality, but would it have been truly egalitarian, an architectural premonition of the Equality proclaimed by the French Revolution? He did indeed propose monumental structures for the most humble dwellings as for the most prestigious; Louis XV rejected the first proposal for the saltworks not only because of the fire hazard it represented but also on account of its unprecedented architectural grandeur, shocking to a king who was used to seeing columns employed for palaces and temples but not

for factories. Ledoux's use of such elements in buildings destined for a variety of functions and occupants may have been perceived superficially as uniformly grand without distinction from one case to another. However, his treatment differed from one particular structure to another. He sought above all to create forms and elements which expressed each building's character, capturing the true essence and purpose of each piece of architecture during a century in which masks and illusions were being peeled away one by one. Ledoux, rather than wanting to eliminate social hierarchy and replace it by an egalitarian society, sought, it would seem fair to say, to glorify every rung of the social ladder without displacing it. On the title plate of the first volume of L'Architecture, he qualified his list of the towns and buildings illustrated in it as a collection of those employed in the 'social order'. The saltworks was organized according to a strict hierarchy. In his theatre at Besançon, he replaced the traditional system of lodges for the nobility and a standing area for the populace in the pit, considered by many to be

a spatial invitation to licentious behaviour, by an amphitheatrical plan with a highly stratified arrangement of places according to rank. Thus members of society could be clearly seen while fully appreciating the spectacle both visually and acoustically.

In the context of this debate about Ledoux's work and its relationship to the changes occurring in France in the later decades of the eighteenth century, the contribution of the architectural historian Emil Kaufmann is of importance. In Von Ledoux bis Le Corbusier. Ursprung und Entwicklung der Autonomen Architektur, written in 1933, Kaufmann set out to establish Ledoux as the principal initiator of autonomous architecture and hence of the Modern Movement. Published in Austria within the context of a neighbouring, burgeoning Nazi regime, this book is testimony to the courage of its author since it endowed contemporary architects such as Le Corbusier and Gropius – whom the National Socialists were to castigate as degenerate – with a historical 'respectability' by placing them within a continuum that included much-admired figures such as Karl Friedrich Schinkel. For Kaufmann, who contributed greatly to Ledoux's reinstatement working from the formal aspects of his production, the Frenchman was the very embodiment of the transition from Baroque to Modern architecture, the built reflection of the social changes brought about by the French Revolution.

Ledoux's architecture represents a melting-pot of old and new, and he was not alone in questioning the tenets of the Baroque. Others, such as Lodoli or Laugier, had already been setting the stage, while Boullée's oeuvre, though he did not design an ideal city strictly speaking, was of comparable stature and significance in this debate. Formally, in his saltworks, despite filling the space with a series of freestanding buildings in a modern manner, Ledoux continued to define a public place not so far from the Baroque through their proximity and arrangement upon the semi-ellipse. Indeed he did so theatrically, creating an urban stage upon which all members of the community visibly acted out the tasks to which they had been assigned. Each element was simultaneously independent and in unison in a manner echoing Rousseau's social contract. He efficiently arranged each of the constituents that enabled the enterprise to function smoothly according to a logic applicable to an entire city or society, and endowed them, by

Jean-Jacques Lequeu, *Monument to the sovereignty of the people*, 1793–94, and *Symbolic order*, 1789. Bibliothèque Nationale de France, Paris, Cabinet des Estampes

A. Entablement et frise ou s'trouvent attachés à demie bosse des Genies fleuronnés entrelassés avec des rinceaux de feuillages, armés de fusils, pistolets, lyres &c. s'bassent ce monstre d'une énorme grandeur et d'une forme effroyable qui parut vers le 14 juillet près le palais du Souverain. Cette Bête hideuse à mille têtes humaines vomissant le feu et la flame, mêlée dans fumée noire, semblait se nourrir du Sang des français.

B. 1 Bustes en rond de bosse qui portent sur un pied-douche et un pied destal, représentant les uns les Seigneurs aristocrates, les despotes fugitifs, les autres leurs Complices Subalternes, tous Criminels de leze-Nation, en Chaines /.

Q. R. Rosette de la culasse du Canon et bombe qui éclattent.

of Independence, 'The Thirteen United States of America' that had secured emancipation from British sovereignty proclaimed: 'We hold these truths to be self-evident, that all men are created equal, that they are endowed by their Creator with certain inalienable Rights, among these are Life, Liberty and the pursuit of Happiness.' Humankind's ability to take events into its own hands and to fashion its future was now proven. The year 1789 saw the outbreak of the French Revolution. Mercier professed to have predicted the events of the French Revolution in his *L'An 2440* (a slightly exaggerated claim since he did not overthrow the monarchy in his book). The Revolution proclaimed its total break with the past in a truly utopian manner with its new calendar, new laws, new celebrations and so forth, but the rupture was relative and Robespierre defended the inalienable right to property. Meanwhile, deep transformation of another nature was under way: the industrial revolution. Though its origins lay in the eighteenth century, its impact on the face of Europe was to be felt primarily during the nineteenth.

removing their masks and revealing their purpose, with an architectural honesty and dignity. His saltworks and his designs for the ideal city are less a premonition of an egalitarian or democratic society than that of an industrialized one intermingled with his dream of accommodating a virtuous, moral world governed according to the laws of nature.

From 1775 to 1781 the American War of Independence was waged, and in 1783, in the Declaration

6

The Search for Order in the Age of Great Cities

'Our age is predominantly the age of great cities,' wrote the British historian Robert Vaughan in 1843.[1] The nineteenth century was characterized by the development of the industrial process and the growth of the large urban conglomeration, primarily in Europe and the United States of America. The city was viewed by many as chaotic, generating an unjust and dehumanized society, to which orderly utopian alternatives were proposed in works of literature, model urban schemes and experimental communities. While a handful of utopians called for a rejection of industrialization itself, most sought to find harmony within its framework.

Philippe Jacques de Loutherbourg,
Coalbrookdale by Night, 1801.
Science Museum, London

Pages 118–120
Paul Signac, *Au temps d'harmonie*, 1893.
Mairie, Montreuil

FROM POLIS TO MEGAPOLIS

During the eighteenth century the European economy was predominantly agricultural, and industry operated along traditional lines. There were few large units of production such as van Robais's textile factory at Abbeville in France or the more substantial iron industry established by Peter the Great in the Urals before the last decades of the century. In England, the first large iron foundries, such as Coalbrookdale, so fascinating to Romantic painters as a symbol of the mouth of hell, appeared around 1780. At the end of the eighteenth century the earlier years of scientific experimentation gave birth to a veritable explosion of new inventions. Among these, Richard Arkwright's spinning frame of about 1770 is generally viewed as the starting-point for mass production: by 1790 England possessed some two hundred and France had eight, while Germany acquired its first in 1794. By the early nineteenth century, with England at its vanguard, the industrial revolution had really kicked into action. The initial enthusiasm with which industrialization had been greeted was soon to be offset by revelations of the darker, dehumanizing aspects of those new 'temples' where, in William Wordsworth's powerful words of 1810, 'is offered up / To gain, the massive idol of the realm / Perpetual sacrifice'.

The working conditions in the factories are well known and it suffices here to mention just one statistic to recall the extent of the horror: in England in 1802, the working day of a child (who was often employed from the age of five) was reduced to twelve hours! It became increasingly evident that the era of universal fraternity and equality promised in 1789 was far from being attained. The growing riches which, as Adam Smith had argued in his *Wealth of Nations*, would be the driving force behind modern society appeared to be reserved principally for those at the top of the social ladder. However, among those figures whom we shall now consider that sought an alternative to the situation around them, few were those who went so far as to criticize industrialization itself: the majority sought to build a new world within its framework. The machine, the epitome of progress, was almost invariably accepted: at worst, acknowledged as an inevitable reality or, at best, welcomed as the key to a better life. As we shall see later, this continued to be the case – indeed it was intensified – during the first half of the twentieth century. The exception to this general rule can be seen in the position of figures such as A. W. N. Pugin, John Ruskin and William Morris. Theirs was an increasingly difficult line to maintain, however, given the veritable tidal wave that industrialization represented. Even Morris, late in life, suggested that the machine should be mastered and used 'as an instrument for forcing on us better conditions of life'.[2]

In its wake, industrialization brought the mass exodus of people from the countryside in search of work and unprecedented urban demographic growth, described, again, by Wordsworth:

> At social Industry's command,
> How quick, how vast an increase! From the germ
> Of some poor hamlet, rapidly produced
> Here a huge town, continuous and compact,
> Hiding the face of the earth for leagues – and there,
> Where not an habitation stood before,
> Abodes of men irregularly massed
> Like trees in forests – spread through spacious tracts,
> O'er which the smoke of unremitting fires
> Hangs permanent, and plentiful as wreaths
> Of vapour glittering in the morning sun.

In the course of the century cities grew at a phenomenal pace, particularly from about 1850. A globe which counted no cities at all with a population of over a million at the century's outset had a dozen by its close.[3] In 1900, the largest were London (whose population topped the million mark in 1811 and had reached 6.5 million by 1900), Paris and New York. Alongside these record-breaking centres were countless others whose populations numbered

hundreds of thousands. Not only did long-established cities experience breakneck expansion, but numerous new towns sprang up around the novel industries, with the factory now replacing the church, palace or town hall as the key building. The growing gap between the bourgeoisie and the working class was reflected in the physical segregation of social classes within cities, as in London's West and East Ends. For vast numbers of urban dwellers, living and working conditions were appalling and overcrowding, pollution and poor or non-existent sanitation went hand in hand with

Gustave Doré, *A Street in Whitechapel*, in Louis Enault, *Londres et les Londoniens en 1875*, Paris, 1876. Bibliothèque Nationale de France, Paris, Département des Estampes

disease and poverty. The professional press, in this case *The Builder* in 1863, described towns in England's industrialized north, 'where the factory smoke pollutes the air, and the dye-houses poison the streams; where streets cannot well be described than as canals in wet weather: where it is difficult to get air at all, and impossible to get it untainted by the chimneys and sewers; where the refuse of a thickly populated district lies rotting in the open streets, and the gutters do duty for more than surface drainage'. During the course of the century, artists such as Gustave Doré used their media to lament this miserable picture. Authors like Charles Dickens, Victor Hugo, Eugène Sue and Emile Zola[4] expressed their outrage in fictional writings, while the situation in England was also described in works such as Sir Frederick Morton Eden's first sociological survey, *State of the Poor*, the 1842 *Report from the Poor Law Commissioners to the House of Lords*, and Friedrich Engels' *The Condition of the Working Class in England* (1845). In order to get to grips with so vast and so complex an urban and social scene, the century saw the development of the census, the survey and statistics. These no doubt helped to record and analyse a situation with the aim of improving it, but they engendered the identification of means and of types, tools which were the delight of the ideal-city planner who most often worked, as we have seen, in an abstract rather than a specific context. Thus, the new metropolises were viewed as chaotic on account of the conditions recounted above. Indeed, they had emerged at lightning speed, which prohibited the application of those ideas about the type of city required by the new industrial world, including functional questions of communications and sanitation, which had been tentatively considered in the eighteenth century, as mentioned earlier. The reality of this new stifling metropolis increasingly distanced from its neighbour, the countryside, proved dissatisfactory to people across a broad political spectrum. It did not even suit the requirements of the capitalist order of which it was the fruit. It is for this reason that, mid-century, Baron Haussmann subjected Paris to major surgery, cutting new axes into the existing fabric to improve communications (as well as facilitate policing) in the France of Napoleon III. He thus superimposed an innovative urban structure adapted to the requirements of the new economic forces upon the existing scene. His

Jean Gigoux, Portrait of Charles Fourier, 1853. Musée du Temps, Besançon

could almost be considered an ideal city, even though it is not a formula devoid of context but a vast programme materialized in stone, for it aimed to bring the existing city into line with the demands of a recently established economic order. We shall not dwell on Haussmann's Paris, however, despite its interest, but will instead consider some of the alternatives by utopian thinkers who sought to provoke changes which were not only urban but also social and economic. In many cases, they were socialists (although it is misleading to seek to establish too close a correspondence between any given political position and urban layout), and often they considered that a fairer distribution of land would provide the key to bridging the gap between rich and poor. The striking contrast between the densely built-up megapolis and the countryside was viewed as a major problem and the panoply of designs we shall consider all tried to install a new intimacy between the two, employing a variety of alternative formal patterns. Whereas Ruskin, Morris and Ebenezer Howard favoured small, dense urban units reminiscent of the pre-industrial town in which functions were mingled,

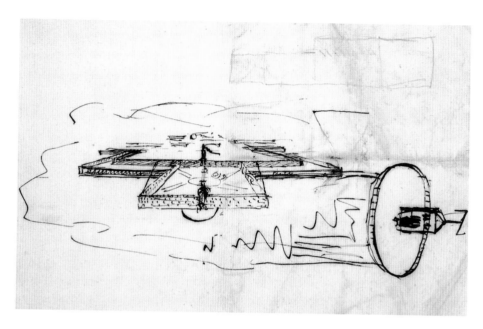

Anonymous, *View of a phalanstery,* 19th century. Musée du Temps, Besançon

Charles Fourier, *Aerial view of a phalanstery, c.* 1814. Archives Nationales, Paris

most were to separate them and to dispose large, individual buildings across the landscape, an autonomous architecture that had been announced by Ledoux's saltworks. The city became increasingly treated as a machine that must operate as efficiently as possible, a tendency which was to be accentuated during the twentieth century. The physical environments projected by the utopian thinkers of the nineteenth century are approached, for convenience's sake, through three groups here: experimental communities, literary descriptions and urban models. They are not to be taken as being rigorously separate, for many utopians followed more than one route. A word is required about Marx, for whom metropolises were the logical reflection of the economic structure, accepted as an intrinsic element of the historical momentum leading inevitably to the advent of communist society, the theatre for revolutionary change. Neither Engels nor Marx saw any merit in predicting or proposing a spatial environment for the world to come; they refused, as Marx said, to 'write cook-books for the kitchens of the future'.[5] Their speculation in this respect was limited to the suggestion that the distinction between town and country would be suppressed.

EXPERIMENTAL COMMUNITIES

In response to the plight of the urban poor, herded together in these cities so often viewed as evil, corrupting places, a number of people proposed, and indeed oversaw, the creation of experimental communities which – rather like some of the religious communities we have encountered previously – existed alongside the dominant structures, combining the source of work, housing and many services on one site. The majority of the experiments we shall consider were model industrial estates where the factory provided the wealth and employment which enabled the entire complex to survive. Many remained on paper, others incomplete or destined for a very short lifespan; very few managed to continue for decades like Godin's *Familistère* at Guise in northern France. Some have been almost forgotten, even though they caused a stir at the time of their conception. Among these lesser-known examples could be included, for example, the large new port at Tremadoc in Wales, the dream of William Madocks. His unsuccessful venture was described in Thomas Love Peacock's novel *Headlong Hall,* in which philosophers visiting his site discuss the pros and cons of industrialization: in as early as 1816, the ability of the industrial process to create wealth, scientific advance and employment was weighed up against the dehumanizing effect which turns people into 'mere automata, component parts of the enormous machines which administer to the pampered attitudes of the few'. Their creators emerged from a variety of backgrounds and intellectual points of departure, and it is obviously difficult to attempt to position them all upon an ideological spectrum. In some cases, their motivation was as much practical as altruistic (if not more so), based upon a belief that better treatment of employees would render them more productive. Such figures showed little more desire to redistribute wealth and transform society than Haussmann. Henri de Gorge Legrand, for example, the capitalist entrepreneur behind the important industrial concern, Le Grand

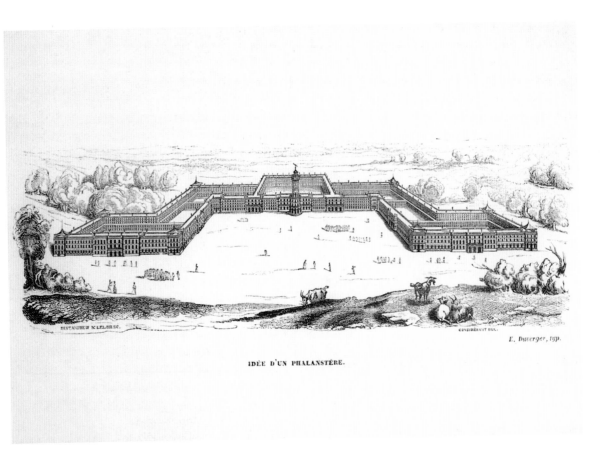

IDÈE D'UN PHALANSTÈRE.

Victor Considérant, *Idea of a phalanstery*, c.1840. Archives Nationales, Paris

Charles Fourier, *Plan of a phalanstery*, c.1814. Archives Nationales, Paris

Hornu, built near Mons in Belgium from 1816, was criticized by Godin as lacking in social ambitions regarding the improvement of the worker's lot.[6] Alfred Krupp, whose huge factory was located close to Essen in Germany, built comfortable homes for his craftsmen from the 1860s but betrayed an instinct for self-preservation when he stated that 'everything I have recommended is necessary, and will be hugely repaid by the results. We still have much to recuperate. Who can say if, in the years to come, when a general revolution sweeps the country and the working classes rise up against the employers, we won't be the only ones to be spared, if we begin everything in good time.'[7] The majority, though, were philanthropists who provided fairer conditions as a result of a personal moral and humanitarian reaction to the consequences of the unequal distribution of wealth. Figures such as

Robert Owen perceived the asphyxiating cities as the physical image of the chaos of a society which they hoped to see profoundly transformed through peaceful reform and emulation of the model communities they described or created. They often conceived their own role as paternalistic, leading their flocks of passive workers and gradually, through education, enabling them to take on greater responsibilities and an increasing share in the benefits brought about by that great march of progress which we have already discussed and in which they believed so resolutely. Engels and Marx labelled the socialism of figures like Owen as 'utopian' – ignorant of the realities of class struggle and the deep-rooted economic causes that the urban situation reflected – and therefore saw it as ultimately ineffective, in contrast to their own 'scientific socialism'. In the *Communist Manifesto*,

Marx condemned Owen and his followers in the following terms: 'Historical action used to yield to their personal inventive action, historically created conditions of emancipation to fantastic ones, and the gradual, spontaneous class organization of the proletariat to an organization of society specially contrived by these inventors. Future history resolves itself, in their eyes, into the propaganda and the practical carrying out of their social plans.... They still dream of experimental realization of their social utopias, of founding isolated "phalanstères", of establishing "home colonies", of setting up a "little Icaria" – duodecimo editions of the New Jerusalem – and, to realize all these castles in the air, they are compelled to appeal to the feelings and purses of the bourgeois.'[8]

Although Charles Fourier failed to meet personally an enlightened sponsor who would enable him to realize his dreams, others were later to attempt to do so. His principal argument, put forward in the *Théorie des quatre mouvements* (1808) and the *Traité de l'association domestique agricole* (1822), was that, whereas previous utopists had suppressed the natural passions, of which he identified twelve, it was precisely these and the attractions between them that should be classified and exploited in order to create the ideal society. By grouping people according to their passions, universal harmony could be achieved. For Fourier, society was evolving through a number of phases and, after its current, industrialized stage of 'civilization', it would proceed next to *garantisme* where institutions ranging from banks to workers' cities to phalansteries would ensure solidarity among members of a state-free society. He envisaged communities based on shared ownership, management and profits and described a model radial city. He imagined the town itself occupying an inner ring, suburbs and large factories a middle one and further suburbs and avenues the outer circle, while the architecture of each would ensure it a certain degree of uniformity. Beyond the three concentric rings, the land is adorned by monuments and colossal statues. Groups of about 1500 to 1600 people (ideally 1620 in order to accommodate all the 810 types of human nature identified by Fourier) live together in phalansteries, whose architectural regularity contrasts with what he viewed as the chaotic little houses of his day. Functions are separated in the phalanstery

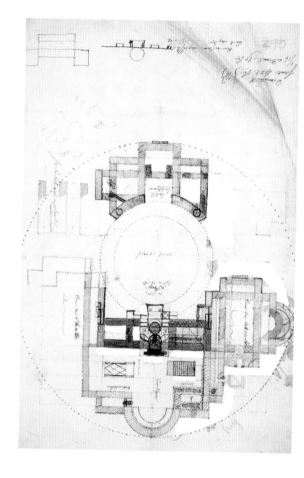

with, for example, the noisy crafts relegated to one wing while another is reserved for guests. The centre contains the *Tour d'Ordre* (the directional nerve-centre of the whole community), temple, dining rooms, library, ceremonial carillon and the carrier pigeons. A large galleried street enveloping the whole façade, underground passages and air conditioning ensure the physical comfort of the residents. Fourier's ideas, which privileged diversity (albeit very codified) above the uniformity characteristic of most utopians, were to inspire many. Victor Considérant, Fourier's principal champion, continued to produce his journal, *La Phalange*, after the master's death and published a description of the phalanstery, *Description du Phalanstère et considérations sociales sur l'architectonique*, in 1840. Proclaiming that architecture writes history, he provided a scathing portrait of the Paris of his day as a dreadful architectural fray, depriving its dwellers of air, light or views and reflecting in relief its social anarchy and incoherence, abhorrent, of course, to a lover of order and harmony. The well-known form of the phalanstery,

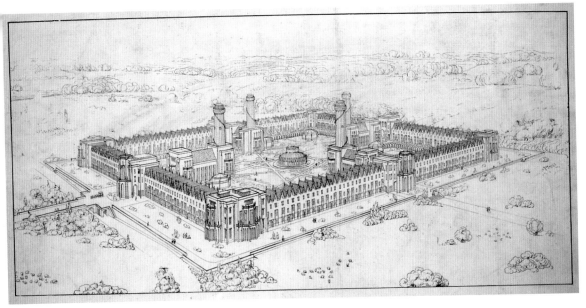

Stedman Whitwell, *Bird's-eye view of one of the communities of Harmony in the State of Indiana...*, c. 1825. New York Historical Society

Robert Owen, *A view and plan of the agricultural and manufacturing village of unity and mutual cooperation.* Reproduced in the pamphlet *New State of Society*, n.d. [c. 1817]. Bibliothèque Nationale de France, Paris, Département des Imprimés

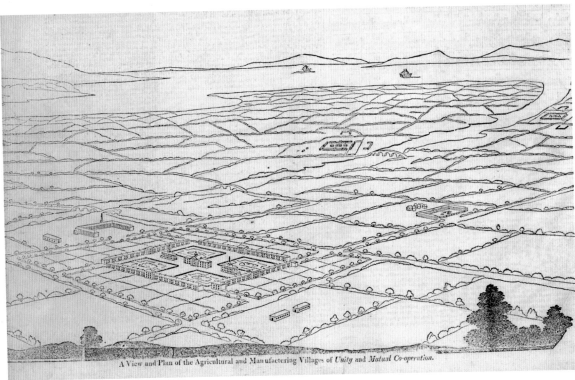

A View and Plan of the Agricultural and Manufacturing Villages of *Unity* and *Mutual Co-operation.*

the palace for humankind, a great three-winged building similar in layout to the royal château at Versailles, is illustrated and described in detail by Considérant (although he does remark that it should be neither authoritarian nor definitive). Short-lived attempts to realize Fourier-style phalanstery communities included Considérant's own at Condé-sur-Vesgres in France in 1832 and in Dallas and Houston,

Texas, in 1853–55, those of the Belgian poet Zoé Gatti de Gamond at Cîteaux in 1841, of Albert Brisbane and Horace Gresley in North America (which saw some 37 examples), of Oliveira in Brazil, and of the agricultural union in French colonial Algeria.[9] The most famous 'utopian socialist' in nineteenth-century England is surely Robert Owen, a successful self-made entrepreneur in the textile industry. He

recalled in his *Autobiography* (1857/8) that at around 1815 he visited many British industrial factories and considered the conditions of slavery there worse than those in America and the Indies (for although the slave trade had been abolished in England in 1807, slavery itself was maintained until 1833).[10] Owen introduced a number of measures in his spinning-mill at New Lanark in Scotland, where he employed some 1000 workers by 1800, including improved working conditions and hygiene, no child labour before the age of twelve, a ten-hour working day and the provision of shops and schools. One of the partners in the enterprise at New Lanark was Jeremy Bentham whose Panopticon has been mentioned earlier. In 1817, Owen published a *Report to the Committee for the relief of the manufacturing poor*, in which he proposed the creation of industrial

villages of 500 to 1500 people on 500-hectare sites. The publication of this proposal includes a sketchy bird's-eye view of the layout of such a plot whose square form is divided into parallelograms. The village contains communal buildings such as the school, library, lecture-room, place of worship, a kitchen and refectory at its centre and dormitories or private lodgings for people with young children at the sides. Primarily agricultural, these villages would include some manufactures which would be located on the periphery of the main square. Owen outlined similar proposals in his *Report to the County of Lanark* and *The Book of the New Moral World*, but in this case adapting them to populations ranging from 300 to 2000 people. It is interesting to recall that in 1819 he reprinted a pamphlet of 1696 by John Bellers which had inspired him. Bellers's proposal,

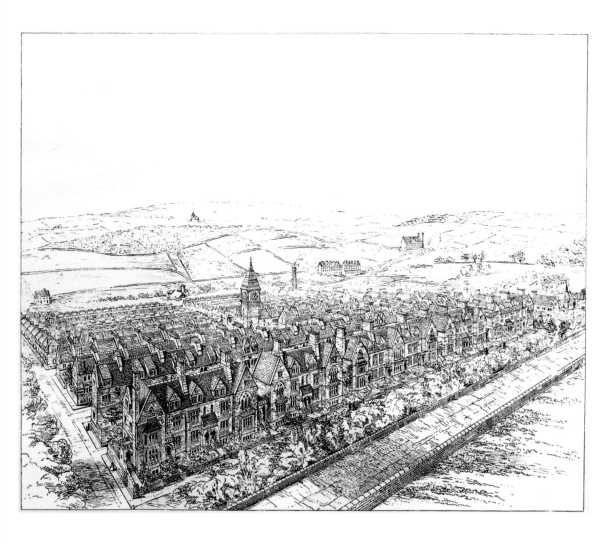

W. H. Crosland, *An Ideal Sketch of 'Akroydon' near Halifax*, in Edward Akroyd, *On Improved Dwellings for the Working Classes, with a Plan for Building them in Connection with Benefit Building Societies*, London, 1862. Bibliothèque Royale de Belgique, Brussels, Département des Imprimés

based upon the contemporary workhouse with improvements, was for a self-supporting college in which education was of prime importance, the creation of 'an Epitomy of the World, by a collection of all the useful Trades in it; so it may afford all the Conveniences and Comforts a Man can want, and a Christian use.... Regular People (of all visible Creatures) being the Life and Perfection of Treasure, the strength of Nations, and Glory of Princes.' Anxious to see his ideas realized, Owen went to America in 1825 where he acquired a village in Indiana, named New Harmony, which had belonged to the Harmony Society led by George Rapp. On the site of the existing chequerboard village, Owen harboured grand but short-lived designs to build a community based on the square scheme he had devised earlier, now drawn up by his architect, Stedman Whitwell, a pupil of John Soane. On his return from America, he made a final attempt to realize an ideal community with 224 adults and 448 children housed in a huge mansion called Harmony Hall, at Queenwood, Hampshire, but the extravagance of his building plans there caused its failure too.

Among the many communities attempted in the wake of Robert Owen's experiences was Orbiston in Lanarkshire where Alexander Hamilton and Abraham Combe entertained ambitious plans to create a settlement financed through agricultural and industrial activities. Only one wing of the projected phalanstery-type construction was completed, containing homes for 300 people, a factory, an inn and other services, as the death of one of the founders rang the knell of the scheme. In 1850 Sir Titus Salt initiated Saltaire, which was a far more ambitious enterprise and is believed to have been inspired by the description of Trafford's factory village in *Sybil* (1847), the novel in which Benjamin Disraeli portrays a model village as he also

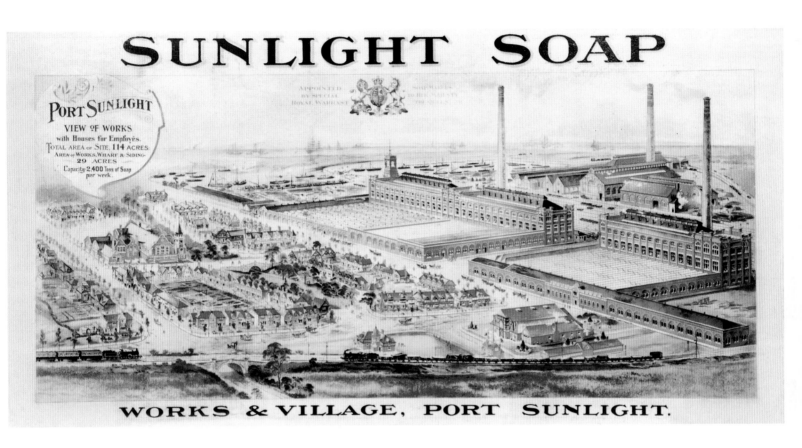

SUNLIGHT SOAP

PORT SUNLIGHT
VIEW OF WORKS
with Houses for Employès.
TOTAL AREA OF SITE. 114 ACRES.
AREA OF WORKS, WHARF & SIDING·
29 ACRES
Capacity 2,400 Tons of Soap
per week.

WORKS & VILLAGE, PORT SUNLIGHT.

Anonymous, *Port Sunlight, Works & Village*, 1905. Unilever Historical Archives, Port Sunlight

had done in *Coningsby* (1844). Designed on a grid plan by the architects Lockwood and Mawson, the alpaca worsted mill and the houses (of which there were 820 by 1872) were supplemented by an institute, almshouses, a park and a steam laundry. Sir Titus is reputed to have wished to acquire the Crystal Palace built by Paxton for the 1851 Great Exhibition and to reconstruct it at the heart of Saltaire. At this time too – and again in England's Yorkshire – a Member of Parliament and textile manufacturer, Edward Akroyd, built the Gothic-style industrial village of Copley in 1847, complete with mill, housing, canteen, school, church, library and allotments, and the larger one of Akroydon from 1859. The latter was built to a typically ideal square plan, outlined by G. G. Scott, while W. H. Crosland was the acting architect. It was Akroyd's desire that a mixture of different grades of housing would cause interaction between social classes which in his view

could only be beneficial to the 'lower' echelons of society. In 1888, work began on the English village of Port Sunlight, founded by the Nonconformist industrialist and campaigner for social issues, William Hesketh Lever, producer of the best-selling Sunlight soap. Although Lever's scheme never fulfilled its creator's full ambitions, it none the less provided workers with homes of a standard previously reserved for the wealthier middle classes. After visiting Port Sunlight, the Belgian monarch, Leopold II, encouraged Lever to build similar settlements in the Congo of which one was named Leverville. The Quaker chocolate magnate George Cadbury planned his influential ideal community at Bournville with W. Alexander Harvey in 1895. It combined low-density suburban villas with more modest terraced and semi-detached cottages within prolific gardens. Convinced, like Richardson, of the benefits of physical fitness, he provided a swimming pool, sports ground and gymnasium for his employees and encouraged the practice of gardening. With insight, Cadbury decided that no more than half of the residents should be employees of his factory, thus attempting to avoid the claustrophobic atmosphere of certain other industrial villages. Although Great Britain provided particularly fertile ground, the founders of model estates were obviously not confined to that land. Jean-Baptiste-André Godin's *Familistère* at Guise in northern France is of importance as an attempt at ideal organization which was economically viable, socially advanced and long-lived (well over a century from its conception in 1858). The son of a provincial locksmith, Godin made his fortune through the invention and patenting of the cast-iron stove. He was stimulated by the ideas of men like Etienne Cabet, Saint-Simon, Owen and Fourier, although he was to abandon the latter's theories regarding the passions. He had contributed financially to Considérant's attempt to establish a Fourierist community in Texas in the early 1850s, and considered one of the causes of its failure to be its lack of clear leadership. In his company, a 'co-operative association of work and capital', which inspired much interest from the international co-operative movement generally, capital and labour shared the profits. The workers enjoyed universal but indirect suffrage and a certain degree of co-management, although they were increasingly disenchanted by overly rigid regulations and the authoritarian attitude of their employer. Even though Godin pragmatically stated that he was alleviating the suffering of the workers and seeking their physical and moral well-being rather than a Fourier-style happiness, he also clearly expressed his wish – like Owen's at New Lanark – that the social advances he instigated would be emulated and would be but one step upon a long road of reform.

On the borders of the town of Guise, Godin constructed, in stages, a *Familistère* (neologism combining 'family' and 'phalanstery') which, by 1880, housed 1170 people and was equipped with common services, co-educational schools, a theatre and a park. Its architecture was profoundly and

H. Demare, *Caricature of Jean-Baptiste-André Godin*, in *Les hommes d'aujourd'hui*, 1880. Musée Municipal, Guise

Perspective view of the Familistère of Guise, in Jean-Baptiste-André Godin, *Solutions Sociales*, Brussels, 1871. Musée Municipal, Guise

intricately linked to the thinking of its creator as he proclaimed in *Solutions Sociales* (1871): 'The social progress of the masses is subordinated to the progress of the social provisions of architecture.' With a layout close to Fourier's phalanstery and hence to the castle at Versailles, Godin described it in the following terms: 'Since it is impossible to make a palace of the cottage or hovel of every working family, we have aimed to place the worker's dwelling in a palace: the Familistère, indeed, is nothing less than that: it is the social palace of the future.' At the *Familistère*, now listed as a national landmark, his workers lived in better and cheaper dwellings than those housed in the neighbouring town and in their well-lit apartments they enjoyed comforts such as lavatories, running water and rubbish chutes, benefits which Godin referred to as

Pages 134–135
Familistère of Guise: elevation, section, plans, n.d. Musée Municipal, Guise

Joseph Gandy, *Plan for a village*, in *Designs for Cottages*, London, 1805. Royal Institute of British Architects, London

LE FAMILISTÈRE OU PALAIS SOCIAL **MANUFACTURE**

| *Ateliers* | *Boulangerie* | | *Écoles* | *Théâtre* | *Écoles* | *Débits* | *Restaurant* | *Boucherie* | *Bains et Lavoirs* | *Bureaux* | *Dessin* | *Sculpture* | *Mécanique* | *Émaillage* | *Fonderies* | | *Ébarbage* |

divers *Café* *Billard* *Écuries Remises* *Basses-Cours* *Gazomètre* *Magasins* *Ajustage et Montage*

La nourricerie est derrière le Pavillon central du Palais.

the 'equivalents of wealth'. However, while its architecture encouraged social interaction and brought light (a symbol, for Godin, of intellectual and moral progress) into the residence, it also encouraged the community members to supervise one another from their apartments overlooking the central courtyards. Emile Zola visited the *Familistère* (and criticized it: 'Order, regulations, mechanism, comfort, but what about the wish for adventure, the risks of the free and adventurous life?'[11]), and it provided inspiration for his novel, *Travail* (1901), which was in turn to influence Tony Garnier's designs for an industrial city in the early twentieth century.

The most famous of the American industrial estates was the 'Manufacturing town of Pullman and car works belonging to Pullman's Palace Car Company' in the suburbs of Chicago, commissioned by George Pullman, the company's president in 1879, and designed by Solon Spencer Beman in collaboration with the landscaper, Nathan F. Barrett. This anglophile architect was inspired by many examples of company towns, including the experiences of

Owen, Akroyd, the Cadburys and, above all, Salt in the United Kingdom. Indeed, the evidence that Pullman and Beman were directly inspired by Saltaire seems overriding, as Thomas J. Schlereth has argued, outlining some of the flagrant similarities between the two schemes.[12] Pullman City became famous on both sides of the Atlantic, partly owing to the presentation of models (even a 30-metre long one) at exhibitions such as the World's Columbian Exposition in Chicago in 1893 and that in Paris in 1889. The precision, order and economy of means and effort with which the manufacturing process was established at Pullman City stimulated the admiration of many contemporaries, and was exemplary of the sort of scientific rationality of organization which men such as Frederick W. Taylor were to extol shortly. Despite its fine architecture, however, the town of Pullman experienced poor labour relations, including a violent strike in 1894, in the face of George Pullman's increasingly autocratic attitude towards his employees.

The urban transformation was indeed spectacular

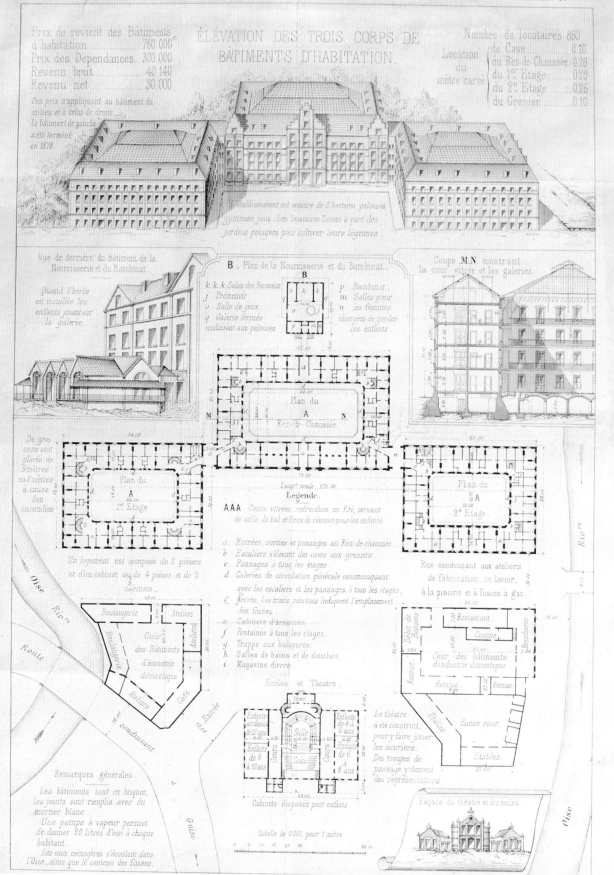

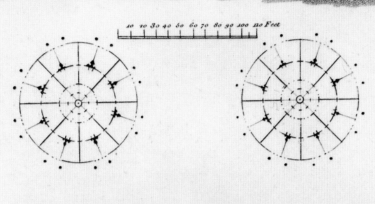

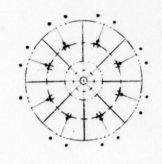

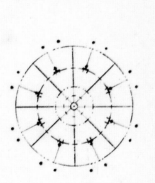

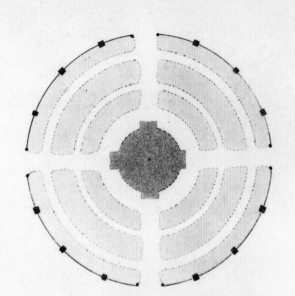

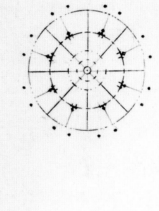

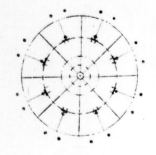

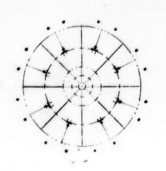

London Published by John Harding 36 S.t James's Street March 1.st 1808.

but should not mask the fact that most countries continued to have a majority of country dwellers throughout the century. England was far from typical in counting as many urban as rural dwellers by 1851; the balance was tipped in Germany only in 1890 and in the United States in 1920. Those people that remained in the country sometimes lived in a squalor comparable to that of their urban counterparts. During the eighteenth and nineteenth centuries dozens of ideal villages were created, and although they are beyond the subject of this book, it is worth mentioning just one design by Joseph Gandy, collaborator of John Soane, in Britain in 1805. Its 64 cottages grouped around a central church or chapel is an extension of his design for a House of the Winds and is interesting, not only because it provides a plan for an entire village, but above all in that it resembles a number of more ambitious ideal-city plans and seems to announce Ebenezer Howard's drawing for his Social City.[13]

LITERARY UTOPIAS

The Frenchman Etienne Cabet was responsible for one of the most important utopian novels of the first half of the nineteenth century: *Voyages et aventures de Lord William Carisdall en Icarie* (1839), republished in 1840 under the title *Voyage en Icarie*. This politically active lawyer and father of utopian communism according to Marx, read Thomas More and met Robert Owen during a period of exile in England after his prison condemnation on account of texts published in the paper he had founded in 1833, *Le Populaire*. The society Cabet described in the novel, written on his return to France, inspired 500 volunteers to attempt its realization at Nauvoo, Texas, from 1848 to 1898. The world of state socialism which he portrays, despite the fictional medium, is pictured in great detail as a veritable blueprint for action. Above all, it is striking on account of its stifling, codified uniformity. Icara,

the capital city of a community, Icaria, of over a million people, is circular with a straightened river and clean, well-lit, covered streets arranged on a grid plan. The river splits in two at its heart to form a round island containing the principal site, a palace and a massive column topped by a statue of its founder. The town also has another two rings of respectively 20 and 40 further sites. The purity of the air is assured by placing hospitals, cemeteries and polluting factories on the outskirts, while the cleanliness of the streets is secured by paving, daily sweeping and washing and a system of fountains and underground canals distributing and collecting water. This familiar nineteenth-century obsession with cleanliness is taken to such a degree here that even the cupboards are hermetically closed to ensure that no dust enters them and moral hygiene is ensured by the exclusion of any cafés, dance halls or gaming rooms. The town is divided into 60 districts, each of which bears the name of a city such as Peking, Jerusalem, Constantinople or Paris, and its monuments and houses are designed in the style of these places to provide a condensed version of the world. Each road has 32 houses with identical façades, five storeys and a terraced roof. Public buildings are placed at their centres and extremities. In this prophetic work, the model house plan is the result of a competition (a bust of the winner is placed in every house); model plans are similarly drawn up for schools, hospitals, farms and even furniture, so that all elements such as window frames can be manufactured in great numbers. It is typical of the interweaving of threads making up the ideal-city fabric that one encounters John Minter Morgan amid the initial sponsors for Owen's aforementioned unfinished scheme at Orbiston. Morgan was a follower of Owen for many years. Amalgamating religious and social ideas, he published major works dealing with utopia, particularly *The Revolt of the Bees* (1826), *Hampden in the Nineteenth Century* (1834) and *The Christian Commonwealth* (1845), in which he reproduced an illustration very close to Stedman Whitwell's design for New Harmony and described a scheme which was physically very

G. Muller, *Bird's-eye view of a utopian settlement*. Frontispiece of John Minter Morgan, *The Christian Commonwealth*, London, 1845. Bibliothèque Nationale de France, Paris, Réserve des Imprimés

similar, housing 300 families in a large square. Though not an architect, he described his communities in great detail, even entering into issues such as the precise number of rooms and costs of construction. Finally separating from Owen, he set up his own organization, entitled 'The Church of England Self-Supporting Village Society', which took on board many of Owen's ideas but with strong religious overtones.

A somewhat atypical figure in this portrait gallery of the nineteenth century is Benjamin Ward Richardson, who was neither architect nor political thinker but an English doctor. His research in the medical field led him to write *Hygeia, a City of Health* (1876), a description inspired by More's *Utopia* and prepared for the Social Science Association for which he was in charge of health matters. It is a hygienist's ideal city criticizing the current urban state of affairs and particularly problems such as mortality rates. In thinly populated Hygeia, 100,000 people inhabit 20,000 houses built on 4000 acres in streets laid out, once more, on a grid. They have access to a wide range of swimming pools, Turkish baths, gymnasia, libraries and schools. The houses have some interesting features, such as terraced roofs (on a gentle slope but not quite flat), internal chimneys connected to central wells in which the smoke is treated, rubbish

chutes and hot and cold water throughout. They are made of glazed bricks which are perforated to allow the air to pass through them! Three years later, in France, Jules Verne published *Les 500 Millions de la Bégum* in which he describes two towns built thanks to the Begum's fortune: an industrial city of steel constructed by a German scientist and a contrasting hygienist's ideal vision of a city planned by a French doctor. Richardson's work clearly inspired Verne as the latter's description of France-Ville is riddled with similarities to Hygeia, from the number of citizens to the layout of the town on a grid with streets of uniform width, the height of the individual houses (two floors), the sloping terraced roofs, the generous size of the bedrooms, the location of the kitchen on the first floor next to a terrace and serviced by a lift, and so on.

In 1888, the American author Edward Bellamy published a utopian novel which was to become an overnight bestseller: *Looking Backward: 2000–1887*. William Morris was not convinced by the economic argument at the basis of Bellamy's book, but it may well have been this that provoked him to respond by writing *News from Nowhere* in 1890. When he reviewed *Looking Backward* for *The Commonweal*, Morris pronounced a somewhat cynical opinion of utopia in general and a slightly condescending one of the American's in particular: 'The only safe way of reading a Utopia is to consider it as the expression of the temperament of its author. So looked at, Mr. Bellamy's Utopia must be still called very interesting ...'[14] Ebenezer Howard was profoundly marked by *Looking Backward*, though critical of the centralized, authoritarian aspect of the society Bellamy devised. He later recalled that after reading it, 'I went into some of the crowded parts of London, and as I passed through the narrow dark streets, saw the wretched dwellings in which the majority of the people lived, observed on every hand the manifestations of a self-seeking order of society and reflected on the absolute unsoundness of our economic system, there came to me an overpowering sense of the temporary nature of all I saw, and of its entire unsuitability for the working life of the new order – the order of justice, unity and friendliness.'[15] The key protagonist, Julian West, wakes up in the remains of his home in Boston in the year 2000, from a hypnotic trance lasting 113 years. During his somnolence, the capitalism of his day has been transformed, peaceably, through fierce competition between companies and increasing monopolization, into a mechanized, bureaucratized corporate state. The nation is responsible for the organization of work, production and distribution, salaries are equal, work is pain-free and a leisurely retirement begins at 45 for all in this vice-free world devoid of banks, police or army. The environment is almost totally urban, a fact William Morris was quick to condemn in his review of the book: 'Mr. Bellamy's ideas of life are curiously limited; his dwelling of man in the future is Boston (USA) beautified. In one passage, indeed, he mentions villages, but with unconscious simplicity shows that they do not come into his scheme of economical equality, but are mere servants of the great centres of civilization. This seems strange to some of us, who cannot help thinking that our experience ought to have taught us that such aggregations of population afford the worst possible form of dwelling-place, whatever the second worst might be.'[16] In a later work, *Equality* (1897), Bellamy thinned down the population to

create 'these modern cities, in which every house stands in its own enclosure', and tells us that, 'Were you to visit Manhattan Island I fancy your first impression would be that the Central Park of your day had been extended all the way from Manhattan to Harlem river, though in fact the place is rather thickly built up according to modern notions, some 250,000 people living there among the groves and fountains.'[17]

The prolific English art critic John Ruskin influenced Morris, Howard and many others in his condemnation of the material and moral misery of the proletariat believed to be the product of industrial capitalism and his nostalgic appreciation of the medieval world as one in which artisans, directly involved in the production process, experienced joy in the creation of beautiful and useful artefacts. He shared his good friend Thomas Carlyle's

France-ville and The City of Steel (Acier-ville), in Jules Verne, The Begum's Fortune (Les 500 Millions de la Bégum), Paris, 1879. Collection Van Loock, Brussels

Cette masse est Stahlstadt, la Cité de l'Acier. (Page 42.)

revulsion towards the industrial machine and free enterprise on social grounds. Ruskin's idealization of the medieval past as a golden age was shared by many who rejected industrialization and the alienation it created. It continued well into the twentieth century, where it appears in the ideas of movements such as German Expressionism. Augustus Welby Northmore Pugin, author of *Contrasts, or a parallel between the noble edifices of the 14th and 15th centuries and similar buildings of the present day* (1836), had already made a plea in favour of the Middle Ages over his own mechanical century. Nikolaus Pevsner has pointed out a confusion between aesthetic and social considerations that characterizes mid-nineteenth-century art criticism.[18] Ruskin's objection was also aesthetically driven as he recoiled before the unsightliness he perceived in the modern world. Both he and Morris saw this ugliness not only in the shoddy design and quality of articles produced by the (still relatively young) machines which underpinned their call for a revival of the craftsman, but also in the transformation of the broader physical environment. Ruskin's prediction concerning England's future, if the forces of industrial capitalism continued unleashed, was nightmarish: '... from shore to shore the whole of the island is to be set as thick with chimneys as the masts stand in the docks of Liverpool: that there shall be no meadows in it: no trees: no gardens: only a little corn grown upon the housetops, reaped and threshed by steam: that you do not leave even room for roads, but travel either over the roofs of your mills, on viaducts; or under their floor, in tunnels: that, the smoke having rendered the light of the sun unserviceable, you work always by the light of your own gas ...'[19] Refusing to accept such an eventuality, he recalled, in the *Crown of Wild Olive* (1866), the universality of the utopian ambition, referred to Plato, More, Bacon and others and quoted the inspiring words of Shakespeare:

> This royal throne of kings – this sceptred isle –
> This fortress built by nature for herself
> Against infection, and the hand of war;
> This precious stone set in the silver sea;

> This happy breed of men – this little world:
> This other Eden-Demi-Paradise.[20]

He extolled the merits of cities such as Venice, Rouen, Geneva and Cologne for their fine architecture and human scale, and sought to re-create the medieval communitarian ethic within a new democratic framework. His vision prefigured the compact town favoured by the garden-city movement.

Indeed, Howard was later to quote the following words from Ruskin: '... lodging people and providing lodging for them means a great deal of vigorous legislature, and cutting down of vested interests that stand in the way, and after that, or before that, so far as we can get it, thorough sanitary and remedial action in the houses that we have; and then the building of more, strongly, beautifully, and in groups of limited extent kept in proportion to their streams and wall around so that there be no festering and wretched suburb anywhere, but clean and busy streets within and open country without, with a belt of beautiful garden and orchard round the walls so that from any part of the city perfectly fresh air and grass and sight of far horizon might be reachable in a few minutes' walk. That is the final aim.'[21]

'How deadly dull the world would have been twenty years ago but for Ruskin! It was through him that I learned to give form to my discontent, which I must say was not by any means vague. Apart from the desire to produce beautiful things, the leading passion of my life has been and is hatred of modern civilization.'[22] Famous Pre-Raphaelite designer and craftsman, militant socialist and founder of the Socialist League in 1885, William Morris thus acknowledged his debt to John Ruskin in 1894. His prologue to *The Earthly Paradise* (1905) again seems to echo his predecessor:

> *Forget six counties overhung with smoke*
> *Forget the snorting steam and piston stroke,*
> *Forget the spreading of the hideous town;*
> *Think rather of the pack horse on the down;*
> *And dream of London small white and clean,*
> *The clear Thames bordered by her gardens green...*
> *A nameless city in a distant sea,*
> *White as the changing walls of faerie.*

Morris shared many of Ruskin's views, such as his nostalgia for the pre-industrial world, but sought to incorporate them within a Marxist framework, believing, optimistically, that revolutionary change was imminent. Unlike Marx, however, he was not reluctant to describe his personal vision of a communist world. He portrayed his ideal city succinctly in a lecture called 'Makeshift' in 1894:

'... contrast such monstrosities of haphazard growth as your Manchester–Salford–Oldham etc., or our great sprawling brick and mortar country of London, with what a city might be: the centre with its big public buildings, theatres, squares and gardens: the zone round the centre with its lesser guildhalls grouping together the houses of the citizens; again with its parks and gardens: the outer zone again, still with its district of public buildings, but with no definite gardens to it because the whole of this outer zone would be a garden thickly besprinkled with houses and other buildings. And at last the suburb proper, mostly fields and fruit gardens with scanty houses dotted about till you come to the open country with its occasional farm steads. There would be a city for you ... what is to hinder such kinds of cities being the type of the future dwelling places of aggregated men? Nothing, it seems to me, if men shall be free to build them; what hinders it being done now, I will tell you.... The reason we put up with all these makeshifts is that we are so poor we cannot help it....What do I say! too poor to make peace in our midst, and make an end at last to the war between rich and poor, between the have-alls and the lack-alls.' Morris developed his dream further in his novel, *News from Nowhere, or An Epoch of Rest, being some chapter from a Utopian Romance*. Far from seduced by Bellamy's 'state communism', which he warned should not be taken as the 'socialist bible of reconstruction', Morris set out to paint his own picture of a communist world in which the state has withered away and projects his utopia one century later than Bellamy's. The protagonist of *News from Nowhere*, the socialist militant William Guest – a fondly caricatural and thinly disguised self-portrait of Morris – discovers England in the year 2102. This is a dream and the atmosphere is hazy, impressionistic. In the post-revolutionary, anti-industrial communist world, work is pleasure, not slavery, individuals are free in intentional contrast to the uniformization and control of so many other utopias, crime has disappeared along with poverty, and the state, still so present in Bellamy's work, has become redundant and withered away. Whereas Bellamy

Frontispiece of William Morris, *News from Nowhere; or, An Epoch of Rest. Being some chapters from a Utopian Romance,* Hammersmith, 1892. New York Public Library

Pages 142–143
Henry Holiday, *Dante and Beatrice*, 1883. Walker Art Gallery, Liverpool

maintained the industrial city in his world of 2000, Morris has replaced it, one speculative century later, with irregular, organically developed towns rich with luxuriant greenery, including the historic heart of London, villages and idyllic cottages scattered amidst the woods. The centuries-old process of rural exodus has been reversed and the townspeople have moved back to the countryside so that, as the respective populations have levelled out, the differences between town and country have diminished. In the British Museum, Guest meets Hammond, an elderly historian who explains: 'This is how we stand. England was once a country of clearings amongst the woods and wastes, with a few towns interspersed, which were fortresses for the feudal army, markets for the folk, gathering places for the craftsmen. It then became a country of huge and foul workshops and fouler gambling-dens, surrounded by an ill-kept, poverty-stricken farm, pillaged by the masters of the workshops. It is now a garden, where nothing is wasted and nothing is spoilt, with the necessary dwellings, sheds, and workshops scattered up and down the country, all trim and neat and pretty.'[23]

URBAN MODELS

Generally speaking, architects seem to have been little concerned by the ideal-city problematic during the nineteenth century: perhaps their creative impulses were too well occupied in the realization of the great constructions required by this age, for it is during periods of architectural frustration that they are often most prolific in this specific field of design. None the less, the century gave birth to a number of novel formal solutions of which the linear city and

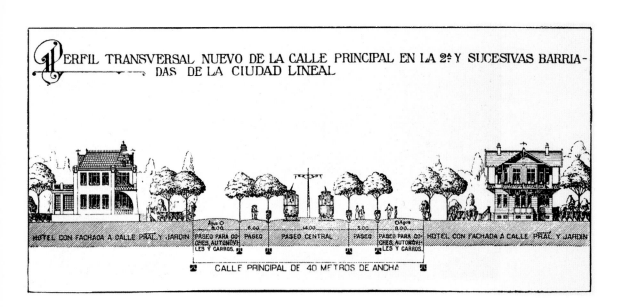

the garden city were to exercise an enduring influence in the twentieth century.

In 1854, when Barcelona, the only Spanish city in which industrialization had really taken root, was shaken by a revolutionary tremor, the progressive Liberals who assumed power called for the demolition of the surrounding walls that had been constructed by Philip V in 1719. When these had been erected, Barcelona had a population of 35,000 which, by 1854, had grown to over 150,000, accompanied by the inevitable problems of overcrowding, insalubrity and disease. Antonio López de Aberasturi has recounted the events that occurred once the destruction of the walls was settled.[24] The question immediately arose – since Spain had a strong inclination for codified town planning (of which the Laws of the Indies regarding new towns in the American colonies that were discussed earlier were a symptom) – of what form the future city should take. A competition arranged in 1858 was won by the architect Antonio Rovira y Trias, who accompanied his project with the (far from utopian!) words: 'The layout of a town is the work of time more than that of an architect.' In a design whose proportions conformed to those of the human body, a central square, representing the head, connected the old to

a new town laid out upon a series of concentric rings. The nobility would reside close to the centre, the bourgeoisie upon the major radial axes and the workers in the peripheral areas near to the factories, an urban segregation reflective of its social counterpart already established in capitalist Barcelona. Meanwhile, the engineer Ildefonso Cerda had formulated a quite different vision of the form he believed the city should take, a truly ideal plan intended to stimulate social transformation. For Cerda, the cities that he saw around him were the product of history, the history of oppression. The way to alleviate the situation was by inventing a new city, the 'ruralized urbanization' that he was to describe in his lengthy publication of 1867, the *Teoría general de la urbanización*, revealing the influence of Rousseau's ideas. Cerda sought to revive 'ruralized urbanization', the fundamental urban organization of primitive man before his true nature had been buried under the effects of civilization, and to combine it with the benefits of scientific and technical progress. His urban plan for New Barcelona was to be the guarantor of a healthy balance between individual freedom and sociable relations within an egalitarian society. This is reflected in his chequerboard plan which aimed to

The principal road in the Linear City, in Arturo Soria y Mata's *Ciudad Lineal*. French translation of the original 1894 edition. Collection Jean Dethier, Paris

View of the Model Town of Victoria set in a landscape. Frontispiece of James Silk Buckingham, *National Evils and Practical Remedies*, London, 1849. Bibliothèque Royale de Belgique, Brussels, Département des Imprimés

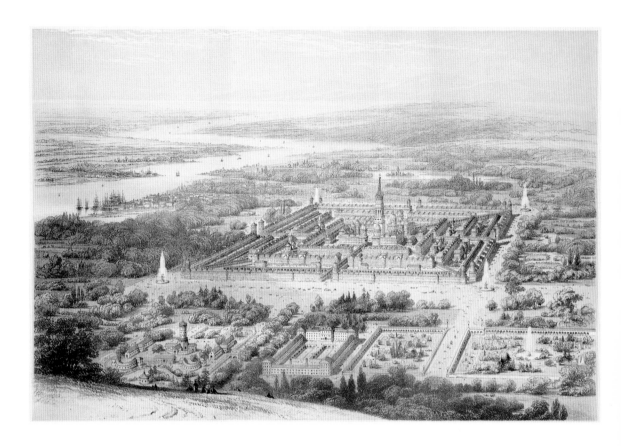

ensure equality, the potential to expand without deformation of the original layout, a facility of communication (to which the addition of a number of diagonal axes contributed further), and a clear distinction between the private, restful domain in the residential blocks and the public areas, places of movement. The desire for fresh air and greenery that is evident in so many utopian schemes, and particularly so in the nineteenth and twentieth centuries after the growth of the stifling metropolis, is satisfied by the fact that each square urban block was only built upon two of its sides and contained a massive garden in its centre (reminiscent of some of the squares built in London around Notting Hill for example, but now developed within a huge isotropic scheme). The length of each block was to measure 113 metres, with cut corners of 20 metres creating a series of squares, and the streets (apart from the even larger main avenues), which replaced the traditional 'corridor-roads', were to measure 20 metres, unusually wide for the time. The old city was not to be demolished initially, but Cerda was convinced that its inhabitants would be so impressed by his system that they would demand to be housed in

such ideal conditions also. With the backing of his political acquaintances in Madrid, he manœuvred to assure his plan's adoption, but as it was applied *in situ* his ideas were seriously disfigured and the generous gardens he had envisaged quickly succumbed to the pressures of building. Cerda was not the only ideal-city planner to end his days virtually forgotten and penniless, but his legacy was to endure. During the nineteenth century, which saw the establishment of sociology and of scientific socialism, Cerda, in his *Teoría general de la urbanización*, introduced the word *urbanización*, urbanization or urbanism, in which town planning is considered a scientific discipline. The word, which was used with increasing frequency in the twentieth century, characterizes the town planning of the industrialized world, in which the ongoing process of utopian detachment from a specific context is not only perpetuated but indeed reinforced.

Another Spaniard, Arturo Soria y Mata, also hoped to 'ruralize the town and urbanize the country', in order to achieve the ideal combination of the benefits of the metropolis with the physically and morally healthy influences of the countryside, when he exposed his original scheme for a linear city, a *ciudad linear*, intended to connect urban nuclei the world over, in the Spanish paper *El Progreso* in 1882. He described his solution as follows: 'A single street of 500 metres' width and of the length that may be necessary – such will be the city of the future, whose extremities could be Cadiz and St Petersburg, or Peking and Brussels.

'Put in the centre of this immense belt trains and trams, pipes for water, gas and electricity, reservoirs, gardens and, at intervals, buildings for different municipal services – fire, sanitation, health, police etc. – and almost all the complex problems produced by the massive populations of our urban life would be resolved at once ... Our projected city unites the hygienic conditions of country life to the great capital cities and, moreover, assumes that the railways, like today's streets and pavements, will carry free or for little all citizens.' In the 1890s, he set up a limited company in order to put his scheme into effect. The first and only segment of five kilometres of an intended 55-kilometre long railway encircling the city of Madrid was built. However, Soria's ambitious project, dogged by economic constraints and the fact that it had been unable to obtain 'public utility' status which would have facilitated land expropriation, failed to progress any further. The city Soria envisaged for the future is of interest, not only on account of its innovative form but above all for the fact that it sought a solution to urban problems on a regional scale. While he did not propose one unity to be reproduced in numerous cloned copies at acceptable distances from one another, he suggested instead a system which could be spread all over the globe and thus satisfy the desire for dissemination in his own way. Soria hoped that his proposition, which was strongly influenced by the doctrine of the American economist Henry George, could accomplish an equitable distribution of land. It was also visionary in its incorporation of new developments in high-speed surface transportation and it had much influence during the course of the next century. One of the most active champions of his linear city idea was the Spanish lawyer and diplomat, Hilarion

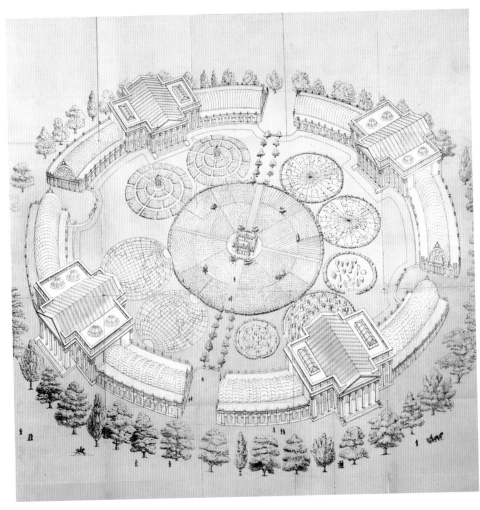

González del Castillo, who planned a linear city for Belgium in 1919 and saw it as an effective method of colonization for Spanish Africa. In Chile, the engineer and urbanist Carlos Carvajal Miranda devoted his life to the promotion of the linear city for his country. Edgar Chambless, inventor in the United States of a linear project called *Roadtown*, proposed an indefinitely long high-velocity railway line surmounted by a continuous concrete house; Georges Benoit-Lévy, the champion of the French variant of the garden city, was attracted by the supranational aspects of the linear city idea in the 1920s; and Le Corbusier also designed a linear industrial city which bore some resemblances to Soria's scheme, although residences and civic buildings were placed apart across a green belt. In post-revolutionary Russia, attempts at realization were made under the first Five-Year Plan of 1928–33 but also in a more diluted form thereafter.

A View of the Colleges for the Happy Colony to be established in New Zealand by the Workmen of Great Britain, in Robert Pemberton, *The Happy Colony*, London, 1854. British Library, London, Printed Books

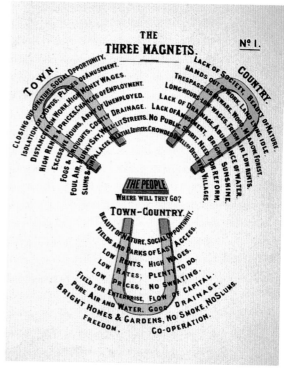

Two schemes that were produced in nineteenth-century Britain were to continue the utopian tradition and to contribute, along with many of the other figures we have mentioned, to the well-known solution projected by Ebenezer Howard at the close of the century. In 1849, James Silk Buckingham, Member of Parliament and social campaigner, designed an ideal city named Victoria which was intended to alleviate the desperate condition of the 'Unfortunate'. Well-versed in utopian practice (he had visited a Quaker community, Zoar, and a Rappite one, Economy, in America) and a supporter of John Minter Morgan, Buckingham was inspired, as he himself stated, by Wren's plan for the reconstruction of London after the great fire and by his visit to America's Circleville for his detailed and illustrated description of an ideal city in *National Evils and Practical Remedies*. His scheme was intended to house 10,000 inhabitants in buildings grouped in series of typically utopian concentric places surrounded by a green belt. The architecture would reflect closely

the social organization with different classes and income groups gathered together in separate areas: in the colonnaded walkway which was attached to each area, the status of the inhabitants was signalled by the architectural order used on the columns, the opulent capitalists being indicated by the Composite order! Another unrealized proposal to be published in England in the mid-nineteenth century was that described by Robert Pemberton in *The Happy Colony* (1854). Pemberton proposed the creation of circular model towns (of which the first was to be called Queen Victoria Town) in New Zealand, where ten 20,000-acre districts could be acquired easily. His scheme incorporates elements of Fourier's ideas concerning the harmony of the passions as well as those of Owen with regard to education. The colony was to contain a number of statues illustrating history as well as huge terrestrial and celestial maps at the heart of the town.
In 1898, Ebenezer Howard, a self-taught stenographer, published, with the aid of a £50 loan,

Diagrams in Ebenezer Howard, *To-morrow: a Peaceful Path to Real Reform*, London, 1898. Hertfordshire Archives and Local Studies, Hertford

a description of his 'invention', the garden city, under the title *To-morrow: a Peaceful Path to Real Reform* (re-edited in 1902 as *Garden Cities of Tomorrow*). It prompted a somewhat patronizing remark when reviewed in *The Times* newspaper of 19 October 1898: 'If Mr. Howard could be made town clerk of such a city he would carry it on to everybody's satisfaction. The only difficulty is to create it; but that is small matter to Utopians.' Linking the nineteenth and the twentieth centuries, Howard's ideas built upon the experience of the utopian socialist tradition and were to have far-reaching impact throughout the twentieth century, from the foundation of the first garden city at Letchworth in England in 1903 to the creation of numerous new towns (and suburbs) worldwide. In the elaboration of his scheme for garden cities, he clearly hoped to bring about a profound transformation in the social structure through change in the physical environment.

During the 1870s and 1880s, Howard had frequented the world of the London Radicals whose members had founded utopian colonies such as Topolobampo in Mexico, while the early 1890s saw him closely involved with the English Nationalisation of Labour Society – the equivalent of Bellamy's Nationalization Party in the USA – which had tried to set up a 500-acre community inspired by *Looking Backward*. Other works that influenced him included Henry George's *Progress and Poverty* (1881) and Peter Alekseyevich Kropotkin's *Fields, Factories, and Workshops* (1899), which announced the arrival of a new era of decentralization in which society would be organized in small-scale 'industrial villages' containing co-operatively owned cottage industries and workers' homes. Convinced that the existing metropolises of the nineteenth century were doomed either to perpetuate the current exploitation of labour or to instigate violent class conflict, Howard concluded that the reorganization of the physical environment would provide the framework for the more civilized stage of social evolution, the co-operative commonwealth. Opposing the increasing monopolization of land (less than 7000 people owned 80 percent of the land in the United Kingdom in 1873), his principal aim was its gradual redistribution, and the garden cities were to be established initially through the support of wealthy philanthropists setting up non-profit companies, raising money by issuing bonds, purchasing the required acreage and building the basic transport, water and power infrastructure. He speculated that rising land values and rental income would enable the company to buy them back from the original investors and to make substantial contributions to the civic life of his towns. Howard's solution was expressed in his 'Three Magnets' diagram in which the people are presented as iron filings and the appeal of the city and the countryside is contrasted with a new attraction, the Town-Country, which combines the urban benefits of employment and entertainment with the rural ones of healthy and spacious living. He envisaged clusters of towns of 30,000 to 32,000 inhabitants, linked to each other and to a larger Centre City with a popula-

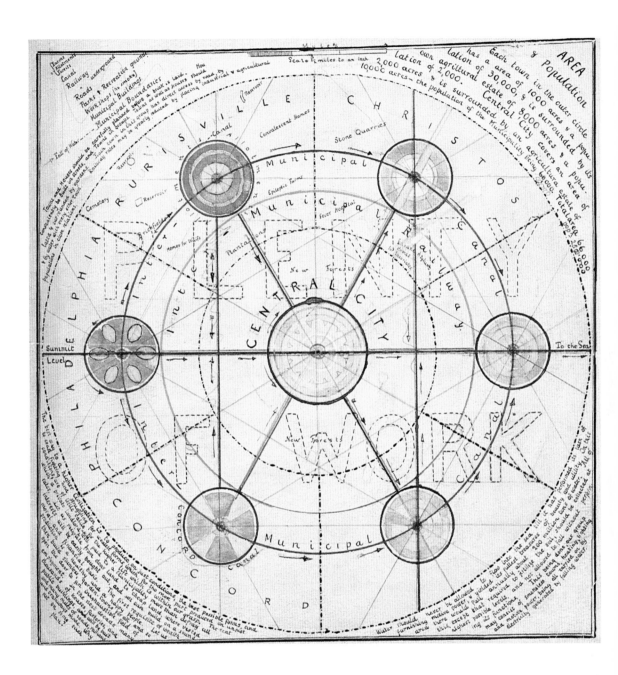

tion of 58,000 by a circular canal, which he changed
to a rapid-transit system in the 1902 edition, the
ensemble making up a diverse and stimulating
entity, the Social City. At the heart of his town, and
symbolizing the importance he placed on civic
affairs and leisure, a Central Park would contain
public buildings such as the town hall, library,
museum, hospital, and concert and lecture hall
surrounded by a glazed arcade, the Crystal Palace,
containing a number of small shops, residential
areas and factories at the periphery of the town.
Radial streets divide the land into six 'wards' of

1000 families living in houses with gardens, neigh-
bourhoods complete with their own local institutions and a school placed along a Grand Avenue.
He specifically stressed, in contrast to Thomas More,
that the design of the various towns should differ
and, at the Bournville Garden City Conference of
1901, he asserted that, 'of course, no actual plan for
the laying out of the town can be presented until an
estate has been selected'.[25] Variety is literally written
into his master plan.
Howard worked tirelessly to witness the realization
of his ideas, giving numerous public speeches with

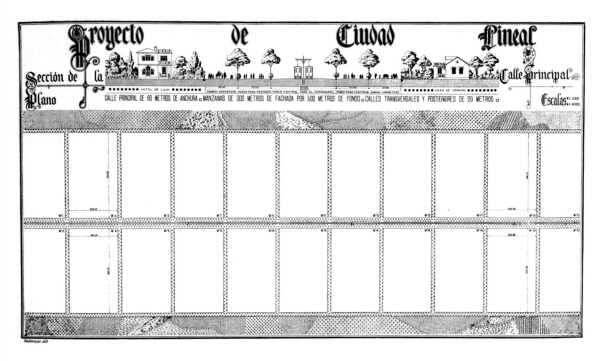

titles like 'The Ideal City Made Practicable, A Lecture Illustrated with Lantern Slides', and he enlisted the support of the Land Nationalisation Society, founded by Alfred Russel Wallace in 1881, which called for state ownership of the land as a remedy to the rural exodus. With its aid, he founded The Garden City Association in 1899, engaged the liberal London lawyer, Ralph Neville, as chairman in 1901, and enlisted the backing of George Cadbury and W. H. Lever. Despite inspiring the interest of thinkers of the calibre of George Bernard Shaw, however, he failed to secure the active support of important working-class organizations such as the co-operative movement. In 1903, the First Garden City Ltd took possession of a plot of over 3826 acres in Hertfordshire, 34 miles from London. It was the future site of Letchworth, the world's first garden city, built upon 1300 acres within a green belt. Howard remained closely involved in the creation of the first garden cities, but the role of the architects, Barry Parker and Raymond Unwin at Letchworth from 1904 and Louis de Soissons at Welwyn Garden City from 1920, now became paramount. Many of

Howard's social ideals failed to come to fruition at Letchworth, due, partly, to undercapitalization from the outset: only one of the planned co-operatively organized quadrangles was realized and the intended mix of social classes was not achieved as the cost of housing proved too high for lower-paid workers. At Letchworth, Howard's geometrical plan was replaced by a more organic treatment which respected the natural form of the terrain and the separation of the industrial from the residential area by rail tracks. Parker and Unwin shared Ruskin and Morris's penchant for the medieval world, while the influence of the German model was evident in the plans of Hampstead Garden Suburb, for which they were also responsible, according to the analysis of Baillie Scott and others writing in *Town Planning and Modern Architecture in the Hampstead Garden Suburb* (1909–10). In *Characteristics of German Town Planning Up to Date*, Bruno Taut wrote that 'the aspects of the mediaeval German towns gave nourishment for romantic sentiments to the cool, organizing English-man'. Parker and Unwin had also been influenced by the ideas of the Arts and Crafts Movement in

Design for a Linear City, in Arturo Soria y Mata's *Ciudad Lineal*. French translation of the original 1894 edition. Collection Jean Dethier, Paris

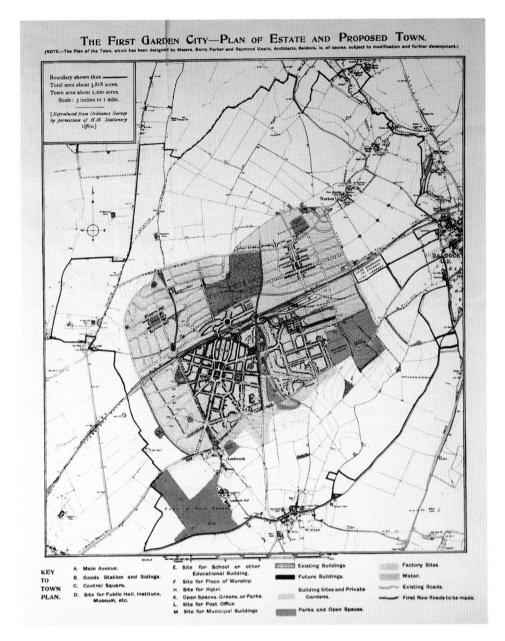

THE FIRST GARDEN CITY—PLAN OF ESTATE AND PROPOSED TOWN.

(NOTE.—The Plan of the Town, which has been designed by Messrs. Barry Parker and Raymond Unwin, Architects, Baldock, is, of course, subject to modification and further development.)

Boundary shown thus ———
Total area about 3,818 acres.
Town area about 1,200 acres.
Scale : 3 inches to 1 mile.

[Reproduced from Ordnance Survey by permission of H.M. Stationery Office.]

KEY TO TOWN PLAN.
A. Main Avenue.
B. Goods Station and Sidings.
C. Central Square.
D. Site for Public Hall, Institute, Museum, etc.
E. Site for School or other Educational Building.
F. Site for Place of Worship.
H. Site for Hotel.
K. Open Spaces, Greens, or Parks.
L. Site for Post Office.
M. Site for Municipal Buildings

Existing Buildings.
Future Buildings.
Building Sites and Private Gardens.
Parks and Open Spaces.
Factory Sites
Water.
Existing Roads.
First New Roads to be made.

Barry Parker and Raymond Unwin, *First plan for Letchworth*, 1904. First Garden City Heritage Museum, Letchworth

offspring of the Englishman's original idea. In 1927, Lewis Mumford, another ardent carrier of the garden city flame, was to express a dream that would surely have rung sweetly in the ears of the by then deceased Ebenezer Howard: 'Saltaire, Pullman, Port Sunlight, Letchworth are drops in the bucket ... the aim of a garden-city movement must be to change the shape of the bucket itself; that is to say, the frame of our civilization.'[27]

England and of Emerson, Whitman and Thoreau in America. Among Unwin's papers in the Royal Institute of British Architects, one finds his transcription of Morris's words: 'We must turn this land from the grimy back yard of a workshop into a garden. If that seems difficult, I can not help it: I only know that it is necessary.'[26] Howard's work inspired the creation of numerous garden cities during the twentieth century – too many to attempt to list them here. However, many garden suburbs, which differed considerably in that they did not contain the many functions of a true city, also claimed to be the

An avalanche of technological breakthroughs, the development of the giant metropolis, the first world conflict and the revolutions in Russia and Germany all gave rise to a sentiment, during the early years of the twentieth century, that a new era was dawning. Although the German Expressionists desired a return to a pre-industrial type of environment where the artisan played a central role in society, the vast majority of avant-garde movements sought to create a city and society that operated along the functional lines which characterized the state-of-the-art factory. These were the early, heady, heroic years that gave birth to the Modern Movement and to new political systems. Well before the middle of the century, however, these were transformed into the academicism of the International Style and the totalitarianism that disfigured several European countries.

Paul Citroën, *Metropolis*, 1923. Rijkuniversiteit Leiden, Prentenkabinet

Pages 152–154
Ludwig Hilberseimer, Hochhausstadt or Highrise City: perspective view of East-West street, 1924. The Art Institute of Chicago, Gift of George E. Danforth

THE URBAN JANUS

Many of the developments discussed in relation to the nineteenth century continued during the first years of the twentieth. Conurbations like London, Paris, Berlin and New York each housed several million people by 1900, and continuing demographic expansion and centralization combined with new factors, particularly the increase of automobile traffic, determined the new cityscapes. Though some of these metropolises, including Paris, Barcelona and Chicago, had undergone specific transformations in an attempt to adapt them to the requirements of an industrial society, most had grown in a more piecemeal fashion, which frequently prompted critics to denounce their chaotic nature. Pressure on land produced tenement blocks devoid of light and fresh air[1] as well as skyscrapers (which were obligatorily terraced in New York from 1916), whose headlong ascent was made possible by advances in the architectural field. These included the growing use of materials such as steel and the newly developed reinforced concrete, the demise of the load-bearing wall, the introduction of the fireproof metallic frame and the hydraulic lift. The polychromic, polyphonic, dynamic urban environment of the early twentieth century, with its waves of crowds, its bright, artificial lights, its cars mingled with horse-drawn traffic and its slogans crying out from innumerable shopfronts and advertising billboards, provided a source of both fascination and horror as revealed in the literature, poetry, photography and painting of the time.

The Western world was being radically transformed by an industrialization which continued to advance at breakneck speed. The end of the nineteenth century and the outset of the twentieth witnessed a veritable avalanche of scientific breakthroughs: the harnessing of electricity, the very force of nature, and the invention of the telegraph, telephone, calculator, typewriter, gramophone, microphone, radio, the automobile, the aeroplane and so on. Technological advance touched the whole of

Western society as every aspect of life became mechanized and human beings themselves increasingly resembled cogs in a massive machine aimed at achieving maximum productivity and guaranteeing future material well-being. In the United States,

before the First World War, the industrial engineer Frederick W. Taylor extolled the merits of 'scientific management' following a tradition in which Bentham and the Panopticon can also be placed. He sought to achieve the most efficient performance of a disciplined workforce by analysing and regulating its every motion. In a similar vein, Henry Ford aired his views on the introduction of the moving assembly line, the standardization of parts and the organization of industrial mass production in his autobiography, *My Life and Work*, in 1923. These years suffered the horrors of the Great War, followed by the turmoil of revolution in Russia and Germany. Unemployment and inflation in the period

after the world conflict led to a growing discontent, accentuated by the shock of the Wall Street crash, with parliamentary democracy increasingly viewed as inoperative and defunct. By the early 1920s currents of thought, which were soon to bring about the totalitarian systems we are so familiar with in Europe, were already fermenting while in the United States many people were tempted by the writings of the economist and sociologist Thorstein Veblen. As early as 1921 Veblen was writing attacks on the disorderly, avaricious way in which he considered the country was being run and calling for rational, organized direction by professional engineers. Veblen's ideas were later to be adopted, during the depression, by the American technocrats who proclaimed that engineers should be given almost dictatorial powers to manage the country in an orderly, efficient, planned manner. This would guarantee jobs, prosperity and, as a result, support from the workers. In France, the Saint-Simonian view that the organization of industry would form the basis of an emerging new order which would be run not by the state but by an élite of *industriels* (industrialists, scientists and artists) was taken up again by neo-Saint-Simonians and a group also called the 'Technocrats', who similarly advocated the rational organization of production and distribution by an élite of technically trained managers. Such ideas tempted architects who dreamed of running the world. To Le Corbusier, for whom the society of administration would supercede political systems, it mattered little whether bourgeois capitalism or communism won the day. As in Frank Lloyd Wright's Broadacre City, where the county architect was to play a similar role, Le Corbusier's universe required an all-powerful master planner who had both the impartial wisdom and the supreme power to assure its realization and successful management. Le Corbusier, who was convinced, with a frightening self-assuredness, that his task was to imagine, for the common good, 'a complete system, coherent, just and indisputable',[2] was evidently candidate for the post. The situation had all the necessary ingredients for a rash of ideal-city design: a stimulating combination

of change and impotency, comparable to that already seen in the early Renaissance in Italy. On the one hand, the social and technical changes, heightened by the experience of the war, engendered an urgent sense of break with the past and of an emerging order whose essence many an architect wished to capture in order to create the environment propitious to the flowering of a new man. On the other, the economic situation often forced him into a frustrating inactivity and obliged him to express his ideas on paper. These realities provoked a variety of responses, which can be broadly grouped, for our purposes, into those that viewed the increasing industrialization negatively and criticized it, often in anti-utopian literature (which we will discuss very briefly), and those who welcomed it as the key to the future. Hannes Meyer, second director of the Bauhaus, was one of many in the latter category, expressing his confidence in the new technology in a manifesto entitled *Die Neue Welt* (1926) in which he enumerated the many inventions which were to benefit the increasingly mechanized planet.[3] Those who, like Wright and Le Corbusier, believed that the industrial era had only undergone its first stage and that the Western world was about to enter a second, liberating phase of the Machine Age, appreciated that industrialization needed to be harnessed like some wild beast in order to truly benefit society. The vast majority of architects and artists, though their political stances may have varied, shared a view of the machine as a social liberator, capable of provoking equality between men, not only by relieving them of physical toil but above all by engendering a universal art and a truly collective society. The work of art itself, previously a unique piece enjoyed by an élite in conditions of exclusive intimacy, was dethroned in favour of the prototype, which could be reproduced *ad infinitum* for the pleasure of the greatest number. This era of idealism – the subject of this chapter – gave rise to the birth of modern architecture, a style of international and universal ambition that claimed to incorporate the new means of production and construction and to suit the requirements of an industrial society. The

Frans Masereel, *Smoke*, 1920.
Museum Plantin-Moretus, Stedelijk
Prentenkabinet, Antwerp

Weissenhof exhibition of 1927 had revealed a certain unity arising from a number of isolated initiatives and this was consolidated in 1928 with the foundation of the Congrès Internationaux d'Architecture Moderne (CIAM). The functionalist orientation of the organization was provided by Siegfried Giedion and Le Corbusier. At the meeting held during a cruise between Marseilles and Athens in 1933, the discussion centred around the theme of the 'Functional City' and led to the establishment of the *Principles of the Fourth Congress* which Le Corbusier revised and published anonymously as *La Charte d'Athènes* in 1943. This identified four principal urban functions – residing, working, cultivating body and spirit and, above all, circulating – and advocated the laying out of cities in functional zones separated by green spaces. The creation of the CIAM and particularly the later international acceptance of the aesthetic of modern architecture are considered by many to have marked its shift into the academicism which is the demise of all avant-gardes. Before considering the enthusiasm of its heroic phase, a few words should be said of the early warnings issued by the anti-utopians.

Karl Steiner, Untitled (The City), 1925. IVAM,
Centro Julio González, Valencia

An ominous shadow had been cast over the almost
unbridled optimism of most architects by writers
and filmmakers from the end of the nineteenth
century. The debate about utopia widened to
embrace not just social and economic issues but
those of a more philosophical nature about
humanity in general. Fearing that a transformation
of human nature might be the prerequisite of an
ideal society, some began to question the desirability of both the means and the ends. Long before the
menace of the totalitarian regimes of the 1930s,
while portraying fictional utopias – which proved on
realization to be dystopias – from the new perspective of within, they cried out against the dangers of
standardization, uniformization, robotization,
eugenics and genetic transformation that such
worlds demanded. 'You must either make a tool of
the creature, or a man of him. You cannot make
both. Men were not intended to work with the
accuracy of tools, to be precise and perfect in all
their actions. If you will have that precision out of
them, and make their fingers measure degrees like
cog-wheels, and their arms strike curves like
compasses, you must unhumanize them. All the
energy of their spirits must be given to make cogs
and compasses of themselves ...,' argued John
Ruskin in the nineteenth century.[4] His words were
just as pertinent in the twentieth century, when
humans were portrayed as automata, as in Heinrich
Hoerle's mechanical men, as collaged amalgams
of machines, as in Umbo's photomontage portrait
Die rasende Reporter (1926), or just deformed by
mechanical movement in Charlie Chaplin's Modern
Times (1936). Jerome K. Jerome also satirized these
tendencies in The New Utopia (1891), where people,
known by numbers, are kept to the same physical
size and mental capacity through surgical intervention and the countryside is levelled to ensure its uniformity also. In as early as 1871 in The Coming Race,
Edward Bulwer-Lytton portrayed a people, the Vrilya,
in whose distorted nature the very passions which

constitute humanity had been suppressed in order to create a new society which they did not even have the capacity to enjoy. Herbert George Wells is, of course, the figure that looms largest in the history of utopian literature at this time, embracing not just social but also eschatological issues. In *When the Sleeper Wakes* (1899), he advances the calendar to the twenty-second century and projects a spatial environment not so far from the reality he observed. A proletariat, hypnotized, exploited and indebted to the point of slavery, works underground and lives in a London boasting 33 million inhabitants, covered by an enormous transparent dome. Even those who work the land reside in the city, for the countryside has been completely depopulated. Technological progress has achieved all Wells's generation could have desired: lifts, travelling and aerial pavements, flying machines, cinema and even television. In *The Time Machine* (1895), set in the year 802,701, the Eloïs, the degenerate descendants of the capitalist masters, live in fear of the subterranean Morlocks, progeny of the proletariat, and the city has vanished leaving only ruins behind. In R.U.R. (1921), an abbreviation of 'Rossum's Universal Robots', the Czech Karel Čapek depicted a world in which all characteristics which do not contribute to work are eliminated in 'robots' (he invented the word based on the Czech verb for 'work') which assume all the tasks but finally rebel and massacre the human race. The Russian Yevgeny Ivanovich Zamyatin mimicked the influence of Taylorism in the Soviet Union in *We* (1920), where in his 'United States', the city of 2920 is a huge mass of geometric forms peopled by 'numbers' and enclosed within a glass wall beyond which the countryside is an untamed forest, shelter to a few thousand refractory 'Mephi'. Glass, as we have seen, has a particular appeal – and one which is intensified during these years – to utopians. Zamyatin caricatures this transparence which discourages dissimulation and nonconformist behaviour by creating a crystalline environment where pavements, façades and partitions are all made of glass, as is the huge dome that covers the city. Although published abroad, *We* prompted the

Soviet critic A. K. Voronsky to respond that Bolshevism desired not the subjugation of the 'I' to the 'We' but their harmonious synthesis and that the communist world, far from exaggerating the divorce between city and nature, would achieve its balanced coexistence. When Orwell confronted the horrors of political totalitarianism in *Animal Farm* (1945) and *1984* (1949), he depicted, in the latter, a world where the surveillance of the individual by the watchful eye of Big Brother was no longer assured by glass alone but by microphones and television screens. The literary ploy of introducing rebellious characters such as Zamyatin's 'Mephi', living outside the dystopian mainstream, recurs often in counter-utopian literature of the twentieth century: in Ray Bradbury's *Fahrenheit 451* (1953) the outsiders each memorize a book to counteract the regime's eradication of the past.

In *Metropolis* (1927), the architectural training of the film's director, the Expressionist Fritz Lang, is

Still from the film Modern Times, *directed by Charlie Chaplin, 1936. The Kobal Collection, London*

Erich Kettelhut, Metropolis, set design, second version: city with tower, 1925. Stiftung Deutsche Kinemathek, Berlin

evident in the powerful urban visions created in collaboration with his three set designers, Erich Kettelhut, Otto Hunte and Karl Vollbrecht. The film's foreboding, striking sets provide an exaggerated portrayal of certain tendencies of contemporary urbanism with its buildings amassed like mountain ranges, its streets like canyons, its aeroplanes, its crowds gushing out of the workplace, its overhead trafficways, its main generator that resembles an altar for human sacrifice, and its underground machine halls where armies of slaves toil under life-threatening conditions. In his preliminary sketches, Kettelhut depicted a more orderly, almost idyllic downtown, dominated by a Gothic cathedral like that of Cologne. It was Lang who insisted that the ominous, nightmarish aspect of the city be emphasized and that a Tower of Babel be placed in the symbolic central location. The cathedral, an image of unity dear to the Expressionists, was retained for the final reconciliatory scene, where it symbolized the heart of the new city based no longer on

exploitation but on a new humanity. (In 1930, in response to Metropolis, the American director, David Butler, released Just Imagine with sets designed by Stephen Goosson, an optimistic vision of New York fifty years hence.) For Things To Come, the 1936 film version of his 1933 book, The Shape of Things to Come, Wells explicitly stipulated that he wanted to produce the exact opposite of Fritz Lang's environment in Metropolis. Following a century of war, disease and despotic rule which had begun in 1936, reason would at last reign again in his fictional, totally rebuilt 'Everytown'. Set designs by Fernand Léger were rejected by Wells; Le Corbusier chose not to participate; László Moholy-Nagy contributed numerous ideas (including creating a transparent world where opaque walls were replaced by glass and plastic); and Vincent Korda finally designed Everytown, an ornament-free, horizontal environment which typified the style of the Modern Movement. But it was, perhaps, Wells who had the last laugh. At the end of Things To Come, his stream-

Schulz Neudamm, *Metropolis*, 1926. Poster for
the film by Fritz Lang. Museum of Modern Art,
New York

Erich Kettelhut, *Metropolis. The Tower of Babel*,
1925. Stiftung Deutsche Kinemathek, Berlin

lined town is razed to the ground. By 2054, Nature has reclaimed the land, the city has moved underground and bemused children watch historical films to discover the skyscraper city that once was New York.

GERMAN VISIONS OF A CRYSTAL PARADISE

In Germany, after the First World War, certain painters, and in particular George Grosz, portrayed a nightmarish urban scene in which the exploitation of man by man seemed to go unhindered. Grosz did not share the widespread hope that the first global conflict had changed the world for ever and that a new, better, era was dawning, as Heinrich de Fries expressed in 1919: 'From the deepest torment, the terrible struggle fought during humanity's blackest hours, arises the dawn of a new world, glowing in the promising light of a new art.'[5] While most idealists during the first half of the century envisaged the future within an industrialized framework, some took a position closer to that of William Morris, picturing a forthcoming, community-oriented world, inspired by the Middle Ages, where the artisan, not the machine, created beautiful and useful objects. This was the case with the German Expressionist architects whose crystal edifices were to induce and celebrate a new civilization in harmony with the universe, sculpted by the hand of its architect creators. This movement, which reached its zenith against the backdrop of unemployment, galloping inflation, the collapse of the building and other industries, and the German revolution of November 1918, emerged shortly before the Great War.[6] In 1914, the Deutsche Werkbund exhibited a glass pavilion, Bruno Taut's 'Glashaus'.[7] This architectural jewel, designed to capture and shatter the light of the cosmos and offer a haven of peace to the purest souls, was a model for the more ambitious glass architecture that Taut soon recommended for all collective buildings. 'The Gothic

cathedral is the prelude to glass architecture,' he wrote on the title page of the pamphlet that accompanied the pavilion, and he inscribed texts by the novelist Paul Scheerbart upon the precious edifice. Scheerbart, in turn, dedicated *Glasarchitektur* (1914) to Taut: a compilation of 111 lyrical texts which argued that for humankind to reach a higher cultural level, it was necessary to transform architecture, creating edifices of clear and coloured glass letting sun, moon and starlight flood through their transparent walls.

Bruno Taut, a pacifist with the drive of a missionary, co-directed a workers council for art alongside Walter Gropius, founded the magazine *Frühlicht*, operational from 1920 to 1922, and was involved with the group around the Expressionist review, *Der Sturm*. The symbolism is crystal clear in the 28 charcoal drawings that make up *Der Weltbaumeister*, a series of theatrical backdrops in which

Still from the film Just Imagine, *directed by David Butler, sets by Stephen Goosson, 1930. British Film Institute, London*

George Grosz, Die Großstadt (Metropolis), *1916–17. Fundación Colección Thyssen-Bornemisza, Madrid*

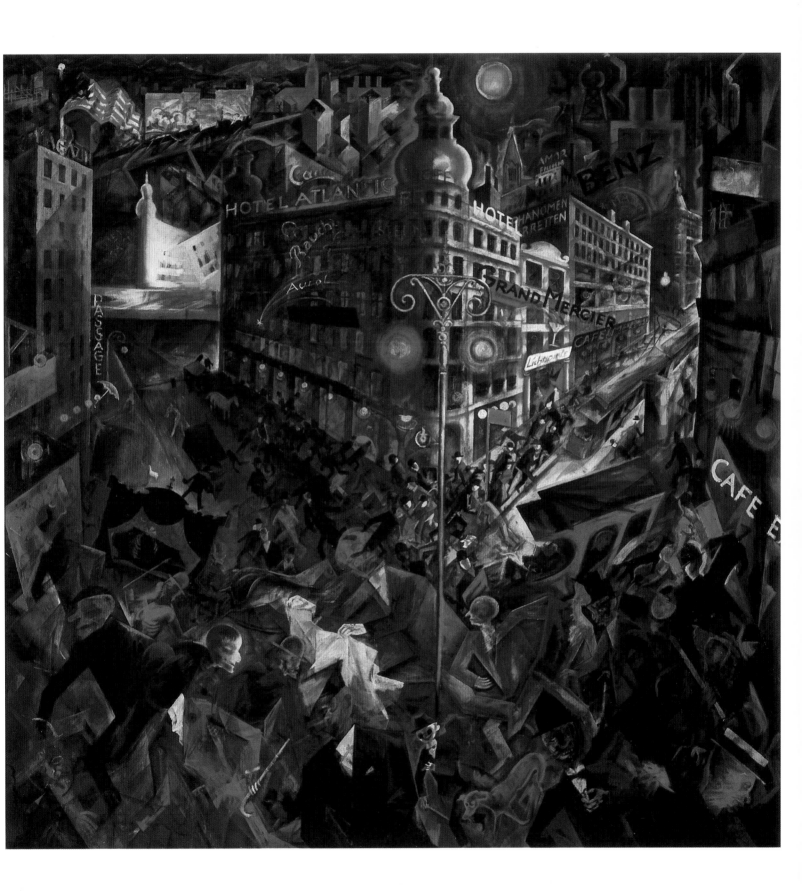

a cathedral rises and falls, a starlit night passes, a radiant crystal edifice appears, bathed in the red light of dusk, and a rainbow unites heaven and earth. Convinced that religious faith was a prerequisite to true culture and well-being, Taut proposed, in *Die Stadtkrone* (1919), that a non- or suprapolitical socialist movement could satisfy such a religious drive in his ideal city, where modest homes nestled around a sacred glass palace, the urban crown. Taut was inspired by the Temple of Solomon in Jerusalem, the Baroque plan of Karlsruhe, Howard's garden city and the project for Friedenstadt designed by Hans Kampffmeyer, General Secretary of the German garden-city movement, and took up the latter's vignette in his drawing of the urban crown viewed from the east, basking in its halo of blazing sunshine. In *Alpine Architektur* (1919), dedicated to Scheerbart, Taut again imagined coloured crystal cathedrals, now glistening among the mountain tops, oases, glowing at night, devoted to beauty and peace, transcending national conflict in protest against the bellicose environment of the time. The act of participating in as monumental a scheme as the transformation of a chain of mountains would, he believed, absorb human energies and redirect humankind's propensity to aggression into one of universal fraternity – ideas of concern to Nietzsche as well as to contemporaries such as Thomas Mann and the architect Otto Kohtz. The cosmic dimension of his ideal is accentuated by the presence of celestial signs, stars and moon crescents in his drawings. In *Auflösung der Städte* (1920), Taut condemned the arachnoid cities where capitalist property speculation ran riot and envisaged a world of huge, low-density garden cities where fertile land is populated equitably and nation states no longer exist. Such movements of population were in fact being encouraged in German legislation at this time in an attempt to alleviate the misery (and perhaps the risk of political radicalization) of the post-war populace. In this work, Taut referred to both Kropotkin, whose world of mutual aid was symbolized by the medieval cathedral and town hall, and Gustav Landauer (who had translated Kropotkin).

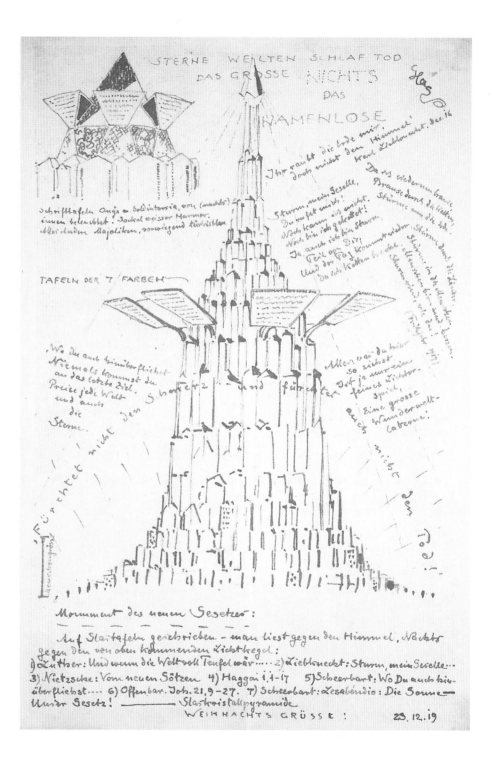

Bruno Taut, *Monument to the New Order*, letter of 23 December 1919. Stiftung Archiv der Akademie der Künste, Berlin

SCHNEE
GLETSCHER
GLAS

Die Ausführung ist gewiss ungeheuer schwer und opfervoll, aber nicht unmöglich. Man verlangt zu selten von den Menschen das Unmögliche. (Goethe)

Illustration from Bruno Taut, *Die Stadtkröne*, Jena, 1919

Frontispiece (detail) of Hans Kampffmeyer, *Friedenstadt*, Jena, 1918

Snow, Glacier, Glass, in Bruno Taut, *Alpine Architektur*, Hagen, 1919. Stiftung Archiv der Akademie der Künste, Berlin

In *Aufruf zum Sozialismus*, Landauer had envisaged a society whose rural communes ensured a harmonious combination of freedom and order, autonomy and independence, whereas Taut now projected a spatial realization of these ideas, imagining town and country blending together in a network of circular villages, each huddled around a central community hall. In 1919, Taut initiated and co-ordinated a secret circle called the *Gläserne Kette* (Glass Chain) whose members, twelve artists and architects grouped around him like apostles in a new church, used pseudonyms: Taut became 'Glas' (glass), Hermann Finsterlin 'Prometh' (Prometheus), Walter Gropius 'Mass' (measure, an identity he had already used previously) and Hans Scharoun 'Hannes' like St John (Johannes). They corresponded about a future city for a humankind yet to be born, a harmonious, paradisaical world, whose perfection and purity were symbolized by crystal. However, in 1920, Taut suddenly abandoned his brotherhood, explaining that he no longer wished to design utopias *in principio* but ones which were rooted in reality.

Wenzel Hablik, a craftsman and collector of crystals, pursued a long fascination with crystalline edifices, aerial architecture and hilltop cathedrals, producing twenty engravings in 1908–09 entitled the *Schaffende Kräfte*, wherein satellites drifted across the universe. Hablik kept a diary of his dreams and in one entry of 1908 describes building, and launching, a flying city, a theme which recurs throughout his work as in that of many others during these years, when air travel was an exciting new prospect. In *The Construction of the Celestial Allotment* a propellor-driven, outer-space Noah's Ark was to contain human samples of different races to be selected, on their return to earth, by the far from imaginary Dr Karl Gmelin, director of a sanatorium on the Frisian island of Föhr, who is reputed to have asked Hablik to build a complete small town for the purposes of experimentation in human selection. He again took up his favoured topics in 1925 in a new portfolio of etchings

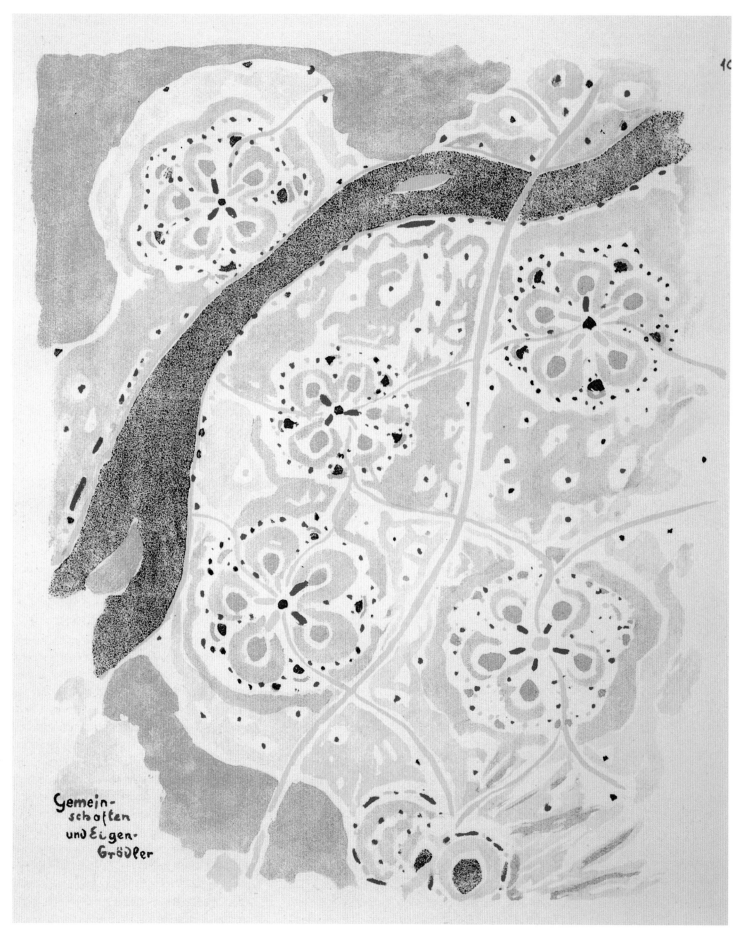

Gemein-
schaften
und Eigen-
Grödler

entitled *Cyclus Architektur* and subtitled *Peoples of the earth! Nations! Ethnic groups! Races!* Here, once more, constructions on and below the land, in the mountains, in the desert, on the sea and in the air were to be the bases of new ideals, a new religion, a new conception of the world and the reunion of the peoples of the earth – but from a political perspective far from the socialism of Bruno Taut. In 1924, by which time the Expressionist movement had almost breathed its last breath, the Austrian graphist and poet Uriel Birnbaum published *Der Kaiser und der Architekt*, an illustrated poetic tale which mocked the messianic attitude of his contemporaries. The emperor, having dreamt of a celestial city, requested that his architect realize his vision for him but, despite 33 attempts resulting in blue, yellow, white, rainbow-coloured, marble, glass, crystal, pearl, gold, silver and kaleidoscopic ideal cities or ones composed of mountains, terraces or bridges, the architect was unable to capture his master's obsession. At last, the emperor decided to give up his quest and to await its apparition beyond the grave. The architect, though, now had the bit between his teeth and, lo and behold, his final attempt produced the celestial city. However, as

though a pact had been made with the devil, he was smothered to death as the celestial belfry collapsed upon him!

When the Bauhaus opened its doors in Weimar in 1919, the school of art and design was steeped in the Expressionist dreams of its first director, Walter Gropius, a participant in Taut's Glass Chain, but within four years these ideals had evaporated. Gropius, it is true, had already displayed a rationalist streak in as early as 1911 when he built the Fagus factory at Aldfeld-an-der-Leine, but he clearly expressed his Expressionist leanings in the school's manifesto of 1919: 'Let us form a new guild of craftsmen, without those arrogant class divisions which have insolently erected a wall separating artists from craftsmen. Let us desire, envisage and create together a new guild, the guild of the future, which will be everything in a single form – architecture and sculpture and painting, which will rise aloft from the hands of a million craftsmen as the crystal symbol of a new faith to come.'[8] 'The ultimate aim of all creative activity is the building,' stated the prospectus, architecture representing the quintessence of 'total art' which united different artistic media, even though architectural training was not

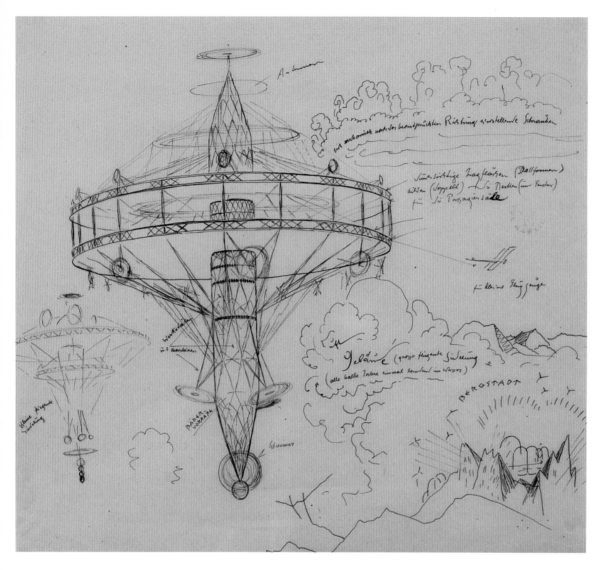

Wenzel Hablik, *Flying Settlement*, 1907–14. Wenzel-Hablik-Stiftung, Itzehoe

Wenzel Hablik, *Flying Colony*, in *Cyclus Architektur*, Berlin, 1925. Wenzel-Hablik-Stiftung, Itzehoe

properly organized at the school in its early years. The Expressionist symbolism is clear in Lyonel Feininger's cathedral illustration for the cover of the Bauhaus manifesto as indeed it is in Walter Determann's unrealized design for a Bauhaus estate, laid out in crystalline fashion and complete with its crystal symbol for the Bauhaus at its heart, in Buchfart, near Weimar. However, other architectural ideas were brewing at this time and Gropius and his school were soon to succumb to their charms.

In 1921, Theo van Doesburg, prominent figure in the De Stijl movement in Holland, entered the Bauhaus circle. Members of this mercurial group included Piet Mondrian, Gerrit Rietveld, Jacobus Johannes Pieter Oud, Bart van der Leck, Vilmos Huszar and Jan Wils. The De Stijl artists believed in concrete and

spiritual regeneration, in the forthcoming advent of a communal world, as the title of their third manifesto suggests: 'Towards a New Formation of the World'. For some, this was connected to a political conviction that capitalism, with its individualistic bourgeois culture, would soon be replaced by communism and a new era of collective art. For most, art, rather than politics, offered the pathway to achieving the new world. Transcending politics, then, their art was intended to act as a harmonious model for future life, defining a universal set of values which humanity could progressively adopt in its increasingly aestheticized everyday life. The logical outcome of this process was, as Mondrian appreciated, the ultimate obsoleteness of the arts as metropolitan life itself became art. Their language

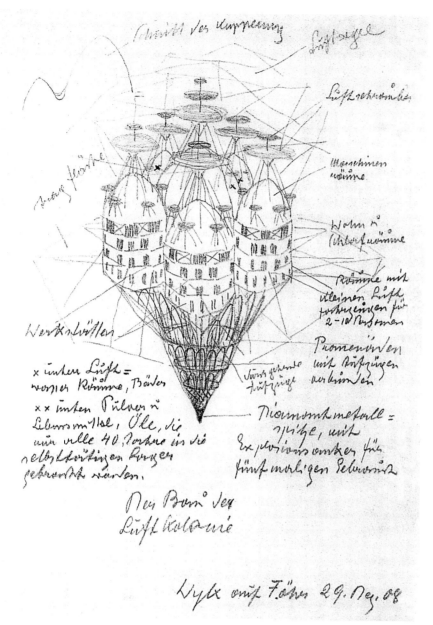

found appealing for, as Mondrian said, 'in the great city, nature is already constrained, put into order by the human spirit'.[9] In reality this proved difficult. It was Oud who recognized that their uncompromising method and syntax, though applied in a few architectural interventions,[10] encountered a major stumbling block when confronted with the city. He wrote of it to Van Doesburg: 'In the modern city we can be pure only in an isolated building. The facts impose an impure, but necessary solution.'[11] Oud's observation is important. He had understood that the profound gulf between the ideal, perfect, static form and the complexity of the urban situation was unsurpassable. Since De Stijl's purism was incompatible with the exigencies of the real city, Oud abandoned the movement in about 1920. Yet the group's work nevertheless exercised formal influence upon urban design. In the drawing for a city plan, entitled *Cité de Circulation*, by Van Doesburg and Van Eesteren whose concern is above all – as its title suggests – that of adapting the city to the problems of increasing 'automobilization', the disposition of the buildings recalls the former's *Counter-compositions*.

In the same year that Van Doesburg went to Germany, the Russians El Lissitzky and Ilya Ehrenburg moved there too and edited three issues of an arts magazine named *Veshch/Gegenstand/Objet* which presented many of the ideas emerging across Europe that were to be the foundation of the functionalist school of architecture and design. Influenced by both Constructivism and Suprematism, El Lissitzky too played an important part in adapting the new languages which had evolved in the plastic arts to architecture. In 1923, he translated the concepts of his *prouns* (signifying 'projects affirming the new in art') into three dimensions in his 'proun space' which was exhibited in Berlin. His work will be discussed again in relation to the Russian scene. In the same year László Moholy-Nagy also brought his very personal vision to the Bauhaus teaching staff, exploring glass architecture as a symbol of a regenerated European's harmonious relationship with a rational, transparent built

was one of absolute abstraction, a natural progression from Cubism, free of any reference to objects in nature, unhampered by the individualistic distractions of external realities. It therefore limited its expression to the use of vertical and horizontal straight lines, in due course organized in a gridiron, and orthogonal blocks of the base colours with black, white and grey. (When Van Doesburg, probably as a consequence of his exchanges with El Lissitzky, introduced diagonals, the result was a major rupture with Mondrian.) The members of De Stijl were keen to act upon the city, which they

dry style of machine forms without the contents. His own chaste taste gave these hollow glass shells a crystalline purity of form; but they existed alone in the Platonic world of his imagination and had no relation to site, climate, insulation, function, or internal activity; indeed, they completely turned their backs upon these realities just as the rigidly arranged chairs of his living rooms openly disregarded the necessary intimacies and informalities of conversation.'[13]

Progressively the Bauhaus abandoned its Arts and Crafts foundations in favour of a *rapprochement* with heavier industry. This shift was complete by 1923, when Gropius had devised the motto 'Art and Technique, a new unity', and a square, white, functionalist model house, the *Haus am Horn*, designed by Georg Muche, was displayed during the Bauhaus exhibition as the optimal example of new living for Germany. Functionalism, inextricably linked with the industrial process and responding to the needs of a country suffering, like Germany after the First World War, from economic hardship and a housing shortage, now provided the school's ideological foundation.[14] Mechanization permitted the mass production of prefabricated, standardized objects and could be applied to almost any element ranging from an item within a house to the components of the house itself and hence to a district or even a complete city. Its influence extended beyond its products to incorporate not only the work process but also the private life of the labourer in its every aspect and thus, just as Ford had rationalized factory production, architects now set out to 'scientifically' analyse the behaviour of the populace in order to establish the most efficient way of organizing the city.

In 1925 the Bauhaus was transferred to Dessau, having been considered too radical by the local right wing, and Gropius designed its famous headquarters there. Its glazed curtain wall prompted Rudolf Arnheim to marvel in 1927 that, 'It is a triumph of purity, clarity and generosity. Looking in through the large windows, you can see people hard at work or relaxing in private. Every object displays its con-

Lyonel Feininger, *Cathedral*. Frontispiece of *Manifest und Programm des Staatlichen Bauhauses*, 1919. Bauhaus Archiv, Berlin

Pages 172–173
Uriel Birnbaum, *The Apparition of the Celestial City*, 1921–22, in *Der Kaiser und der Architekt*, Leipzig and Vienna, 1924. Graphische Sammlung Albertina, Vienna

Walter Determann, *Plan of the Bauhaus Colony, south of Weimar*, 1920s. Kunstsammlungen zu Weimar

environment. Glass, which had so fascinated the Expressionists, now appeared in new forms, such as Ludwig Mies van der Rohe's design for a glass office tower for Berlin's Friedrichstrasse (published in *Frühlicht*, 1922). Mies, who was later to become the school's third and final director, was another purist and was convinced that the architect could define the Platonic universals which suited the spirit of his age and thus instil order and harmony into a chaotic world. 'True architecture,' he claimed, 'is always objective – the expression of the inner structure of the age out of which it has grown.'[12] Lewis Mumford's criticism was caustic: 'Mies van der Rohe used the facilities offered by steel and glass to create elegant monuments of nothingness. They had the

ÉTUDE POUR
LA CITÉ DE CIRCULATION
ECHELLE 1:400 VOIR DÉTAILS
PARIS 1924-1929 ARCHITECTE

Theo van Doesburg and Cornelis van
Eesteren, *The City of Circulation,* Paris,
1924–29. Instituut Collectie Nederland,
Rijswijk

struction, no screw is concealed, no decorative
chasing hides the raw material being worked. It is
very tempting to see this architectural honesty as
moral, too.'[15] Two *siedlungen* (workers' housing
districts) created under Gropius's aegis – Dammer-
stock at Karlsruhe (1927–28) and Siemenstadt in
Berlin (1928) – confirmed the school's new
direction. A complete architectural department was
finally created at the Bauhaus in 1927 under Hannes
Meyer, who had spent a brief spell as Georg Metzen-
dorf's assistant for the planning of the Margareten-
höhe garden city from 1909. During World War I,
when the Krupp firm had as many as 167,000
employees, Meyer had worked in its building department under Robert Schmohl. His later recollection
of those days requires no comment: 'We had to build
the so-called "menage" for 5000 workers with
canteens and dormitories. The workforce was standardized by number and type: every day each

received 2 litres of food with x calories, slept in two
square metres of surface and had some rest in a
courtyard of two square metres for each worker.
In 1918 we finished building a huge "menage" for
27,000 workers with annexed dormitories, where
54,000 meals were distributed each day. Hugen-
berg, the director of Krupp's at that time, said that
with such structures the German people could make
the world war an eternal institution.... I myself was
Employee Meyer no. 16824 and every Wednesday of
the war period I received an extra ration of 2 metres
of horsemeat sausage.'[16]
In 1928 Meyer succeeded Gropius as director and
recruited Ludwig Hilberseimer, who was to be
responsible for urban design at the school. In the
early 1920s, Hilberseimer had developed two
projects for ideal cities, and in 1929 he attempted
to adapt his basic concept to the specific context of
central Berlin, which he proposed razing in a
manner similar to Le Corbusier in his 'Plan Voisin'
for Paris. He considered the development of large
urban agglomerations to be the natural consequence of global capitalism and industrialization[17]
but criticized the manner in which they had grown
during the nineteenth century. Taking the problem
of circulation as their point of departure, the ideal,
rational conglomerations of the future should, he
argued, be divided into functions, with work and
residential areas clearly distinct and planned
according to basic geometrical principles upon an
orthogonal grid. In an article entitled 'Grossstadtarchitektur', Hilberseimer explained his use of basic
forms, the desired domination of chaos by a general
law: 'The need to model a mass of material which is
often enormous and heterogeneous according to a
formal law which is equally valid for all its elements
supposes that the architectonic form be reduced to
the greatest generality. A limitation to geometrical
cubic forms: the fundamental elements of all architecture.... Modelling great masses following a
general law and repressing diversity is what
Nietzsche means, when all is said and done, by
"the style": the general case, the law is honoured
and elevated, whereas the exception is, on the

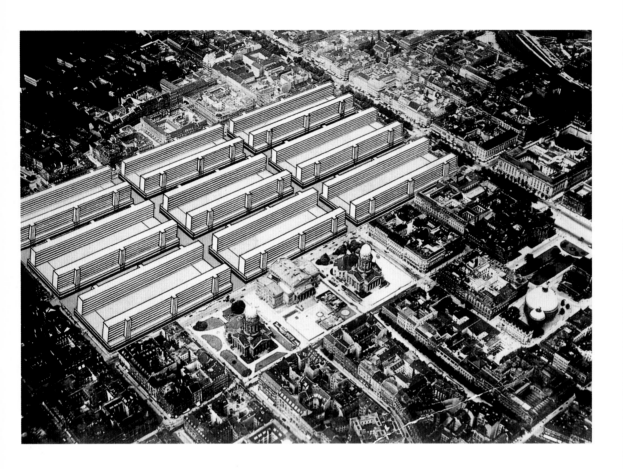

Ludwig Hilberseimer, Berlin Development Project: Friedrichstadt District, Bird's-eye view perspective, 'Applying the Principles to Berlin', c.1928. The Art Institute of Chicago, Gift of George E. Danforth

contrary, pushed aside, the nuance obliterated; measure imposes itself as the master, chaos is forced to take form: logic, clarity, mathematics, law.'[18] The first of Hilberseimer's ideal-city designs was for a series of residential satellite towns housing populations of 125,000 each, to be built around a central city which would fulfil the economic, administrative, cultural and industrial functions, and to which access would be provided by rapid rail transport. He made reference to Letchworth and Welwyn garden cities in England, and his project has been described as a rational, modernist variant of Ebenezer Howard's scheme for garden cities. The layout of the model satellite city is as follows: 78 long, rectangular residential blocks with terraced roofs, placed upon a grid and making up a rectangular plan, are divided by north–south axes running along their lengths; the central axis contains a

railway line with stations spaced one kilometre apart. Commercial roads run east–west along the widths of the buildings flanked by shops and, at the extremities of these streets, hospitals and schools occupy the outskirts of the towns. His second ideal-city plan was drawn up after a journey in 1924 which included a visit to Le Corbusier's office, where he saw the latter's drawings for his 'Ville contemporaine de trois millions d'habitants'. In this vertically layered city of towers, again laid out upon a rectangular plan, Hilberseimer superimposes a series of residential fifteen-storey towers upon a broader five-storey business district. The difference in width between the upper and lower blocks allows for the provision of 10-metre wide pavements upon the roofs of the inferior buildings, which are, in turn, separated by 60-metre wide streets reserved for automobiles. Provision is made for metro and rail

Ludwig Hilberseimer, *Hochhausstadt* or
Highrise City: perspective view of North-South
street, 1924. The Art Institute of Chicago, Gift
of George E. Danforth

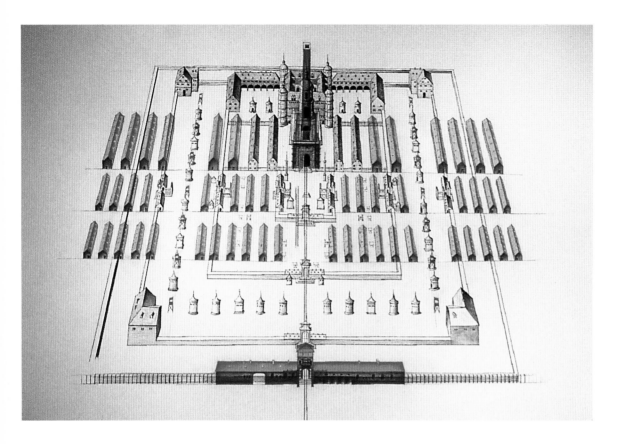

Melvin Charney, *Visions of the Temple (After Matthias Hafenreffer's Reconstruction of the Temple of Jerusalem, Tübingen, 1631)*, 1986. The National Gallery of Canada, Ottawa

transportation upon a further four underground levels. Hilberseimer's oft-reproduced monochromatic drawings for this project offer a spine-chilling, dystopian rendering of the architect's intentions and almost a caricature of the Functionalist city. In 1963, in a rare and surprising *mea culpa*, Hilberseimer described this ideal city of towers, designed some forty years earlier, as inhuman in every regard, a completely sterile landscape of asphalt and cement, resembling a necropolis more than a metropolis.[19] The crystal dreams of a pure, new, socialist or communist world of many of the Expressionists and the Functionalists around the Bauhaus soon shattered like so many windows during the infamous Night of Crystal, when the Nazis ransacked the shops belonging to Jews. The Gestapo and the S.A. forcibly closed the Bauhaus definitively in 1933, and many of its key players emigrated to America, promised land once again. The architectural expression of the National Socialist government – whose ideology contained, at least in conception, its own strong utopian element[20] – can be found in the grand plans of Hitler's architect and Minister for Armaments and War Production, Albert Speer, for

Berlin. By means of an enormous north–south axis, public squares and monumental buildings, Speer's megalomaniacal scheme was designed above all to provide a setting for a display of totalitarian power and its planned completion in 1950 would have been the occasion for a universal exhibition and the rechristening of Berlin as 'Germania'. Functionalism may not have been the style Speer chose to employ here but the regime did not entirely ignore it, reserving it instead for its most dystopian realizations: the concentration camps and the complete city of Auschwitz.

Italian Futurists: Cities that Rise and Re-arise

'We affirm that the world's magnificence has been enriched by a new beauty: the beauty of speed. A racing car whose hood is adorned with great pipes, like serpents of explosive breath – a roaring car that seems to ride on grapeshot is more beautiful than the *Victory of Samothrace*...

It is from Italy that we launch through the world this violently upsetting incendiary manifesto of ours. With it, today, we establish *Futurism*, because we want to free this land from its smelly gangrene of professors, archaeologists, *ciceroni* and antiquarians... Take up your pickaxes, your axes and hammers and wreck, wreck the venerable cities pitilessly!'[21]

Such were the words French readers could discover on opening their newspaper, *Le Figaro*, on 20 February 1909, when Filippo Tommaso Marinetti published the first Futurist manifesto. The Italian Futurists made an important contribution to the history of ideal-city design by introducing the fourth dimension as a central feature (even though this also became an element as rigid as those of other, less hectic, models). Their movement exalted war ('the world's only hygiene'), aggression, militarism, patriotism, speed, technology, massed crowds, metamorphosis and the city: not the historical towns but the modern metropolises, buzzing with life, glistening with steel and throbbing to the vibrations of the motor car. The vision of the painter Umberto Boccioni, who had previously depicted cities like Milan in paintings that conveyed a sense of melancholy and the isolation of humankind lost within the great industrial urban complex, changed dramatically in 1910, as though he were victim of some contagious disease, in this case Futurism. Now, he was elated by the emerging city. The role of the citizen, indeed but a cog in the urban machine, a cell within a larger living organism, was enviable, thrilling. In *La Città che sale* (1910), the city can be perceived in the scaffolding and the new constructions rising in the background, while the foreground is occupied by the symbolic figures of two horses engaged in a battle for domination: the stronger, red beast, representing the Futurist revolution, is clearly taking the place of the white animal, whose domain is that of the past. Scaffolding plays a major role in many of Boccioni's canvases. Marinetti declared in his book on Futurism of 1911, that there existed nothing finer than the scaffolding of a house under construction, for it symbolized the state of flux the Futurists extolled so passionately. Cities, like people, were but elements within the greater cosmic scheme, reflections of a universe which was in continual movement. Asphyxiated by the rich cultural heritage of their homeland, yet not satisfied with the newly emerging metropolis as a finality, the Futurists proclaimed that every generation should tear down the existing cities and build its own. Marinetti took transformation to an extreme in his novel, *Gli Indomabili* (1922), where the urban environment foreshadowed ideas developed from the 1950s: now the incessantly changing object of its inhabitants' desires, it was a city of Light, accessible to people whose hearts were pure, welcoming and familiar like a long-lost mother, constantly moving like the sea, with houses created out of hitherto unknown, vaporous materials in forever changing shapes and dimensions. The idea of a Futurist reconstruction of the universe was taken up again by Virgilio Marchi and Vincenzo Fani (who used the pseudonym VOLT) after the First World War. Fani's descriptions in his 1919 manifesto seem to verge on delirium when he describes dynamic flying houses taking off from the ground, congregating to form huge cities which then unite with the inhabitants of Venus and Mercury to wage war on Mars.

In 1914, the Futurists were joined by the architect Antonio Sant'Elia, their most prominent urban visionary, mortally wounded at war in 1916 and later described by Marinetti as a pioneer of Futurist-Fascist architecture. Sant'Elia's influences included the writings of Jules Verne and Emilio Salgari as well as developments in the American metropolises. His *Città Nuova* drawings, exhibited in 1914, conveyed the atmosphere of his ideal city. The exhibition

Virgilio Marchi, *Futurist City, Building for a Square*, 1919. Private collection, Rome

Umberto Boccioni, *The City Rises*, 1910–11. Museum of Modern Art, New York, Simon Guggenheim Fund

catalogue contained a *Messaggio* explaining his views on modern construction amplified in a 'Manifesto of Futurist Architecture' of the same year. Considering that a reinvented architecture could express most accurately the mechanical essence of his contemporary world, the emphasis in Sant'Elia's environment is on technology and dynamism but also, once more, the promise of the building site. Sant'Elia proposed tearing down vast areas of urban slumland and erecting a monumental, multi-levelled ornament-free city in which the communications system has pride of place, composed of hotels, docks, power stations, tall but set-back buildings, external elevators and escalators and railway stations, all of steel, glass and reinforced concrete. 'The problem posed in Futurist architecture,' he wrote, 'is a question of tending the healthy growth of the Futurist house, of constructing it with all the resources of technology and science, satisfying magisterially all the demands of our habits and our spirit, trampling down all that is grotesque and antithetical (tradition, style, aesthetics, proportion), determining new forms, new lines, a new harmony of profiles and volumes, an architecture whose reason for existence can be found solely in the unique conditions of modern life, and in its correspondence with the aesthetic values of our sensibilities. This architecture cannot be subjected to any law of historical continuity. It must be new, just as our state of mind is new.'[22]

Virgilio Marchi, *City*, 1919. Private collection, Lugano

Virgilio Marchi, *Fantastic City*, 1919–20. Private collection, Rome

Mario Chiattone, Constructions for a Modern Metropolis, 1914. Università di Pisa, Gabinetto Disegni e Stampe

Antonio Sant'Elia, The New City: building with external elevators, multi-level traffic circulation, 1914. Musei Civici, Como

CONSTRUCTING A COMMUNIST WORLD

With the Russian Revolution of 1917, the overthrow of bourgeois capitalism and the transfer of power to the proletariat, those living in the fledgling Soviet Union believed that they were experiencing the birth and formation of a completely new world. Artists who had felt isolated within the capitalist system greeted the revolution with open arms, ready to put all their energies and the ideas that they had been working on in the previous years to the service of their new leaders, exuberant in their conviction that they would at last be assimilated into society and that art would once again become an integral part of life. While artists, in general, enthused about their increasingly active role in society, architects, in particular, considered that their domain extended beyond mere physical construction for the benefit of individual clients. They were called to embrace the whole of the emerging society and to organize it through architectural and urban structures. A now familiar messianic note rings clearly in the words of the Vesnin brothers: 'A new era in the history of

mankind had begun, and everything that impeded the development of the new life had been swept away by the impetuous wave of the Revolution. Architects were confronted with the task, as it applied to the realm of architecture, of marching in step with the builders of the new life, ... through the realistic reflection and organization of the new living processes.'[23]

Constructivists (Tatlin and others), Suprematists (Malevich and others) and Rationalists (Ladovski and others), non-hermetic groups rooted in pre-revolutionary artistic developments, expressed – mainly on paper – the utopian enthusiasm for the arising society during the early years after the revolution. As the 1920s advanced, and opportunities to build increased, two main camps emerged: urbanists and disurbanists. In 1932, however, Stalin put a stop to such debate among informal art groups by decreeing their dissolution, proclaiming Soviet Socialist Realism as the only acceptable artistic style and gathering architects within the Union of Soviet Architects.

In order to understand the ideas that emerged after the 1917 revolution, it is instructive to take a quick look in the rearview mirror at developments in previous years. The latter have been considered predictive of the forthcoming socio-economic changes (as has been suggested about the forms explored by Boullée and Ledoux prior to the 1789 revolution in France). This was certainly the view of some of the key figures of the period as the respective words of Malevich and Tatlin testify: 'Cubism and Futurism were the revolutionary forms in art foreshadowing the revolution in political and economic life of 1917',[24] and 'The events of 1917 in the social field were already brought about in our art in 1914 when "material, volume and construction" were laid as its "basis".'[25] Russia witnessed a feverish bubbling up of artistic creativity prior to the Great War with its own complete array of 'isms' including Cubism, Futurism (of a variety different from that of Italy), Cubo-Futurism, Rayonism (short-lived and described by Mayakovsky as a Cubist interpretation of Impressionism) and Suprematism. Kazimir Malevich and Vladimir Tatlin – whose relationship was stormy and competitive – were among the most influential figures on the Russian art scene both before and after the revolution. At the end of 1913, Malevich designed a backcloth depicting an abstract black-and-white square for a production of the opera *Victory over the Sun*: to this he dated the origins of the abstract school of painting known as Suprematism. February 1915 saw the first Futurist exhibition entitled 'Tramway V' in St Petersburg as well as its sequel, '0.10. The Last Futurist Painting Exhibition', in December. It was during the latter that Malevich publicly presented Suprematism. Tatlin, who is generally considered as the father of Constructivism, had participated in the 'Tramway V' show, displaying *Painting Reliefs* which resulted from his struggle with concepts such as the presentation of real space. The origins of the Constructivist movement lie in Tatlin's search to replace the painterly representation of an object (considered bourgeois after the revolution) by a volumetrical complex, that is, illusion by essential form. It is already evident in the jutting, intersecting, angular planes of Tatlin's 'corner reliefs' of 1915–16, in which

he banished frame and background altogether in his conviction that they divorced the work of art from the real world. In his interior design, assisted by Aleksandr Rodchenko and Georgy Yakulov, for the Café Pittoresque of 1917, the orthodox notion of a room was thrown into question by a dynamic, disconcerting array of constructions. Although created before the October Revolution, it forms a clear link with the architectural designs of the post-revolutionary period, lacking only real movement, the movement of the miraculous machinery which was to play so vital a role in the creation of the new world. The quasi-religious faith in the potential benefits of mechanization, efficiency and management that engulfed America and Western Europe has been mentioned already, but it is worth underlining the passionate, utopian strength of similar sentiments in Russia. Here the promise of industrialization was viewed as the means of liberating this still predominantly rural country from backwardness and the uncontrolled forces of nature. With the revolution, Bolshevism became equated with this aspired-to modernity. Despite the fact that most labour movements opposed Taylorism, the American's methods were taken on board by Lenin and referred to as NOT (*Nauchnaia organizatsiia truda*, the Scientific Organization of Labour) in the Soviet Union from 1921. Lenin explained his views in this respect as follows: 'The war taught us much, not only that people suffered, but especially the fact that those who have the best technology, organization, discipline and the best machines emerge on top; it is this the war has taught us. It is essential to learn that without machines, without discipline, it is impossible to live in modern society. It is necessary to master the highest technology or be crushed.'[26] The roles of Alexei Gastev, inventor of the term 'social engineering', and Platon M. Kerzhentsev demonstrate Russia's continuing romance with American industrialization. In *Express – a Siberian fantasy*, written before the revolution, Gastev described a super-urbanized, industrialized Siberia whose territory is covered with geometrically shaped megapolises, called Energy City or Steel City, stretching far above

Konstantin Youon, *The New Planet*, 1921.
State Tretyakov Gallery, Moscow

and below the ground. The ultimate quest in *Express* was the conquest of nature to link Russia and America in one continuous continent. After the revolution, he entertained dreams of the entire globe as a non-stop mechanized city in which a levelled-out society succumbs to the dictates of the tentacular machine. A similar vision appeared in Yakov Okunev's utopian novel *The Coming World* (1923), in which, two centuries hence, all the islands and continents have been linked together in continuous urbanization. Gastev devised a system, derived from the theories of Taylor and Ford, which was actually put into practice in the new Central Institute of Labour in Moscow and its local branches, where hundreds of thousands of workers were taught machine-like gestures by 'hammer-teachers'

attached to their arms. Kerzhentsev, rather than restricting Gastevist theories to the workplace, applied them to every aspect of human activity with a view to completely refashioning human behaviour. He even founded a successful League of Time in 1923 with its own journal, *Time*, which, far from being a marginal affair, counted Lenin, Trotsky and the theatre director Meyerhold among its supporters in a frenetic drive to save time, energy and space! Zamyatin, who despised the de-individualizing effect of both the factory and the city, was quick to condemn Gastevism in *We*, one of the rare – and chilling – anti-utopian novels to come out of Russia at this time. Examples abound to illustrate the extent of the popular excitement about industrial and American ideas in all fields: as illustration, it suffices

Nathan Altman, *Design for the decoration of Uritskii Square, Petrograd, for the first anniversary of the October Revolution*, 1918. State Russian Museum, St Petersburg

to mention aspects of its impact on music and dance. Russians in the 1920s discovered two revolutionary new 'concert halls': the factory and the city. In a symphony performed in Baku in 1922, for instance, industrial sirens and whistles, nautical foghorns, cannon and machine guns were all employed to perform a moving rendering of *The International*. In the field of dance, both Valentin Parnakh, who introduced jazz to Moscow, and Nikolai Foregger surprised spectators with their latest choreographical inventions: machine dances. In these immensely popular dances, which had names like *Taylor-jest* and *Us and Henry*, dancers enacted the working processes of pistons, locomotive wheels, transmission bands and so forth to the rhythms of the modern factory. It was within this cultural climate that similarly empassioned artists and architects sought to bring about the harmonious fusion of architecture and industry, to define a new urban portrait worthy of a modern, mechanized, egalitarian, communist society.

At the watershed of October 1917, avant-garde artists descended into the streets, leaving their easels to create socially active art which would have an impact on the real world. The city was the theatre of the revolution and buildings and prop'art trains carried its message. In 1918, Lenin himself instigated a monumental propaganda plan, inspired by Campanella's 'City of the Sun' (*Civitas Solis*, 1623), to enlighten the predominantly illiterate society. Hundreds of statues and plaques bearing Marxist inscriptions were to be erected – and indeed up to sixty were unveiled – but the project was abandoned in 1921 as many of the plaster figures crumbled, were dynamited or just ridiculed publicly. Lenin also replaced the tsarist inscription on the Romanov Tricentennial Obelisk near the Kremlin with the names More, Campanella, Winstanley, Fourier and Chernyshevsky! Street celebrations played a highly important role at this time and among the earliest and grandest of these was that for the first anniversary of October when Nathan Altman decorated the square in front of the Winter Palace in Petrograd (until 1914 St Petersburg), covering all the buildings along its sides as well as the central obelisk with dynamic Cubist and Futurist designs and construc-

Vladimir Tatlin
Moderna Museet, Stockholm

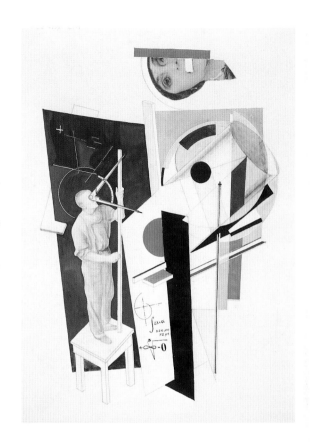

Vladimir Tatlin standing in front of the model of the *Monument to the Third International*, 1919–20. Moderna Museet, Stockholm

El Lissitzky, *Vladimir Tatlin at Work*, 1920. Illustration for Ilya Ehrenburg, *Six Tales with Easy Endings*, 1921–22. Property of the Dessau Trust

tions. In 1919, the Soviet Department of Fine Arts commissioned Tatlin to design a monument to the Third International. The following year, in Moscow, he unveiled a sensational model, paraded through the city, for a tower which was designed to reach a height of about 800 metres and whose open, transparent structure contrasted sharply with the closed aspects of traditional monuments. It was composed of an iron spiral framework on an asymmetrical axis parallel to that of the earth which supported internal glass bodies, a cylinder, a cone and a cube, intended to revolve (annually, monthly and daily respectively) like the revolutionary movement that was transforming Russia. They were to house lecture and congress facilities, executive activities and a news information centre, and boast the latest in technological prowess including telegraph, telephone, radio, loudspeaker, an open-air screen for nocturnal use and even a system of projecting texts onto the sky in cloudy weather. Though never realized, Tatlin's tower became a symbol of the revolutionary leaders' dreams of a new society and faith in the promise of industrial technology. 'My monument is a symbol of the epoch,' Tatlin explained. 'Unifying in it artistic

and utilitarian forms, I created a kind of synthesis of art with life.'[27]

In 1918, Tatlin's supporter, the art critic Nikolai Punin, announced the constructivist approach when he proclaimed that, 'The proletariat will create new houses, new streets, new objects of everyday life.... Art of the proletariat is not a holy shrine where things are lazily regarded, but work, a factory which produces new artistic things.'[28] It was only in December 1921, however, that the term itself, 'Constructivism', was used in a talk by Varvara Stepanova. Its ideology was formulated when the First Working Group of Constructivists was created under Rodchenko's leadership, and one of the earliest texts published on the movement was Alexei Gan's *Constructivism* of 1922. It is something of an umbrella term within which many artists have been grouped, but its advocates included Tatlin, Rodchenko, Stepanova, Liubov Popova, Klutsis, Aleksandr Vesnin and Moisey Ginzburg. (Tatlin was soon to diverge from other Constructivists in, for example, his preference for a natural organic basis for his designs as opposed to ideal geometric proportions.) They sought to build an ideal, new, egali-

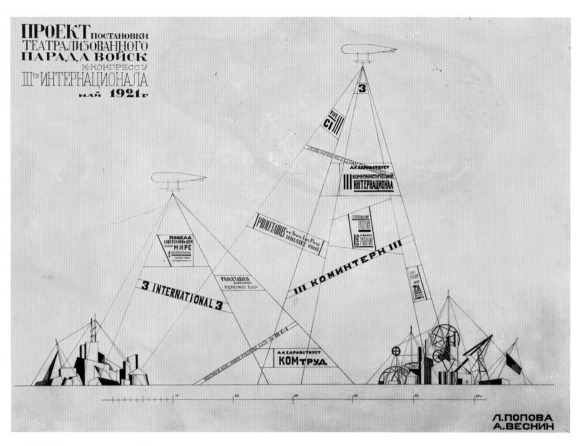

Liubov Popova and Aleksandr Vesnin, Set design
for the mass festival *The Struggle and Victory of
the Soviets*, on the occasion of the Congress of
the Third International, Khodinskoe Field,
Moscow, 1921. State Tretyakov Gallery,
Moscow

Liubov Popova, Set design for
The Magnanimous Cuckold, 1922.
State Tretyakov Gallery, Moscow

Photograph of a performance of
The Magnanimous Cuckold, with set design by
Liubov Popova, 1922. A. H. Bakrushin State
Central Theatrical Museum, Moscow

Photograph of a performance of *The Man who
was Thursday*, with set design by Aleksandr
Vesnin, 1923. A. H. Bakrushin State Central
Theatrical Museum, Moscow

tarian world within the parameters of socialism through the harmonious marriage of art and technology. Rejecting notions such as taste and composition as outdated bourgeois criteria and positioning themselves on a plane not of stylistic trends but of method, they argued along with Rodchenko that the new technological age required an art of organization and real construction. Tatlin's famous expression 'Art into Life' became their rallying cry; Rodchenko proclaimed the end of easel painting in 1921; and the Constructivists called for 'production art', the creation of industrially produced, utilitarian objects. Vesnin explained that the elements of works of art must be as dynamic, functional and essential as the parts of a machine, aiding humankind in the structuring of its new life.

As the ultimate means of giving form to the post-revolutionary world, architecture held a privileged position within the Constructivist movement. For Ginzburg, author of many key texts and particularly *Style and Epoch* (1924), architecture was the rational expression of a system of fundamental laws, and each great architectural style (by which term he went far beyond the visual aspect) was determined by the specific conditions of a given epoch. It was the task of the architect to understand these and to give them shape. Convinced that the industrial and the Russian revolutions had provided the circumstances necessary for the birth of a new architectural style embodying socialist ideals in a mechanized world, he found inspiration in the organizational ideas expressed by Taylor and Ford, quoted them in his writings, and sought to apply them to the architecture not just of the industrial factory but of modern buildings in general. New built environments were to be created not only using the most up-to-date materials and techniques but also applying what Ginzburg called the 'functional' design method. This involved the scientific analysis of every element of the users' requirements and movement in order to establish the separate functions that a building must fulfil and the optimal way of arranging these. Armed with this knowledge, architectonic prototypes which could be mass-produced using standardized components would then be designed in order to satisfy every type of constructive need as efficiently and economically as possible. The Constructivist solution thus came to involve the complete rationalization of the architectural – and living – process, its separation into functions, pre-fabrication and the standardization of the components of construction.

In the early years after the October Revolution, Constructivist architects expressed themselves in a veritable explosion of imaginative designs on paper. Their buildings conveyed information in a manner that recalls the *architectures parlantes* of Boullée or Ledoux with which they were probably familiar. As the new world was expected to be proletarian, communal and industrial, projects relating to all aspects of the life and labour of the proletariat abounded: for communal housing, palaces of labour, industrial concerns, amphitheatres, tribunes, leisure parks and so forth. Stage design provided a particularly fruitful terrain as, unlike paper projects, it enabled experimentation with space and movement. In 1921, in a design for *Struggle and Victory of the Soviets*, the revolutionary theatre director Vsevolod Meyerhold's rehearsed but unrealized mass pageant for the Congress of the Third International, Liubov Popova and Aleksandr Vesnin contrasted a formless 'Citadel of Capitalism' with a dynamic, Constructivist 'City of the Future'. In 1922, Popova, who was very active in the Constructivist movement and a keen advocate of 'production art' (like Stepanova, she went to work in a textile factory), designed a set for Meyerhold's production of *The Magnanimous Cuckold* in which a construction, consisting of a scaffolding with one large and two smaller wheels, was erected upon a bare stage but could also be rebuilt in the open air. This on-stage construction device symbolized, for the Constructivists, the new world then being built. Meyerhold complemented the Constructivist sets which he had commissioned by his introduction of Biomechanics, a system of gestures closely inspired by the theories of Gastev, into the theatre. Vesnin created another urban landscape for the 1923 stage version of G. K. Chesterton's novel, *The Man Who Was Thursday*: the whole proscenium was occupied by a multi-levelled, mechanized, imaginary metropolis, complete with three working lifts, three rotating billboards, an escalator and a swing crane. A similar

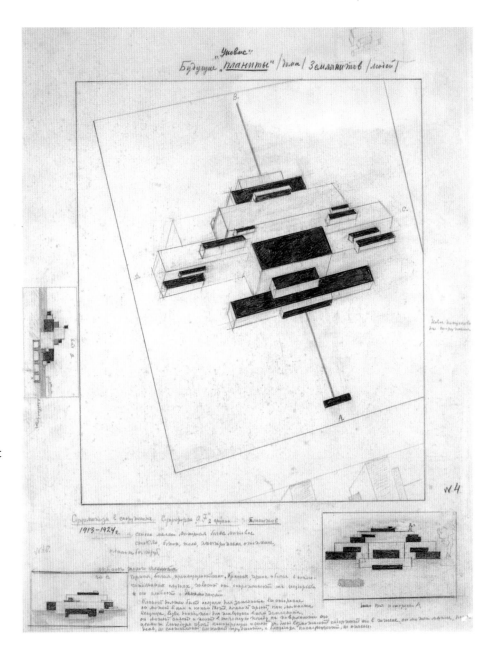

Kazimir Malevich, *Future 'Planits', Homes for Earth Dwellers*, c. 1924. Stedelijk Museum, Amsterdam

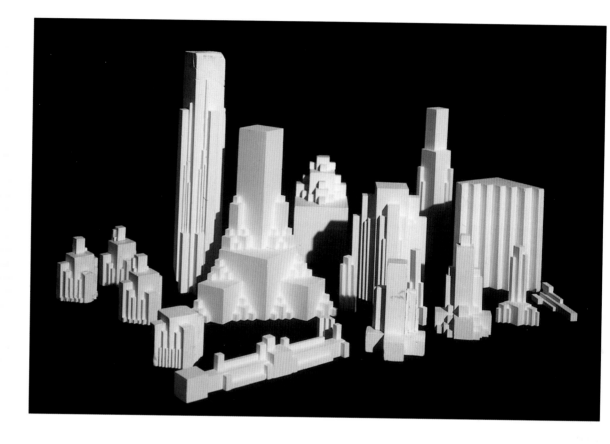

Aleksandr, Viktor and Leonid Vesnin, *Pravda Tower*, 1924. Architectural Museum, Moscow

Kazimir Malevich, *Suprematist Ornaments, City*, 1927. Reconstruction composed of 7 original pieces and 11 reconstituted by Paul Pedersen, 1978. Centre Georges Pompidou/MNAM-CCI, Paris

dynamism to that shown in his stage design characterized the unrealized architectural projects that Aleksandr Vesnin prepared with his brothers, Viktor and Leonid, notably those for the Moscow Palace of Labour and the offices of the *Leningrad Pravda* newspaper.

According to Kazimir Malevich, Suprematist painting died in 1919 with his one-man show entitled 'From Impressionism to Suprematism', and the realm of pure sensation moved with the artist from the easel, which he virtually abandoned, to the compass. In fact, by 1915, he had already begun to explore volume graphically in idealized drawings called *Planits* or *The Contemporary Environment*. A cosmic dimension is conveyed by their apparent suspension in a weightless atmosphere, although these designs were also intended to provide practical inspiration for real building as words on his *Future planit for inhabitants of the earth* of 1923–24 indicate.

During the 1920s, he continued his exploration in three dimensions in models known as *Architectonics*, *Ornaments* and *Monuments*, a variety of parallelepipeds made initially in cardboard but later in plaster. They sought to express the quintessence of a new universal Suprematist architectural or urban order, acting like models waiting to be adopted by builders once the opportunities finally arose. It seems most probable that a familiarity (albeit unacknowledged) with the ideas of Nikolaï Fedorov lay at the heart of Malevich's work.[29] This Russian philosopher, active in the second half of the nineteenth century, had argued that, rather than contemplating the existing natural world, humankind must replace it by a new universe whose order would be determined by the human mind. Fedorov assigned to architecture the task of representing symbolically the transformed matter of the universe and to the artist-architect that of modelling its

forms, in order to master and overcome the natural laws. This restructuring of the cosmos would entail humankind's colonizing outer space and creating new living environments both on earth and throughout the solar system. The influence of Fedorov explains Malevich's quest (and also that of others) to invent a new, in this case Suprematist, order, and helps to explain the particular excitement – which went beyond the more generalized enthusiasm inspired by science fiction – over outer-space projects in Russia at this time.

Lissitzky explained: 'Suprematism having itself traced the true way of the creative process, "the composition" of the new nature, our painting has become a symbol, and the realization of that new nature will be our task in life. Once we have assimilated all the experiments in painting, including that of Cubism, which frees us from rigidity, once we have understood the aim and the system of Suprema-

tism, then we shall give the earth a new face, we shall rebuild it in such a way that the Sun will no longer recognize its satellite. We have given ourselves the task of creating the city ... the new city will not be the chaotic city of modern America, it will present the clear and logical organization of the beehive.'[30] He pursued the search for a Suprematist order in a series of paintings and graphic works which he called *Prouns*, signifying 'projects affirming the new in art', from 1919, and these were transformed into three dimensions in his 1923 Berlin exhibition mentioned earlier. He described these model painting-projects in a lecture delivered in 1921 as 'a changing-trains between painting and architecture'. These designs – for the city, the bridge or the intersection, for instance – proposed ideal solutions to typical problems free of any specific physical context. The most famous of Lissitzky's limited number of architectural schemes for specific sites is

El Lissitzky, *Proun 1E: Town*, 1919–20. Private collection

El Lissitzky, *New Man*. Design of a figure for the opera *Victory over the Sun*, Hanover, 1923. Stedelijk Museum, Amsterdam

El Lissitzky, *Skyscraper by the Nikitskii Gates, Terskii Boulevard,* preparatory drawing for the *Stirrups of the Clouds,* 1924. State Tretyakov Gallery, Moscow

his 1923–25 *Stirrups of the Clouds* design for seven identical horizontal skyscrapers in Moscow, a new world dominating the old city which it would have been quite simply impractical to raze, at least in the short term. In his 1928 diploma project, explicitly entitled *The Future City. Analytical study of the Essential Questions about Architecture,* but also referred to as *A City on Aerial Paths of Communication,* Georgy Krutikov, a student of Ladovski, proposed that industry be situated on earth but that structures in outer space accommodate residents who would reach them in individual plug-in flying-living units.

This was just one among a myriad of projects for aerial or spatial cities that emerged at this time, reflecting the ambitions of an age when even the skies were no longer the limit.

Futurist, Suprematist and Constructivist theories are all evident in the work of the highly prolific Yakov Chernikov who produced some 17,000 drawings and projects and has been dubbed the Soviet Piranesi. His three most important publications include *Osnovy sovremennoï arkhitektury* (1930; 'Foundations of Contemporary Architecture') in which he analysed general concepts such as space, harmony, function-

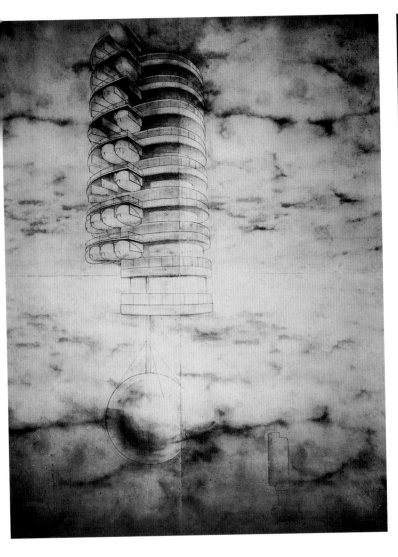

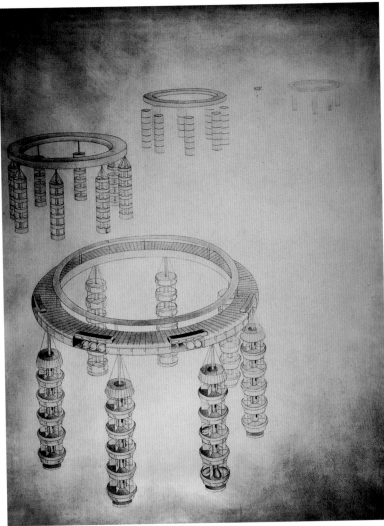

Georgy Krutikov, *A City on Aerial Paths of Communication:* communal house and organization of the city, for 'City of the Future', Vhutein Diploma project, 1928. Centre Georges Pompidou/MNAM-CCI, Paris

ality and applied a system of geometrically based spatial organization to building types such as a radio station, a stadium or an amateur flying club-museum. In the introduction, he wrote that, 'A new content and needs, a new condition for mankind create a new architecture.' In *Konstructsii arkhitecturnykh i machinnykh form* (1931; 'The Construction of Architectural Forms and Machines'), the importance of the machine – 'symbol of the dynamic of the twentieth century' – is stressed and its constructive force is analysed in order to ascertain its architectural equivalent. The 101 compositions that make up his *Arkhitecturniye fantazii* (1933; 'Architectural fantasies') employ the basic geometric forms of the square, the circle and the rectangle to project a series of ideal constructions including skyscrapers, factories, monuments and towns in which not only

the three expected dimensions are present but time/movement is also suggested.

As the 1920s advanced, opportunities for realization increased as the Soviet Union experienced rapid urbanization and a building boom, helped by the influx of foreign capital following the introduction of the New Economic Policy in 1921. Large new socialist towns with populations of up to 100,000 were planned to be dotted across the surface of the Soviet Union. Towards the end of the 1920s a clearly impressed Le Corbusier described the situation: 'Moscow is a factory of plans, the technicians' promised land. The country is being equipped. The flood of plans is astonishing: plans for factories, dams, housing, entire cities. All under one sign: *anything that brings progress.*'[31] Moreover, many of the difficulties people like Soria y Mata had experienced

'Composition no. 58, original exaggerated axonometric of a new industrial town with marked main road', in Yakov Chernikov, *Arkhitecturniye fantazii (Architectural Fantasies)*, 1933. Centre Georges Pompidou/MNAM-CCI, Paris, Gift of Andrey Chernikov and of the Yakov Chernikov International Foundation

Valentina Kulagina, *We are Building*, 1929. Merrill C. Berman Collection, New York

due to land ownership were overcome in Russia through land nationalizations. The absence of any clear model in Marx's writings regarding the form the communist built environment would take obviously left plenty of room for invention. In *Literature and Revolution* (1923), Trotsky announced the replacement of the old cities by new 'city-villages', created by the people themselves on land whose natural conditions had been restored thanks to the prowess of new technology. United in their conviction that the existing city was inappropriate for the new communist man whose ideal environment they were to create, city planners of the 1920s were divided, broadly speaking, into two main camps: the urbanists and the disurbanists, whose champions were, respectively, L. Sabsovich and M. Okhitovich. In an ambitious text entitled *The U.S.S.R. in Ten Years*,

Sabsovich outlined an urbanist vision in which – within the space of ten years – the current cities and villages would be replaced by a series of towns containing 25 to 50 residential units, each housing 1400 to 2000 people and providing well-developed communal facilities. The urbanists considered the city to be a 'social condenser', well adapted to instilling people with the communitarian attitudes which the new world required. Communal dwellings were of great interest to post-revolutionary town planners. One can see evidence of links with ideas, in the monastic and phalansterian traditions, that Le Corbusier was exploring regarding the combination of individual dwellings with communal services such as laundering or catering. The Vesnin brothers, in projects for Kuznetsk, Zaporoje and Stalingrad (where they proposed five towns along the Volga),

collapsible residential units. One of the most interesting competitions at this time was that for a Green City for 100,000 inhabitants outside Moscow, launched, in 1929, by the journalist Mikhail Koltsov. The brief had been for a city in which Muscovites would reside in rotation. Among the entrants, Konstantin Melnikov proposed a recreational city with a sort of sleep laboratory that recalled Hugo Gernsback's fiction *Ralph–124- C41+* (1911) and prefigured Aldous Huxley's *Brave New World* by three years. Ginzburg put forward a project with Mikhail O. Barsh in which, once Moscow had been gradually evacuated and transformed into a sort of leisure park, its industrial and administrative buildings were to be arranged along a series of linear routes lined with factory-produced housing units assembled on site. Ginzburg and Barsh's ideas raised much interest and prompted the socialist Settlement Section of the State Planning Commission to pursue them, resulting in further unrealized schemes for a complete network made up of small towns, industrial estates and highways flanked by family-sized prefabricated homes (the communal blocks were not maintained here) covering the entire country. Numerous and varied schemes were proposed for new towns, but this is not the place to recount them in detail. In 1928, the first Five-Year Plan called for the construction of new industrial enterprises which were intended to create close to a million new jobs: this obviously called for urgent measures regarding housing. Dreams such as the evacuation of old cities appeared as an unrealistic luxury under these conditions. The regime of the 1930s was obliged to reinstate the existing cities, but it also promoted a more academic approach to architecture and quelled the earlier utopian inventiveness displayed in the search to define the ideal accommodation of the new communist man.

envisaged urbanistic solutions. In their 1930 design for Kuznetsk, family homes were replaced by a series of dormitory buildings with extensive communal installations arranged within park space. 35,000 people were thus to be housed in grouped units which, typically, were made up of four identical three-storey blocks for 1100 people each. The factories would form the northern limit of the town, the railway line the southern boundary, a main street would connect the factory entrance to the station, and a leisure centre with a park and cultural house would be situated close to the centre. Disurbanization, which tended to incorporate a diluted mix of linear-city and garden-city theories, represents a response to the vague but recurring reflection that the new communist society would see the suppression of the sharp distinction between town and country. Okhitovich called for the redistribution of the inhabitants of cities like Moscow within continuous linear cities in which residents working in industry or agriculture shared communal facilities and prefabricated, portable and

IDEAL-CITY PLANNING IN FRANCE

Tony Garnier, a Frenchman on a scholarship at the Villa Medici in Rome and later architect for the city of Lyons, broke with tradition when he sent the Ecole des Beaux-Arts in Paris an initial set of drawings dated 1899–1900–1901 for an ideal city, along with

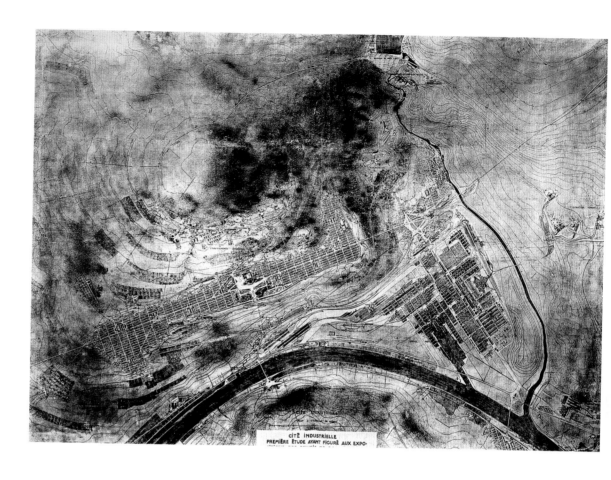

CITÉ INDUSTRIELLE
PREMIÈRE ÉTUDE AYANT FIGURÉ AUX EXPO-

his archaeological study of the Tabularium (on the Roman Forum) in 1901 and again in 1904. These early drawings established the bases of his industrial-city plans, although he was to rework the architectural aspects of the project up until 1917 when he published it, along with 164 plates, as *Une Cité industrielle. Etude pour la construction des villes*. This was the most complete scheme for an ideal city since Ledoux's publication of 1804, which it also echoed in its incorporation of buildings he had designed for actual construction (in this case in Lyons). He envisaged a population of 35,000 but, atypically, allowed for its eventual expansion. One of the most influential aspects of his city on later town planning was its organization into zones according to function. He placed the industries close to the river, the public buildings (including an assembly hall, museums, libraries, theatres and sports centres, all designed in glass and concrete) further uphill in the heart of a residential area which was composed of one- or two-storey flat-roofed houses aligned amid generously planted parkland, and he moved the schools and the hospital even further up. The streets

follow a grid pattern and enclosed areas such as courtyards and patios are prohibited. The architecture of his city is simple, standardized and ornament-free (works of art being kept firmly distinct from construction).

Garnier believed that his industrial city would be home to a radically new society, one in which land was publicly owned, food and medicine supplied by the state, and churches, prisons, law courts and police stations superfluous on account of the just and peaceful way in which it operated. His sources of influence probably include Bellamy's *Looking Backward* and Morris's *News from Nowhere* as well as Anatole France's *Sur la pierre blanche* (1905). The latter proposed a veritable rejuvenation of Antiquity in an ideal world (which none the less contained, like many a utopia, its hidden mechanistic alter ego) – an association of social with classical harmony which also pervades Garnier's work. Indeed, his classical references have been portrayed as a part of the ideological convict's ball and chain which retained him in the nineteenth century despite the forward-looking aspects of many of his concepts.

An Industrial City: metallurgical factories, blast furnaces (top) and public services, 1917, in Tony Garnier, *Une ville industrielle, étude pour la construction des villes*, Lyons, 1919

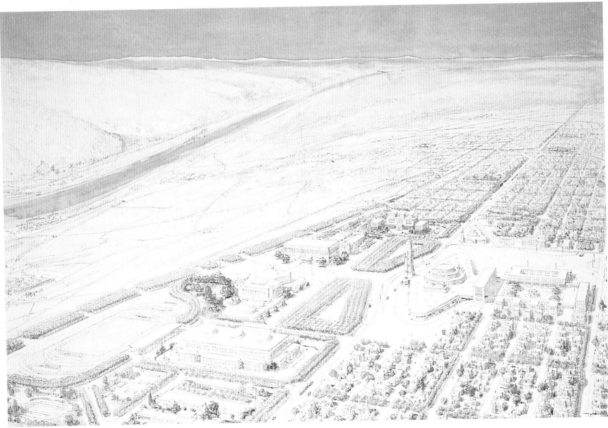

Garnier's project was inspired most directly and profoundly by Emile Zola's novel *Travail* (1901), of which it can be considered an architectural transcription, albeit one which surpasses the physical ambitions of the novel, and from which he anticipated inscribing excerpts upon the façades of his city's assembly rooms. In *Travail*, partly written in response to the Belgian poet Emile Verhaeren's *Les Villes tentaculaires* (1895), Zola describes the replacement of an old town, L'Abîme, by a new one, La Crêcherie, under the aegis of Luc, an engineer deeply marked by the doctrines of Charles Fourier. Zola's society is united around the organization of work, the regulator of the world, a joyful communion undertaken, like a new religion, by its citizens. The town contains a glass and iron factory (whose state-of-the-art technology increases the workers' output while reducing the effort invested), theatres, swimming pools, isolated hospitals for different illnesses, a gymnasium, department stores, laboratories, a covered market and a Communal House containing schools, a nursery, library, meeting rooms and public baths. Unlike Fourier, Zola leaves the workers free to determine the architecture of their residential city of white façades nestled amidst luscious gardens. The difference between the old and new societies is symbolized by the transformation of key buildings: the tribunal has become a museum, the prison a bathing house.

Le Corbusier[32] was familiar with the design solutions of his predecessors and contemporaries. Their traces can be detected in his grandiose, rational schemes to transform not only the spatial but also the social face of the world. His power to assimilate ideas, condense, transform, express fluently and propagate them was unsurpassed. The Swiss theoretician had been profoundly impressed by his discovery in 1907 of the medieval monastery of Ema in Italy: 'I saw a modern city, crowning the hillside in the harmonious landscape of Tuscany,' he wrote, 'I thought I would never again encounter so joyous an interpretation of habitation.'[33] He incorporated this impression into his own personal vision along

Attributed to Charles Imbert, Study for a City of Towers in Paris for the Perret Agency, 1922–32. Institut Français d'Architecture, Paris

with both formal and social elements from Fourier, Howard, Garnier, Soria y Mata, Eugène Hénard,[34] Auguste Perret (whose 1905 scheme to encircle Paris with towers was familiar to his part-time draughtsman of 1908, still known in those days as Charles-Edouard Jeanneret)[35] and many others. Le Corbusier formulated two grandiose ideal-city schemes – a *Ville contemporaine pour trois millions d'habitants* and *La Ville radieuse* – as well as a later linear city. These high-rise, high-density, highly controlled Cartesian places were designed to run as smoothly as machines. Thanks to structural prowess, millions could enjoy the benefits of rational planning in skyscrapers that resembled, in many ways, vertical phalansteries.

In 1920, the first issue of *L'esprit nouveau*, the journal that he edited with Amédée Ozenfant, announced: 'There is a new spirit: it is a spirit of construction and

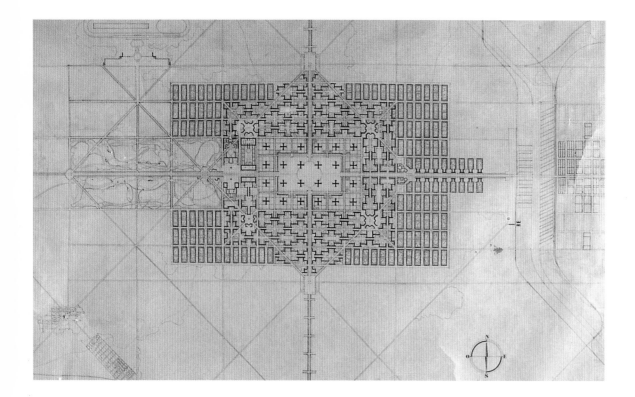

synthesis guided by a clear conception ... A GREAT EPOCH HAS BEGUN.' For Le Corbusier, the first global conflict had created a *tabula rasa* for a new age which would be classical and orderly in accordance with scientifically established rules of harmony. The role of the artist, and particularly the architect, was to interpret the fundamental truths in order to give form to this harmonious new industrial world and to avoid the revolution which risked arising from the lack of coordination between society and the physical environment. The architect alone had the talent to combine the imaginative sensitivity of the artist with the functional progress brought about by the engineer and the machine. In *Vers une architecture nouvelle* (1923), Le Corbusier described architecture as a 'pure act of creation' which puts us 'in tune with a universe whose laws we respect, recognize and obey'.[36] The secret of these universal laws could be found in the study of geometry, for 'Geometry is the basis,' he proclaimed. 'The whole contemporary era is geometrical – eminently so.'[37] The basic forms he exalted, particularly the rectangle, were those that had fascinated the Cubists, De Stijl and the Purists, and he developed a proportional system based on the human body to be used in calculating the proportions of building units, the *Modulor*. While he

abhorred the chaos of the established city, which he called 'a menacing disaster on account of its not having been animated by a geometrical spirit',[38] Le Corbusier did not reject the industrial process or the large urban concentration of citizens which he considered an essential element of the machine age, but one which required radical and thoroughly planned transformation.

The 'contemporary city for three million people' was presented in a 100 square-metre diorama at the Paris Salon d'Automne in 1922. Imagined on a flat plain, its plan is symmetrical with two super-highways intersecting at the heart of the street grid in a massive multilevel terminus; below them at this point, a station links all the subway lines, while above, another connects the mainline trains while the roof serves as a runway for aeroplanes. In the modern world, the nucleus of society would thus no longer be a palace or a place of religious worship but one of transportation, communication and interchange, working like a heart to pump the blood around the body. This focal feature is surrounded by a series of 24 sixty-storey skyscrapers providing a business district for 500,000 to 800,000 workers and social gathering places such as shops, restaurants or cultural amenities. 'From its offices,' Le Corbusier

Le Corbusier, *A Contemporary City for 3 Million Inhabitants,* plan, 1922. Fondation Le Corbusier, Paris, FLC 31006

Le Corbusier, *A Contemporary City for 3 Million Inhabitants,* perspective view, 1922. Fondation Le Corbusier, Paris, FLC 29711

said of this administrative city, 'come the commands that put the world in order. In fact, the skyscrapers are the brain of the City, the brain of the whole country.'[39] Here was a headquarters for the captains of industry, finance and politics and the leading intellectuals of this bureaucratic and hierarchical new world. This élite would live in a series of luxurious high-rise apartment blocks around, and similar in design to, the office towers: a collection of two-storey mass-produced maisonettes slotted into the basic reinforced concrete frame. Each tower would boast a sports gymnasium on the top floor, a running track on the roof, and laundry, maid and kitchen services. Locating high concentrations of people vertically, these towers occupied only 15 per cent of the ground area, so that traditional streets were eliminated and occupants provided with large areas of parkland at ground level as well as the benefits of sunlight and little noise pollution in the upper floors. The residential towers were to be owned jointly and run as non-profit-making co-operatives by their white-collar inhabitants. Blue-collar workers would be housed in garden apartments in the satellite towns on the outskirts and here, after the toils of the working day, they could find everything they required to relax: facilities for sports and hobbies, cafés, dance halls and so forth. Le Corbusier proposed many of the ideas of the Contemporary City for specific sites, including Paris, Algiers, Barcelona, Buenos Aires and São Paulo. The 'Plan Voisin' of 1925 for Paris received its name on account of the fact that, after the car manufacturer André Citroën turned a deaf ear to these grandiose plans, the automobile wing of the Voisin aircraft company agreed to back it by financing printing and exhibition costs. Claiming to be following a tradition set by Louis XIV, Napoleon and Haussmann, Le Corbusier proposed demolishing an area of almost two square miles on the Right Bank close to the Ile de la Cité and replacing it by eighteen skyscrapers surrounded by parkland with a motorway running through the heart of the site. Amid the skyscrapers, three levels of elevated pedestrian malls were to be flanked with shops and cafés; the highest of these would reach close to the tree tops, thus surrounding strollers with an ocean of greenery. His failure to muster up support from the business magnates on whom he had counted for the achievement of his scheme led him to despair of corporate enterprise as a force of change.

Le Corbusier's disappointment at his inability to find backing from capitalist enterprise led to a crystal-

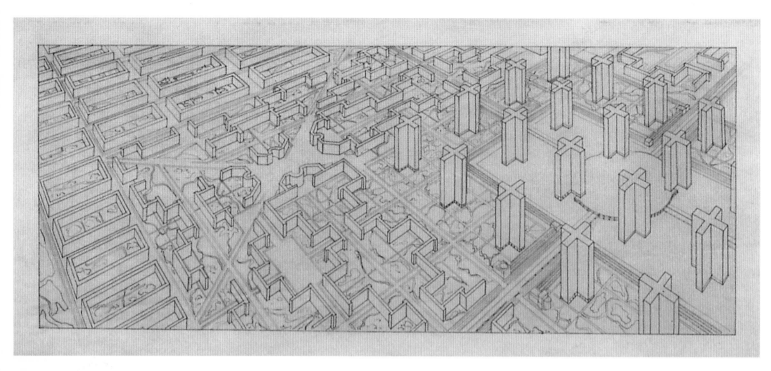

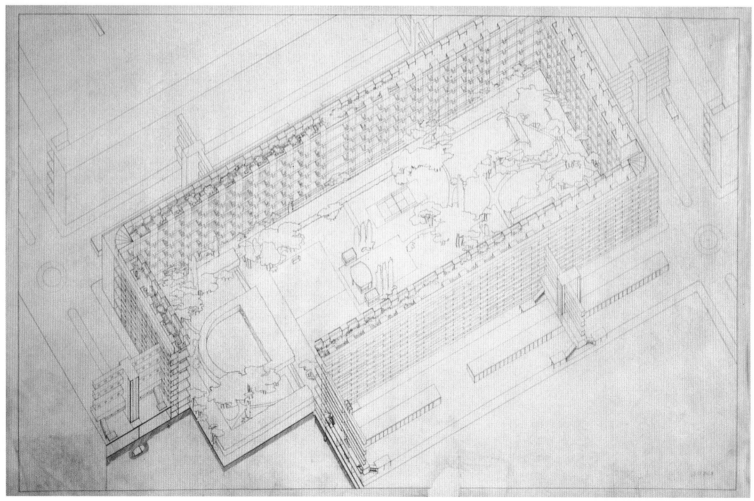

lization of his ideas about organization which were to be reflected in his other model plan, the Radiant City. No longer simply satisfied that a change in the urban structure would dictate a new social one, he demanded first a new political set-up to render these transformations possible. The new, standardized world, where individual initiative would be subjugated to the overall scheme, required a centralized industrial structure, a strong state in which party politics would have faded into virtual irrelevance and administration would have become all-important. A military-style organization with the equivalent of a general at its head, a powerful suprapolitical leader, a Minister for Public Works, who could enforce the realization of the new order which would put society and the city in tune again with the modern world. Le Corbusier became involved with the French syndicalist movement, and authoritarianism, be it of the left or the right, seemed to be the only way to achieve the new world he envisaged. Significantly,

he dedicated his publication of 1935, *La ville radieuse*, quite simply 'To Authority'. In a pamphlet written in 1928 to supplement the bulletin of the right-wing group, the Redressement Français, he called for the expropriation of landlords whom he esteemed a hindrance to the necessary urban transformation and proclaimed that it was the task of authority to put us 'in accord with a situation that has been revolutionized. If this accord is not reached quickly, the sickness that already threatens society will disorganize social life and produce these evils: confusion, incoherence, chaos, all leading to mental disarray and panic: the revolution.'[40] In *La ville radieuse*, a photograph of an Italian fascist rally is captioned as follows: 'Little by little the world approaches its destiny. In Moscow, in Berlin, in Rome, and in the United States, the masses gather around a strong idea.'[41] Although he submitted ideas to the Soviet government in 1928–29, to Mussolini in 1934 and to the French Vichy government in 1941, he never did

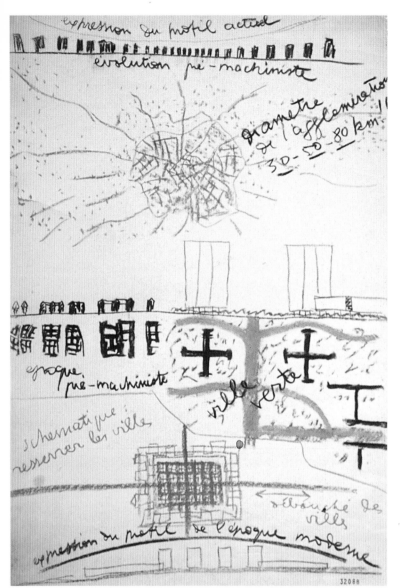

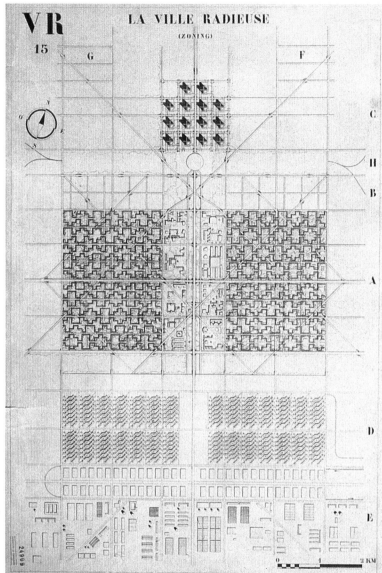

Le Corbusier, *The Radiant City*, plate showing the zoning scheme, 1930. Fondation Le Corbusier, Paris, FLC 24909

Le Corbusier, *Buenos Aires: the existing city, the modern city*, 1929. Sketch made during a conference. Fondation Le Corbusier, Paris, FLC 32088

find, like Albert Speer in Adolf Hitler, the dictator who would turn his dreams to reality. For Le Corbusier a new syndicalist world would be structured like a pyramid with blue- and white-collar factory workers at the bottom, managers, regional and then national leaders at the top of the hierarchy. This organization would be practical, based on ability, and social class distinctions would no longer exist. This is reflected in the fact that the housing in the Radiant City, now placed in the centre, is no longer segregated into zones of luxury towers and more modest garden apartments. Everybody resides together in the high-rise towers, the *unités*, which contain meeting rooms, cafés, restaurants, shops,

crafts workshops, swimming pools, gymnasia, tennis courts, laundries, nurseries, cleaning services and schools, and whose apartment size is a factor not of wealth or social position but of family requirements.

After the Second World War, Le Corbusier suggested that a great industrial linear city should cross Europe in two major north–south and east–west axes linking urban nuclei and ignoring national borders. Towards the end of his life he had the opportunity to witness the partial realization of his ideas when he built a first *Unité* at Marseilles from 1947 and planned the state capital of Punjab, Chandigarh, in India from 1950. But, as is so often the case with

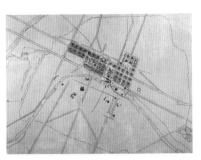

Le Corbusier, 'Plan Voisin', plan and model showing the projected site in Paris, 1925. Fondation Le Corbusier, Paris, 29722 and FLC L2(7)2−2

ideal cities, the latter proved ill-adapted to the context in which it was applied.

CONTRASTING VISIONS IN AMERICA

American planning in the first half of the twentieth century was characterized by an almost unadulterated enthusiasm for the material benefits brought about by technological breakthroughs and industrialization. The experience of the Great Depression seemed only to accentuate this trend, with science and the machine perceived as the keys to salvation, promising a life free of want. The schemes we shall now encounter all shared this attitude. While most contemplated the future from a comfortably apolitical position, Frank Lloyd Wright swam alone against the current in his challenge of the existing economic and social order.

The pharaonic ascension of the high-rise, particularly in New York and Chicago, had become a symbol of American modernity and progress by the early twentieth century, appearing, along with overhead streets and urban air transport, in a popular press which sought inspiration in the repertory of the architects (and vice versa) and contributed to the tantalizing attraction that it exercised upon the public imagination on both sides of the Atlantic. When the setting back of skyscrapers to ensure the street's exposure to sunlight was rendered obligatory in New York's Zoning Laws of 1916, Harvey Wiley Corbett enthused that the style would go down in history along with the Gothic, the Classical and the Renaissance, while Francisco Mujica in his 1929 *History of the American Style* identified the sources of this 'Neo-American style' in pre-Columbian architecture.[42] An intermittent collaborator of Corbett's, Hugh Ferriss, sought a formal ideal in response to the very real issues of civic design in New York in *The Metropolis of Tomorrow* (1929). Firstly, he analysed

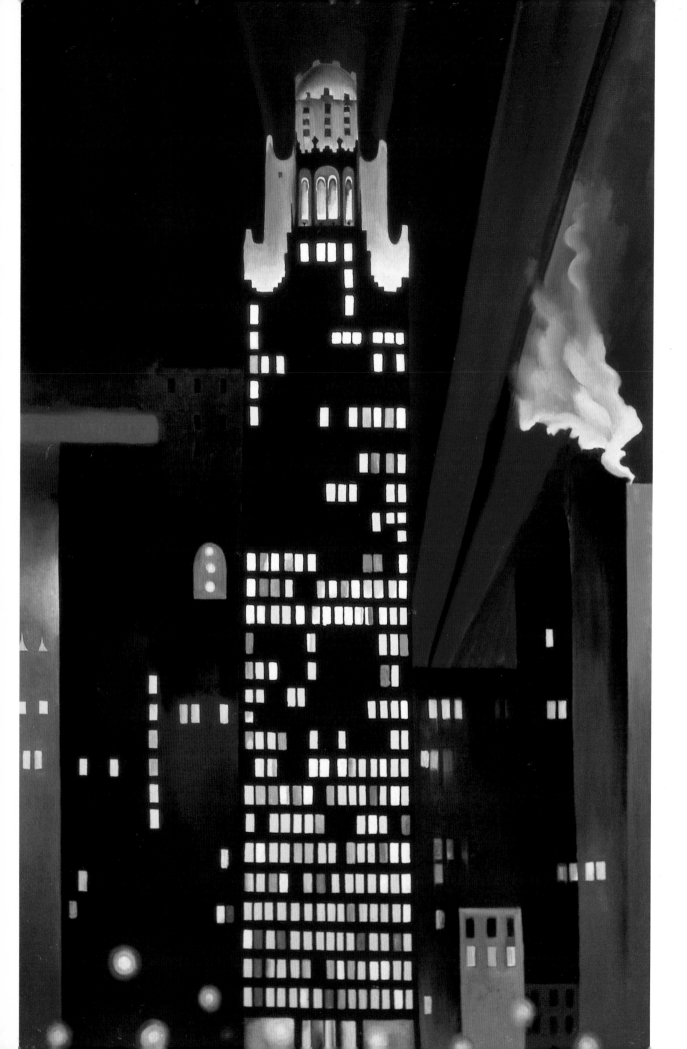

Future circulation and skyscrapers in New York, in l'Illustrazione italiana, 31 August 1913. Biblioteca Nazionale Centrale, Florence

Georgia O'Keeffe, Radiator Building, New York, 1917. The Alfred Stieglitz Collection of Modern Art, Fisk University, Nashville, Tennessee, Gift of Georgia O'Keeffe

a number of recent American buildings and trends. Though disapproving of the use of conventional forms, styles or materials within the context of the modern city, he viewed vertical traffic segregation or bridges carrying apartment buildings[43] with a favourable eye. Then, working from a basic mass which conformed crudely to the Zoning Laws, he arrived at a formal redisposition of the same cubic content in something approaching the Assyrian ziggurat, a harmonious marriage of the dignified individuality of the pyramid with the practicality of the cube. His ideal city would resemble, he ex-

plained, a plain dotted with mountains: its massive 'centres', spanning many blocks, would boast broad six-storey bases with abundantly planted roofs and majestic towers soaring some thousand feet high. The tri-focal city would contain Business, Art and Science Centres surrounding a recreational Civic Circle of parkland. Despite references to the effect of form on humankind and his inclusion of a 'clue' which hinted at an alternative system, Ferriss did not enlarge on questions of social, political or economic organization.

Writings by figures such as Taylor or Ford in the United States had, as we have seen, a strong influence on architecture and urban planning in Europe, to which the 'scientific' methods of Taylorism were applied during the first decades of the century. Another example of the intercontinental cross-fertilization of ideas can be seen in a project by the Viennese-American architect Richard Neutra, who emigrated from Europe in 1923. Like many ideal-city planners, he re-worked his scheme, entitled Rush City Reformed, over many years (c. 1923–35). Once more efficiency and transport were kings in Neutra's zoned plans, which aimed at facilitating motorized circulation by proposing a major central axis and a grid system and segregating different types of transport vertically, while maintaining a human scale by including one- or two-storey family homes, drive-in markets or schools with parking access. His project integrates a shakerful of ingredients from the two continents: alongside obvious resemblances to Hilberseimer and Le Corbusier (the rigid alignment of the downtown building blocks), Soria y Mata (a central linear axis), Sant'Elia (the multi-level railway terminal, itself influenced by New York's Grand Central Station), the verticality of Chicago or New York recurs in the business district while the residential areas recall the horizontal drive-in character of a city like Los Angeles. In 1932, when the recently built Museum of Modern Art in New York presented the latest in vanguard architectural design in its first architectural exhibition, curated by the critic Henry Russell Hitchcock and the architect Philip Johnson, Richard Neutra's work was featured. Other architects to be included were Peter Behrens, Adolf Loos, Auguste Perret, Antonio Sant'Elia, Frank Lloyd Wright and Le Corbusier and Pierre Jeanneret, Walter Gropius, Ludwig Mies van der Rohe,

Julian S. Kupra, *Cities of Tomorrow*, in *Amazing Stories*, August 1939. Musée d'Histoire Contemporaine-BDIC, Paris

Hugh Ferriss, *Vista in the Business Zone*, in *The Metropolis of Tomorrow*, New York, 1929. Reproduced with kind permission of Princeton Architectural Press, New York

Richard Neutra, *Rush City Reformed*, 1923–27. UCLA, University Research Library, Los Angeles

J. J. P. Oud and Gerrit Rietveld. The ambitious title of the exhibition was to go down in history: 'The International Style'.

Frank Lloyd Wright was dismayed at the large industrial cities of his day – whose plan he evocatively likened to the cross-section of some fibrous tumour[44] – and sought to devise a scheme which would provide a universal remedy and engender the creation of a new civilization. The artist, and particularly the architect, should play a key, almost prophetic, role in society, according to Wright, for he alone was able to detect underlying developments and express them in a physical form, acting thus as midwife of another, nascent society. 'A good plan is the beginning and the end,' he wrote, 'because every good plan is organic. That means

that its development in all directions is inherent and inevitable.'[45] Wright's highly personal scheme is, in many respects, a true offspring of the pioneering spirit that had conquered the frontiers of the Wild West, for it captures the American traditions of individualism and love of nature within the famous grid that had shaped the continent's face since the early colonial period.

In Wright's view, the industrial city was the symbol of the exploitation of humankind. There, everyone, rich and poor, was robbed of his true nature which could only be satisfied in a harmonious relationship with the countryside. 'We of these United States,' he wrote, 'have neglected to build a life – therefore a city – natural to us. A natural architecture of a natural economic order of the natural state.

Frank Lloyd Wright, *Broadacre City*, 1934–35. Reconstruction of the original model, 1990. On permanent loan to Arizona State University, College of Architecture and Environmental Design, from The Frank Lloyd Wright Foundation, Scottsdale, Arizona

Frank Lloyd Wright, *Two views of Broadacre City*, 1934–35. The Frank Lloyd Wright Foundation, Scottsdale, Arizona

Organic.'[46] Considering unjust landownership to be the cause of massive inequality, Wright echoed the views of Thomas Jefferson in his conviction that true democracy would be achieved when everyone was a landholder. 'When democracy triumphs and builds the great new city, no man will live as a servile or savage animal,' he proclaimed. The fair allotment of land would be ensured by a 'county architect', who would be responsible for the physical environment and, hence, the *de facto* leader of a world where government would be reduced to a mainly administrative function. Reaping the potential benefits of industrial progress, every 'Usonian' citizen[47] would own a piece of land of at least one acre upon which they would farm and build their homes, while also, if required, working part-time in an industrial or other professional concern of limited size and still having time to spend on intellectual pursuits.

In Broadacre City, Frank Lloyd Wright exploded the city, 'bringing it into the countryside', as he put it, shattering it with a thundering shiver into a series of homesteads scattered throughout the landscape. 'Broadacre City,' he wrote, 'is everywhere or nowhere. It is the country itself come alive as a truly great city.'[48] The urban agglomerations of his day were to be replaced by a completely decentralized system of contiguous plots of land destined most frequently to house the individual families which represented the backbone of his society. 'Automobilization' provided the driving force behind his layout, for, thanks to the proliferation of the car, Wright concluded that people no longer needed to live in compact urban units as they could all travel freely and quickly over long distances (he even defined the financial resources of his potential residents in terms of the number of cars parked in front of their homes: more or less than between one and five would imply excessive wealth or poverty). Unlike the traditional cities, his world would have no urban centre or axial symmetry to physically represent feudal or other forms of power. A community centre would provide cultural entertainment, an unfinished cathedral (the ghost, again, of medieval times), placed adjacent to it in his

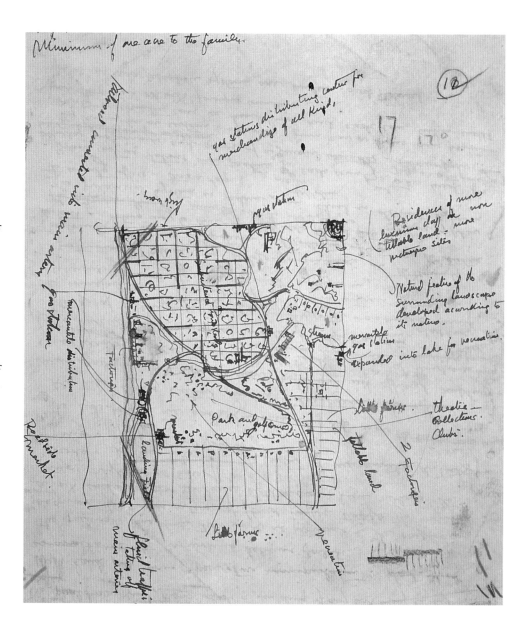

model, would be the place of worship, and industrial concerns and schools would be drastically reduced in size and disseminated throughout the scheme. The fact that America remained deaf to his plans for Usonian man was a source of disappointment to Wright but did not discourage him from pursuing his dream throughout his life.

The mainstream scientific idealism, utopian in its dream of a better world but not in its acceptance of the political and economic social order, was epitomized in exhibitions such as the 1933–34 Century of Progress Exhibition in Chicago or the 1939–40 World's Fair in New York, industry-sponsored platforms for exploring the not-so-different nor

Frank Lloyd Wright, *Broadacre City*, annotated plan (sketch), 1934–35. The Frank Lloyd Wright Foundation, Scottsdale, Arizona

Your World of Tomorrow, pamphlet from the 1939 World's Fair in New York, showing model of Democracity. New York Public Library, Manuscripts and Archives Division

despite the overriding presence of motorways in 'Futurama', the general impression was of a small-town America, healthy and fun to live in thanks to the benefits of science. However, during the years of the New York fair, a great black cloud was to darken this mood of optimism about the future, as the Second World War broke out in Europe.

so-distant future. Later, in *The Living City*, Wright, now in his nineties, could not resist a dig, labelling the 'performance in New York City to call worldwide attention to our "greatness" ... a confession of impotence'.[49] Official themes at the Chicago fair were 'Science Finds – Industry Applies – Man Conforms' and 'The transformation of life through the ministrations of science'. The New York fair, initially entitled 'The Fair of the Future', aimed to 'stress the vastly increased opportunity and the developed mechanical means which this twentieth century has brought to the masses for better living and accompanying human happiness'.[50] In the General Motors pavilion, called 'Highways and Horizons', Norman Bel Geddes stole the show with 'Futurama', an exhibition that transported visitors above a giant model of an urban planning scheme dominated by the automobile. On the same occasion, Henry Dreyfuss's 'Democracity' exhibition showed a 'perfectly integrated future metropolis', a cultural and business centre surrounded by a green belt and commuter suburbs beyond, whereas Lewis Mumford presented an enthusiastic view of life in the green-belt town in the film *The City*. In all these,

8

The Revolt of the Citizen

By the middle of the twentieth century, utopianism
and ideal-city design had displayed their dystopian
aspects. Dreams of realization upon a universal
scale had produced nightmare scenarios.
In response, the period after the Second World War,
and particularly the 1960s, experienced a reaction
against authority and uniformity. Amid the
explosion of urban schemes that dated from these
years, many were utopian, attempting to transcend
and seeking to reverse – at least partially –
the current dominant trend and to reinstate the
individual citizen as master of his environment.
Others were counter-utopian, condemning the
rigidity of the Modern Movement in projects that
exaggerated its characteristics in a manner inspired
by the long-standing literary tradition established
by writers such as Zamyatin and Orwell.

Le Corbusier, *Project A, Fort l'Empereur, Algiers*, 1931. Fondation Le Corbusier, Paris

Pages 214–216
Constant Nieuwenhuys, *Homo ludens*, 1964. Stedelijk Museum, Amsterdam

STRUGGLING WITH THE CHAINS OF UTOPIA

The years before the second world conflict had been characterized by the crudescence of totalitarian systems in many parts of the world. Utopia may have been attempted in the political sphere but it had revealed its dystopian face. Increasingly, the individual had been reduced to the level of a pawn on a gigantic chessboard, a cog in a massive machine, an alienated, expendable spare part. Millions lost their lives in the names of Communism, Nazism, Fascism. In the years after World War Two, faith in ideology was profoundly shaken and the role of authority brought into question as citizens, hitherto subjugated to a system in which they were no more than 'types', sought to reassert their personalities and to master their environment once more. The 1960s witnessed an explosion of self-expression and reaction against authority and the status quo in North America and Europe, culminating in France in the revolutionary events of 1968. In the United States, thousands of hippies moved to California or

New Mexico to set up hundreds of alternative, intentional communities – Drop City founded in Colorado in 1965 and Morning Star near San Francisco in 1966 being among the earliest – which rocked the traditional American way of life. In many cases, private spaces were banished from these communities which privileged the collective and most often rejected the nuclear family unit. The Europeans were quick to follow the American example and the most famous such community is no doubt Christiana, a free commune established in 1971 within 170 military buildings in the heart of Copenhagen.
In the domains of architecture and town planning, the pre-war years had seen the fruits of the early years of heady idealism – when new worlds-just-around-the-corner were formulated with excitement – slowly merge into a rigid solution. Modernism's major language, the 'International Style', progressively dominated the scene; it was a doctrine that preached uniformity and universal applicability, ironing out spatial and temporal differences and leaving little if any room for change, variety or individual initiative. After the war, the pressing need for rapid and economical reconstruction on an unprecedented scale led to the adoption of its ethos, for its methods of mass production and prefabrication appeared to suit the urgency of the situation so well. Eastern Europe and France, whose large Sarcelles estate in the suburbs of Paris gave its name to the term *sarcellite*, designating the malaise experienced by the residents of these monotonous blocks, were particularly avid consumers of this housing of emergency. It was physically more comfortable, without a doubt, than the shanty towns and other miserable lodgings that it replaced but none the less open to criticism by comparison with what might have been realized in its stead.
Indeed, the first critical voices soon began to rumble. In the architectural field, the words of just

one architect, Aldo van Eyck in 1959, expressed the discontent of a number of his generation regarding the functional housing going up around him: 'Instead of the inconvenience of filth and confusion, we have now got the boredom of hygiene. The material slum has gone – in Holland for example – but what has replaced it? Just mile upon mile of organized nowhere, and nobody feeling he is "somebody living somewhere".'[1] The reaction against the modernist credo took many guises of which only a few will be discussed here. The Megastructuralists, although often failing, in their colossal structures, to shed the basic, domineering rigidity of their predecessors, sought to provide for greater flexibility and freedom for the citizen and their schemes represent a sort of half-way house between two eras. They harboured, and illustrated spatially, characteristics of the pre-war utopias alongside those of the New World, highlighting the conflict between the general will and the requirements of individual members of society. Metamorphosis, already explored by the Italian Futurists, became a major issue at this time, particularly for groups such as the International Situationists. The reaction also found a voice in the work of those groups that sought to re-empower citizens in the decision-making process such as the advocacy planners active in cities like Brussels or in New York's Harlem, but their methodology is beyond the scope of this work. By 1975, when the critic Charles Jencks first employed the term 'post-modern' to describe the contemporary architectural tendency he observed around him, particularly in the work of architects such as Robert Venturi, the domination of the avant-garde-turned-academicism of the Modern Movement was spending its last breath. The post-modern movement rejected the *tabula rasa* attitude and the functional zoning of the modernists and called for a return to the integration of historical sources and traditional forms and materials in architectural and urban design.

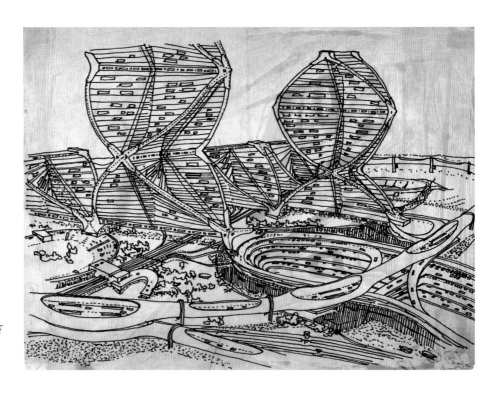

MEGASTRUCTURES: SWANSONG AND SEED

Kisho Kurokawa, Helicoids project, 1961. Centre Georges Pompidou, Paris

In reaction to the straitjacket of the pre-war period, the late 1950s and particularly the 1960s saw a rash of designs for alternative cities which aimed to guarantee greater individual freedom than the utopian designs of the previous generation, yet which still contained, to varying degrees, residues of Modernism. The cities proposed were actually buildings-cum-cities: single, giant structures loosely grouped under the term megastructures and their generally acknowledged ancestor dates in fact from before the Second World War.[2] It is a design by Le Corbusier, who was assuredly a step ahead of everyone else all the time: the *Fort l'Empereur* project from his 1931 plan for Algiers. Its huge, seemingly endless elevated super-highway snaking its way across the landscape is packed with two-storey homes decked out in accordance with the desires and tastes not of the architect but of the inhabitants. The megastructure was defined by Ralph Wilcoxon in 1968 as follows:

> not only a structure of great size, but ... also a structure which is frequently:
> 1 constructed of modular units;
> 2 capable of great or even 'unlimited' extension;

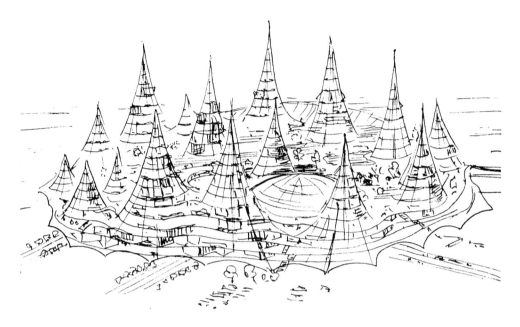

Frei Otto, *Suspended City*, 1960, illustration
from *Architecture d'aujourd'hui*, no. 102,
June 1962

3 a structural framework into which smaller structural
units (for example, rooms, houses, or small buildings of
other sorts) can be built – or even 'plugged-in' or
'clipped-on' after having been prefabricated elsewhere;
4 a structural framework expected to have a useful life
much longer than that of the smaller units which it
might support.[3]

The schemes of the Megastructuralists harboured
the fundamental tension between the basic
structure, the general – 'hard', permanent, rigid,
domineering, and under the control of the architect
(the master planner) – and its units, the particular –
'soft', flexible, transient, and the responsibility of
the users. Some architects swung upon a pendulum
between the two, but as time progressed the production of cumbersome structures that paid lip
service to individual expression became the
privilege of the establishment, while the avant-
garde pursued the unitary path. Among the
proposals in which the hard structure acquired proportions of considerable immoderation, it suffices
to mention that two Englishmen, Mike Mitchell and
Dave Boutwell, devised a *Comprehensive City* in 1969,
a single building crossing North America from New
York to San Francisco. On the other hand, certain
architects took the 'soft' route to its logical conclusion, rendering the megastructure itself increasingly

redundant and so moving from the dominance of
one utopia to that of another. Thus, the Dutch
architect Nicholas Habraken, who had accepted the
support structures as an essential feature in 1961
when he wrote *De Dragers en de Mensen*, came to reject
their necessity as the decade advanced. Among
those that pursued the flexibility and nomadism of
the 'infill' road, some, like Archigram, favoured a
high-tech, spacesuit-inspired version, while others,
such as Yona Friedman, preferred a lower-tech way.
That the majority of the Megastructuralists still had
a foot touching the soil of Modernism is demonstrated not only in the scale and rigidity of the
support structure but also in their acceptance of the
basic premises of an industrial consumer society
and their faith, shared with preceding generations,
in the benefits of material progress. Theirs was a
world in which increasing mechanization was still
expected to produce a fairly-shared reduction of the
workload and increased leisure time for all (rather
than the social exclusion since witnessed), during
which city-dwelling shoppers could select among
mountains of available items with little if any
thought for the dangers of pollution. Many
envisaged the prefabricated plug-in elements
overflowing with expendable mass-produced items.
These objects were now seen as being created in
response to the desires of would-be consumers prior
to their realization, their form being the result of a
complex fantasy/technology symbiosis rather than
the expression of universal, ideal machine-age
forms established by all-knowing designers. These
years represented the heyday of Pop Art which
veritably rejoiced in the world of expendable
consumer goods and mass culture, epitomized in
Richard Hamilton's famous collage of 1956, *Just what
is it that makes today's homes so different, so appealing?*
What were the social ambitions of the Megastructuralists? Did they, like many of the early ideal-city
designers of the Renaissance, seek merely to create
a new city in line with recent or imminent technological, social and other developments? Or did they
hope to provoke profound social and political transformation? The responses to these questions are

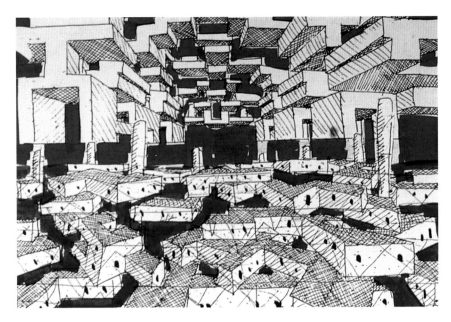

often vague and differ from case to case. The Japanese Metabolists would seem to have been closer to the former.

Archigram's position was suggested by Warren Chalk who, writing in *Archigram 3*, explained that, in the second half of the twentieth century, the old idols, precepts and dogmas were outdated, poorly adapted to contemporary circumstances and, therefore, collapsing. The team sought, he argued, the new idea and vernacular language that could coexist with the space capsules, the computers and the throw-away packaging of the atomic and electronic era.

The International Situationists, however, had a more clearly expressed political agenda and were particularly active during the May 1968 uprisings in Paris. Believing in architecture's ability to promote change, the society they hoped simultaneously to induce and accommodate was that of a post-industrial *homo ludens*, the successor of industrial *homo faber*. Paolo Soleri, too, convinced that function follows form, took a proactive stance, seeking to create a new society through the construction of his 'arcologies'.

The Metabolists – who included the Japanese architects Kiyonuri Kikutake, Kisho Kurokawa, Fumihiko Maki and Masato Otaka, the designers Kenji Ekuan and Kiyoshi Awazu and the architectural critic Noboru Kawazoe – introduced growth and a clear distinction between the permanent and the temporary into their urban plans. Kikutake expressed their point of departure: 'The megapolis of Tokyo is now tired and sick. ... A cancerous and harmful tissue is covering the city.'[4] Aiming to find solutions to the rapid development of cities, perceived as chaotic, and rooted in the tenets of the Modern Movement, although wary of taking them on board lock, stock and barrel, the Metabolist credo stressed flexibility and metamorphosis on account not only of the observation of biological patterns but also of Japanese traditions such as that of the Shinto shrine which involved periodic reconstruction. One project was to have a strong impact on the thinking of the Metabolists: this was Tokyo

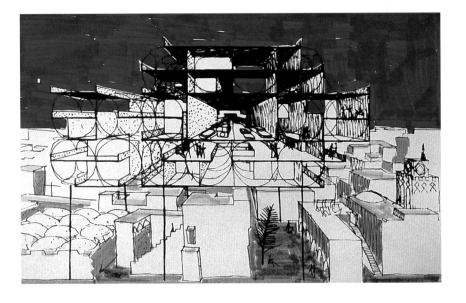

1960, Kenzo Tange's proposal for an extension of the city into the bay in the form of a linear axis (linking Tokyo to Kisazaru) onto which vertical cities could be grafted. Kikutake worked on projects for mobile self-propagating *Marine Cities* complete with reefs for fish on their undersides from 1958. 'When we look at the history of man,' he wrote, 'we cannot help but wonder if man has truly found happiness and hope. The answer is no. Continental civilization has constantly spread bloody strife among that mankind fated to live on land. It may not be too much to say that continental civilization has been no more than a history of conflict. And today the world is being daily threatened with the final confrontation between the two continents.... The marine city is a proposal to build the world of tomorrow.... Fresh air, a healthily mild climate, grand natural scenery, a horizon giving a global feeling, the blessings of the sun from sunrise to sunset, the feeling of humanity liberated from race and national boundaries, an orderly social life – the marine city will be born as, and must be made into, a city truly contributing to human society.'[5]

The French Megastructuralists were presented virtually 'live' in Michel Ragon's *Où vivrons-nous demain?* (1963). Ragon quotes the editor of the French magazine *Architecture d'aujourd'hui* Alexandre Persitz's description of *urbanisme spatial*: 'Imagine, not a single Eiffel Tower, but ten, twenty or even more, like an immense metal forest, connected by bridges, roads and platforms. Within this gigantic "three-dimensional" spider-web are ranged dwellings, schools, theatres, commercial enterprises.... The structure is lighter and more transparent than Eiffel could have dreamed in 1887.'[6] The impression of extreme superstructural lightness that was dreamt of but never realized can be seen in the *Suspended City* project designed by the German Frei Otto in 1960. Yona Friedman, founder of the Groupe d'Etude d'Architecture Mobile (GEAM, Group for the study of mobile architecture), which counted Paul Maymont, Frei Otto and Masato Otaka among its adherents in 1959, hoped to restore true individual initiative, as words extracted from

a series of illustrated comments demonstrate:
> The expert's errors can be prevented if the expert has time to discuss with the future user.
> But if there are many future users, it is no time for anyone to express his wishes.
> Then the expert will invent 'average man', an imaginary being.
> He will make his plans for the use of 'average man'. Obviously, the *real* future users will not be satisfied by these plans, and 'average man' (for whom they were made) does not exist. The actual crisis of planning is the result of the impossibility to communicate between user and expert.
> So what should one do?
> The future user *learns, himself*, an interpersonal language.
> This language shows him what consequences to expect from his project....
> Thus the future user will be able to *plan for himself* without any expert.
> The expert can keep for himself the technician's job.[7]

With this purpose in mind, he formulated two concepts which form the very foundation of his work: *urbanisme spatial*, described by Persitz above, and *architecture mobile*. Friedman explains: 'The essential for the spatial town is what I call a "spatial infrastructure": a multilevel space-frame grid supported by pillars separated by large spans.... This infrastructure represents the *fixed* part of the city; the *mobile* part consists in the walls, floorslabs, partitions, which make possible individually decided space arrangements: the "filling in" within the infrastructure. Thus all elements which are in *direct contact with the user* (i.e. those which he sees, touches, etc.) are mobile, as opposed to the infrastructure which *serves for collective use and is fixed*.'[8] In Friedman's scheme of things the skeletal three-dimensional grid structures would exist way above ground level, thus reserving the latter for historic buildings and vegetation. They were considered suitable for all conditions and climates and were suggested for a variety of sites such as Paris or Tunis or as giant bridge-cities, crossing the English Channel or even, by 1963–64, linking up all five continents. By reducing

the preconceived plan of the architect to a structural minimum, Friedman thus sought to liberate the individual, and this approach soon led him to consider issues of autoconstruction for the developing world. The utopian element of Friedman's work is conveyed in the words of the art critic Pierre Restany in 1968:

> The aerial structures of Yona Friedman
> astride History
> correspond perfectly
> to the organic mobility of a revolutionary society. . . .
> Mobile architecture implies
> the necessary
> abdication
> of the architect in favour of the inhabitant
> in the general interest of the community.[9]

Paolo Soleri is a key figure in the period after World War Two for he combines megastructural urbanism with a strong ecological position in his 'arcologies' (a Soleri neologism combining architecture and ecology), which are designed to accommodate between 500,000 and 8 million people and to eradicate crime and ethnic segregation. 'A social pattern is influenced, if not directed, by the physical pattern that shelters it,' Soleri has claimed.[10] He expressed his opinion about his particular *bête noire*, urban sprawl, as follows: 'The natural landscape is thus not the most apt frame for the complex life of society. Man must make the metropolitan landscape in his own image: a physically compact, dense, three-dimensional energetic bundle, not a tenuous film of organic matter.'[11] In his Veladiga Arcology project, he imagined a giant dam which would form a basic support structure that could be filled with habitations. Soleri still devotes much energy to realizing his ideas and his ambition at Arcosanti, currently under construction, is to group together 5000 people in a high-density, solar-powered structure occupying 14 acres on a site of 3000 devoted primarily to agriculture. Soleri's utopia

Paolo Soleri, Hexahedron, 1970. The Cosanti Foundation, Mayer (Arizona)

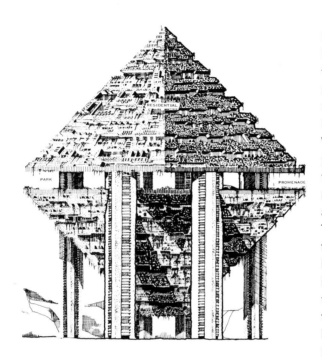

stands out in its respect for the environment,
a feature that was not of great concern to most
Megastructuralists of the 1960s, but which has since
proven to be essential as the effects of our disdain
for nature and our arrogant desire to exploit it
in the name of our ideals have become increasingly
evident.

PLAYGROUNDS FOR HOMO LUDENS

Like Soleri, Constant Nieuwenhuys and the group
named the International Situationists (IS) sought
clearly to bring about profound and mutually
provoked urban and social change, creating the
environment suitable for post-industrial man,
Homo ludens. The IS was founded in 1957, a merger
between Asger Jorn's International Movement for an
Imaginist Bauhaus (IMIB) and Guy-Ernest Debord's
Lettrist International (IL). Until its auto-dissolution
in 1972, Debord was the leading protagonist in this
movement which attracted around seventy mainly

European, short-term members and helped precip-
itate the uprisings of May 1968 in France. At its
founding conference, Debord, convinced of the
mutually determinant relationship between
urbanism and human behaviour, proclaimed: 'We
believe, above all, that the world must be changed.
We want the most liberating transformation
possible of both society and of the life in which we
find ourselves incarcerated.... We must construct
new ambiances that are simultaneously the product
and the instrument of new modes of behaviour.'[12]
The International Situationists were among the first
to question the tenets of Functionalism, responsible, in their eyes, for the alienation of the individual
in society, in texts such as Asger Jorn's *Contre le fonc-
tionnalisme* of 1954. They were marked by the ideas of
the Dutch historian Johan Huizinga, who traced the
historical importance of play in *Homo ludens*, of Henri
Lefebvre who condemned the Functionalists'
dogmatic and arbitrary zoning of the city, and of
Georg Lukács, with whom they shared a belief that
the city could provide the theatre for a veritable
challenge of the capitalist division of labour and life.
The modern city, the space of late capitalism, that of
the 'society of spectacle' as Debord called it, was
suffering from increasing unification and homoge-
nization which the Situationists proposed replacing
with a heterogeneous, rebellious and liberating
series of *unités d'ambiance* (units of ambience).
Before outlining an urban framework for a forthcoming communal, socialist and post-industrial world,
the Situationists sought to analyse the existing city.
They explored the different emotions provoked by its
various districts through *dérive*, drifting, in a manner
similar to the wanderings of the Surrealist group
around André Breton in the 1920s. The experiential
data thus gathered was recorded in texts and in a
new form of cartography, examples of which include
Debord's psychogeographical maps of Paris, *Guide
psychogéographique de Paris* (1957) and *Naked City*
(1958). Debord defined the new science of psycho-
geography, a Situationist neologism, as 'the study of
the precise laws and the exact effects of the geo-
graphic environment, built or unbuilt, in terms of its

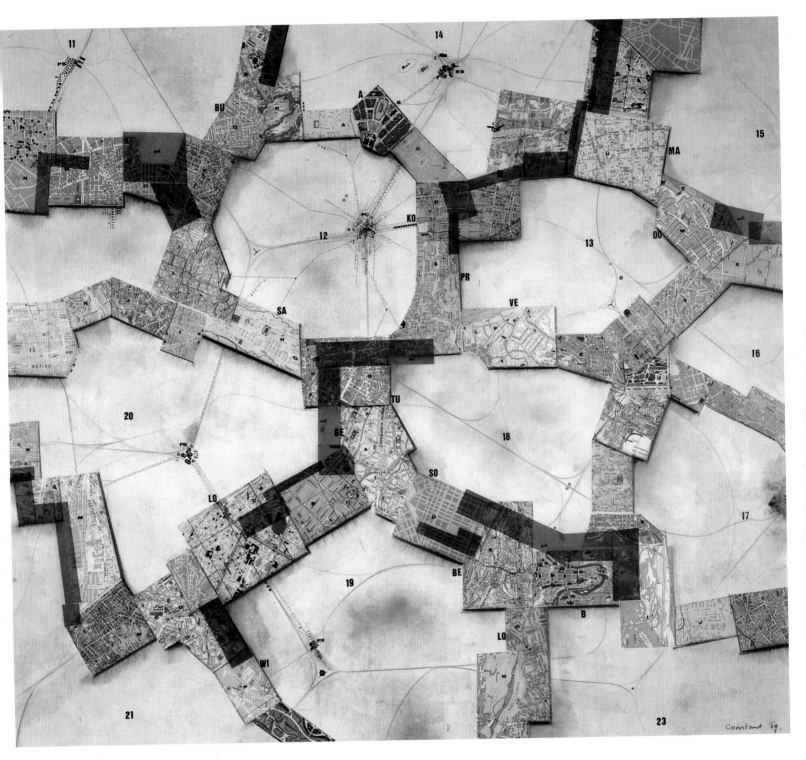

Constant Nieuwenhuys, *New Babylon*,
symbolic representation, 1969.
Gemeentemuseum, The Hague

Constant Nieuwenhuys, *New Babylon*, photomontage, 1971. Gemeentemuseum, The Hague

direct influence on the affective behaviour of individuals'.[13] Again like the Surrealists, the Situationists also practised *détournement*, whereby pre-existing elements were recontextualized. This disorientating strategy included reusing phrases from unacknowledged sources, reassembling film footage or reproducing part of one city in another. The *Palais Idéal* created by the rural postman Ferdinand Cheval from 1879 to 1912 out of recuperated elements such as discarded china provided an archetypal example of architectural *détournement*.

The famous cry of May 1968 '*Sous les pavés, la plage*' might be interpreted as a form of urban *détournement* as the revolutionaries tore up the city's paving stones in search of the beach below. The industrial paintings of Pinot Gallizio, which transformed the machine into an object of play and art into an ephemeral, collectively appropriated environment, can also be situated within this context. Using rudimentary painting machines, the Italian artist transformed huge rolls of canvas measuring tens of metres in length, which were intended not to be

admired like traditional painting but to be taken and used for clothing, housing and so forth. Gallizio's words of 1959 have the ring of the Italian Futurists: 'Still powerful lords of the earth, sooner or later you will give us machines to play with, or we will build them ourselves to occupy the free time which you, with insane eagerness, wish to see us occupy with trivialities and gradual brain death. We will use these machines to paint motorways, to produce the most fantastic fabrics which the happy masses will wear with great artistic feeling for a single minute. Kilometres of printed, engraved and painted paper which will exalt the strangest acts of folly firing enthusiasm. Houses of painted, worked, lacquered leather, houses of metal and alloys, resins and vibrating foundations, will create an unpredictable, constant moment of shock.... Everyone will enjoy the delight of colour and music; the architectonic airs of the coloured gases, the warm walls and infrared rays which an eternal springtime will give us ... poetic coloured signs will produce emotive moments and give us the infinite joy of the magic moment of collective creativeness, a platform for new myths and new passions ... we are close to the primitive state but equipped with modern means: the promised land, paradise, eden can only be the air we breathe, eat, touch, invade.'[14]

Thanks to the liberation from work resulting from increased mechanization, the Situationists believed that the citizen of the future, no longer *Homo faber* but *Homo ludens*, would require a new spatial environment, a series of situations, a construction of momentarily lived atmospheres. The Situationists' position was generally more critical than constructive, but they none the less dreamed also of building cities and their urban theory was embraced by the term 'unitary urbanism'. The cities they envisaged took the forms of nomadic metropolises in a state of perpetual transformation or giant frameworks within which individuals could create their own environment. Parts of the series of models and drawings entitled *New Babylon* by Constant Nieuwenhuys (known as Constant), representing what he referred to as 'a different city for a Different Life',[15] were first exhibited in 1959 at the Stedelijk Museum in Amsterdam. *New Babylon* was the closest the International Situationists got to projecting an ideal city, to depicting the everyday spaces that would both reflect and induce the desires of *Homo ludens*. (The task is obviously difficult due to the inherent contradiction between a desire for perpetual transformation and the fixity of any representation of it, even though it may be understood that any drawing or model only captures a fleeting potential moment.) *New Babylon* was designed to provide 'the environment the homo ludens is supposed to live in. For it should be clear that the functional cities that have been created during the long period of history in which human lives were consecrated to utility, would by no means suit the totally different needs of the creative race of homo ludens. The environment of homo ludens has first of all to be flexible, changeable, assuring any movement, any change of place or change of mood, any mode of behaviour.'[16]

Constant Nieuwenhuys, *New Babylon*, sectors in the mountains, model, 1967. Gemeentemuseum, The Hague

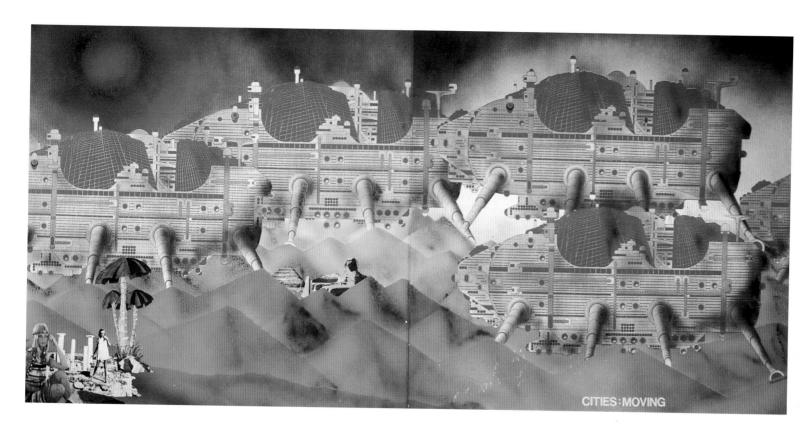

CITIES:MOVING

Constant's space is labyrinthine, indicative of the infinite number of possibilities with which each and every space and moment is pregnant. Already in his painting *Ode à l'Odéon* (1969), in memory of the Parisian Odéon theatre's central role in the revolts of May 1968, the labyrinth is present. His lightweight megastructure in *New Babylon* would be laid out in a dense, multi-levelled, modifiable manner in order to encourage play, social interaction and *dérive* amidst an explosive and unpredictable cocktail of transient ambiences.

The International Situationists were not alone in seeking to invent stimulating places for *Homo ludens* to play in at around this time. In America, Richard Buckminster Fuller designed a World Game while, in England, Joan Littlewood worked with the architect Cedric Price, the engineer Frank Newby and the systems consultant Gordon Pask to invent a Fun Palace whose main structure of five rows of fifteen towers would have a lifespan of nine or ten years and would support a daily-changing multitude of entertaining and educational environments. Such incessant fun and flexibility also implied expendability. In British avant-garde architectural circles during this period the discussions of the Independent

Group (IG) gave birth to Pop Art at London's Institute of Contemporary Arts (ICA) in the 1950s. Lawrence Alloway recalled: 'Expendable art was proposed as no less serious than permanent art; an aesthetics of expendability (the word was, I think, introduced by Banham) aggressively countered idealist and absolutist art theories.... In one way or another, the first phase of Pop Art in London grew out of the IG.'[17]

The union of Pop Art and architecture was to be consummated in the work of the English team Archigram, which united Warren Chalk, Peter Cook, Dennis Crompton, David Greene, Ron Herron and Mike Webb. *Archigram* (a combination of the words 'architecture' and 'telegram') was the name given to an information sheet but it was soon extended to incorporate the team of architects who were responsible for its contents. Mingling sci-fi images, cartoons, photomontage, onomatopoeiae, bubble texts and so forth in nine issues spanning the years 1961 to 1970, completed by issue nine and a half in 1974, they presented a panoply of projects designed by the editors themselves, their contemporaries and selected twentieth-century predecessors. Employing the novel terms of 'hardware' and 'software' to define structure and infill, they proposed skeletal megastructures that provided basic services such as electricity or water supplies and into which commercial, residential or office units could be plugged, their insertion and removal facilitated by the integration of cranes into the megastructure.

In the 'Living City' exhibition at London's ICA in 1963, they pursued some of the concerns of the International Situationists. Here they did not explore static architecture ('hardware') or make concrete urban design proposals, but they expressed their faith in the real city as a living organism, attempting to capture the enigmatic essence of urban vitality in its 'software', the infinite series of situations that it harbours. Both Brasilia and Chandigarh were criticized as not being 'living' cities. In 1964, Warren Chalk began to explore the idea of capsule habitation, inspired by space exploration: adapting an industrial design process previously reserved for consumer items such as automobiles, the units would be composed of a number of independent, interchangeable prefabricated elements and could be piled up upon one another to create a tower. At the same time, Chalk, Cook and Crompton were developing the *Plug-in City* (1962–66), a structural network, placed upon any type of territory and providing services and access, which could accommodate visiting units and in which the lifespan of every element would be predetermined. In *Computer City* (1964) and *Control and Choice* (1967), the concept of the inhabitants' constant determination and transformation of their urban environment was pursued further, introducing computer technology and creating an electronic city that could be incessantly adapted to the users' requirements. *Walking City* (1963–64) and *Instant City* (1969–70) explored the idea of complete urban sections moving from place to place rather like an extension of the principle of the travelling circus. Archigram's interest in continual change and nomadism led to concentration on the facilities provided by the units as shown in Chalk's *Capsule Homes* of 1964 and David Greene's *Living Pod* of 1966, an auto-environment

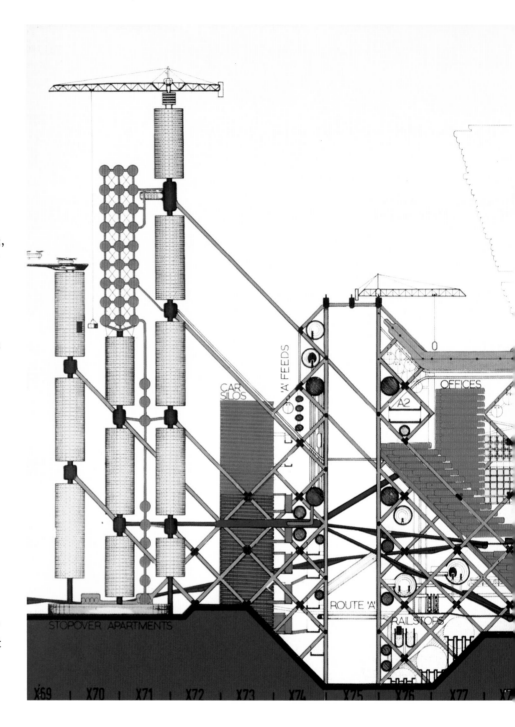

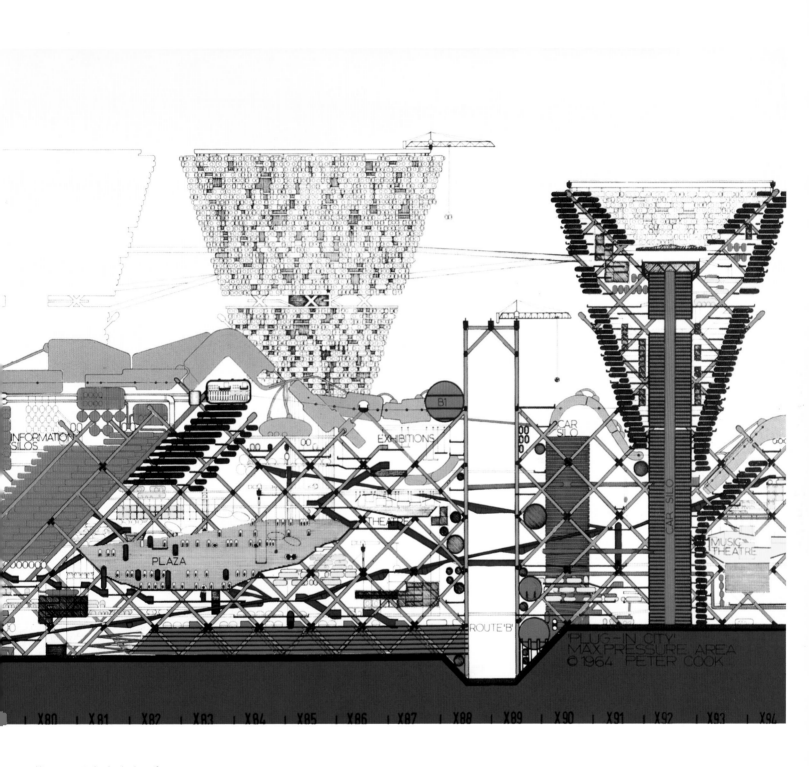

Archigram: Peter Cook, *Plug-in City*, 1964.
Centre Georges Pompidou, MNAM-CCI, Paris

Archigram, *Instant City*, collage, 1969. Centre Georges Pompidou, MNAM-CCI, Paris

Archigram: Peter Cook, *Instant City*, the dirigible in Lancashire, 1970. Archigram Archives, London

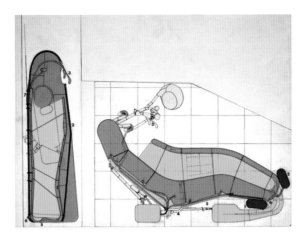

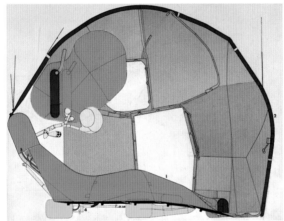

behind it: 'When your house contains such a complex of piping, flues, ducts, wires, lights, inlets, outlets, ovens, sinks, refuse disposers, hi-fi reverberators, antennae, conduits, freezers, heaters – when it contains so many services that the hardware could stand up by itself without any assistance from the house, why have a house to hold it up?' He went on: 'But a properly set-up standard of living package, breathing out warm air along the ground (instead of sucking in cold along the ground like a camp fire), radiating soft light and Dionne Warwick in heart-warming stereo, with well-aged protein turning in an infra-red glow in the rotisserie, and the ice-maker discreetly coughing cubes into glasses on the swing-out bar – this could do something for a woodland glade or creek-side rock that *Playboy* could never do for its penthouse.... From within your 30 ft. hemisphere of warm dry lebensraum you could have spectacular ringside views of the wind felling trees, snow swirling through the glade, the forest fire coming over the hill or Constance Chatterley running swiftly to you know who through the downpour.'[18]

ARCHITECTURAL COUNTER-UTOPIAS

which could either be plugged-in or remain autonomous. In the same year, Michael Webb designed not only the *Cushicle*, a portable, foldable and inflatable dwelling inspired by the car, with built-in water and heating supplies, food, radio and television transmission but also the *Suitaloon*, literally a residential costume, reminiscent of the spacesuit but composed of a network of tubes intended to satisfy the wearer's energetic, vehicular and other requirements.

The concept of the environment as a vital extension of the citizens' desires and actions and the fascination with the portable and increasingly sophisticated gadget were also being pursued at this time by Reyner Banham and François Dallegret in their *Un-house* of 1965. Banham described the reasoning

Modernism received one of its harshest stings from two Italian radical architectural groups founded in Italy in 1966, who also reserved some of their venom for the Megastructuralists. Archizoom and Superstudio did not employ the utopian method preferred by almost all architects, whereby an existing situation is countered by the projection of an alternative, positive model, but adopted instead an approach which parallels that found in counter-utopian literature, depicting provocative, exaggerated visions of existing trends, envisaging the nightmare world they believed lurked just around the corner but had not yet come into view. Andrea Branzi, Gilberto Corretti, Paolo Deganello and Massimo Morozzi founded Archizoom Associati in Florence

Archigram: David Greene, *Living Pod*, 1965.
Archigram Archives, London

Archigram: Warren Chalk, *Capsule Homes*,
1963–66. Archigram Archives, London

Hans Hollein, *Urban Construction above Vienna*, collage, 1963. Centre Georges Pompidou, MNAM-CCI, Paris

in 1966 and were joined by Dario and Lucia Bartolini two years later. Their name recalls Archigram (the fourth issue of the latter's magazine was entitled *ZOOM! Amazing Archigram*) and they readily recognized the English team, along with the Austrians Hans Hollein and Walter Pichler, as an influence on their work. Hollein and Pichler had been criticizing the Megastructuralists from the late 1950s in anti-utopian manifesto-projects such as Hollein's *Urban Construction above Vienna* (1963) in which the city's skyline is dominated by bulbous concrete excretions. The supermarket was a particular *bête noire* for the Archizoom members, who viewed it as the banal, characterless, monofunctional space *par excellence*. In *No Stop City* (1970), they imagined an endless subterranean, artificially lit, monofunctional, multilayered city from which an infinity of lift shafts provide access to the ground-level, a nature reserve protected by a great glass dome.

Superstudio was founded by Adolfo Natalini with Cristiano Toraldo di Francia in 1966. In the years up to 1972, they were joined by Roberto Magris, Gian Piero Frassinelli, Alessandro Magris and Alessandro Poli. In 1969, in their disturbing *Continuous Monument* project, Superstudio presented a dramatic attack on the arrogant, expansionist attitude of urban planning as practised, in their view, by both Mod-

ernists and Megastructuralists. In this 'Architectural Model for Total Urbanization', the world is covered by a three-dimensional isotropic grid of identical reflective glass cubic cells. The series of drawings which represent the *Continuous Monument* show the application of their caricature of the pure language and the global ambition of Modernism to a wide variety of sites, superposed upon existing cities or invading virgin areas such as the Arizona Desert. In 1971, they produced a series of twelve ideal cities, in which their approach is again anti-utopian: isolating a number of characteristics of modern urbanism, such as the industrialization of construction, zoning, uniformity and so forth, each city offers an extreme version of an individual feature. In the *2000 Ton City*, the territory is broken up into an endless series of square cells and the title refers to the heavy ceiling which will fall on the heads of any dissidents that might dare to question this 'perfect' world. In *Vita Educazione Cerimonia Amore Morte* (1972), Superstudio complement their derision of Modernism with new elements, mocking recent dreams of nomadism and a freedom from material ties which indeed appears here, as in the words of the song, like 'nothing left to lose'. In this Cartesian environment, naked families no longer enjoy the protection of roofs, walls or even residential costumes (in the manner of, say, Archi-

gram's *Suitaloons*) yet they are at complete liberty to camp anywhere they wish upon this glazed two-dimensional object- and labour-free network of energy and information.

Finally, let us mention two projects by Rem Koolhaas. *Exodus*, done in association with Elia Zenghelis (1972), follows in the same vein as that of the Italian radical groups of the 1960s, intensifying and thus criticizing aspects of the modern city, of functionalism and of capitalism. Presented like a tale, *Exodus* recounts the creation of a metropolitan ideal – an exaggerated vision of Leonidov's linear city – to which the inhabitants of the real city – a dilapidated London – are deeply attracted (despite its echoes of the concentration camp) and desire to move, but to which access is restricted by two straight, insurmountable walls. In his project for the *City of the*

Captive Globe, Koolhaas recalls the influence upon his thinking of Oswald Matthias Ungers (who had explored the issue of the city within the city in his study on Berlin) and rejects the notion of universality. Upon a grid resembling that of Manhattan, a number of massive, heterogeneous constructions, each spanning an entire block, pay homage to different programmatic responses in the recent history of architecture and town planning. Recalling the phalanstery, their scale is that of the city-state and a wide variety of functions cohabit within each autarchic unity. This is indeed both an echo of the territorial organization that Thomas More introduced on his famous island as well as being a far cry from his 54 cloned copies of a single urban model.

Superstudio, *Vita Educazione Cerimonia Amore Morte*, photomontage, 1972. Centre Georges Pompidou, MNAM-CCI, Paris

Superstudio, *Continuous Monument*, 1969. Superstudio Collection, Florence

Rem Koolhaas and Elia Zenghelis, with Madelon Vriesendorp and Zoe Zenghelis, *Exodus, The Voluntary Prisoners*, photomontage, 1972. Centre Georges Pompidou, MNAM-CCI, Paris

9

In this survey, I have attempted to trace a brief history of those cities which – rather than being apparently chaotic, ever-changing works of art created by entire communities over generations – have been invented in the nebulous realms of the human intellect. The notion that there exist ideal prototypes of which the essence could be captured by philosophers or artists was formulated by Plato. From that spring flowed many of the numerous attempts cited in this book to draw up the perfect plan for the city and society. Particularly from the Renaissance onwards, architects and others joined in this arrogant quest to draw up the perfect design. Most plans, from the *Citte ideale* of the fifteenth century to Le Corbusier's *Contemporary City for 3 Million Inhabitants*, remained on paper.

Others, however, were reproduced *in situ*: for some, specific authors are known, for others, an individual planner may not have been identified, their invention being linked instead to a particular regime or religious group, such as many of the towns built by colonial authorities.

Most of the models we have examined shared a number of common features, as already discussed. One particular characteristic, however, deserves further comment, for it is one whose consequences are of considerable importance today, indeed forming the very problem to which contemporary ideal-city planners should surely address their attention. Almost all the urban blueprints we have reviewed represent examples of humankind's quest to dominate nature, and in this way they have all contributed to our increasing divorce from it. 'Tabula rasa' has been the rallying cry of these planners who, taking a delight in flattening uneven land and straightening rivers, and revelling in the order of geometry, have condemned and attempted to master the apparent chaos of the natural world. In so doing they have contributed to the problems arising from our failure to be receptive to the natural – rather than universal – wisdom. They have taken the world so many steps closer to destroying the habitat upon which humanity is dependent and without which it cannot survive. Already in Antiquity,

the Roman veterans who built some 500 new towns in North Africa impoverished the land that they had appropriated from the local tribes and altered the climate by causing deforestation, salination and reduced soil fertility.[1] Similarly, and much more recently, the cities designed by Le Corbusier, Hilberseimer, Frank Lloyd Wright and other twentieth-century planners, called for the destruction of existing urban creation and projected a world dominated by the automobile, thus threatening the exhaustion of fossil fuel resources and wreaking hazardous effects upon the environment.

The picture that emerges from this book may seem a very grim one, for it is indeed a survey of numerous plans for *utopia* that harboured the seeds of *dystopia*. Certainly, towards the close of the twentieth century, a certain reticence with regard to utopian and ideal-city design became apparent. On the one hand, this can be considered the expression of a fear resulting from the horrors experienced during that violent century in the name of so many promises of better worlds. On the other hand, it is due to the fact that, in the post-industrialized Western world, liberal capitalism, which has become so firmly established as the dominant ideology – a victory apparently crowned by the recent fall of the Berlin Wall – meets, for the meantime, with insufficient dissatisfaction to encourage or sustain a very lively utopian sentiment.

Should we conclude that projecting ideal cities is a dangerous exercise and one that, now discredited, should be avoided? Surely not. As Lewis Mumford recommended on the title page of his work, *The Story of Utopias*, 'A Map of the World that does not include Utopia is not worth even glancing at'. This history may look black, but the places from which these utopias and ideal cities are projected were far from rosy. For they are the fruit of our dissatisfaction with reality, of social and political turmoil, of a pendulum which is considered to have swung too far towards the freedom of individuals, allowing them to exploit one another. They are the expression of a sentiment of revolt against the status quo, of a desire to transcend it and hence promote its improvement,

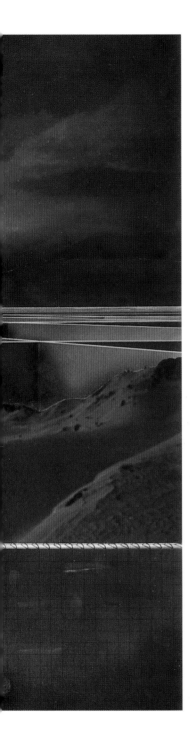

Superstudio, *The Twelve Ideal Cities,*
Città 2000, 1971. Centre Georges Pompidou,
MNAM-CCI, Paris

also of optimism and hope for a better future.
It suffices to recall, by way of example, that Plato
prescribed solutions at a time when Athens was
suffering defeat in the Peloponnesian war, that More
reacted to the consequences of the decline of the
feudal economy, that Leonardo da Vinci sought to
find urban solutions to the overpopulation and
sickness that plagued cities such as Florence, that
Ledoux imagined his ideal city during the period of
flux which gave rise to the French Revolution, that
Robert Owen set up alternative communities in
response to the sufferings of the English workforce,
and that the German Expressionists sought to
counteract the consequences of the First World War,
unemployment and inflation. Thomas More's *Utopia,*
though it may seem unattractive viewed from the
comfortable perspective of today's post-industrial
reader, was intended to appeal to his contemporaries as being infinitely preferable to the sufferings
he observed around him.

At the outset of the twenty-first century, though it
may seem easy, at least in the near term, to ignore
certain problems, they are evidently in far from short
supply and offer a fertile ground upon which
utopians may operate. For planners, the most
pressing issues of all are surely environmental. The
city itself is now firmly established as the predominant form of settlement, with around three-quarters
of Australians, Europeans and North and South
Americans living in urban conglomerations, while
Africa and Asia are becoming increasingly
urbanized. All these cities affect the environment
negatively, exploiting enormous amounts of the
world's resources and generating masses of urban
waste and pollution.[2] Future urban development has
to be sustainable – that is to say, we must preserve
our host planet for the benefit of future generations.
I would suggest that the *sine qua non* for utopianism
to go beyond the impasse in which the experiences
of the twentieth century trapped it lies in its ability to
moderate its ambition. In that century, the scale of
intervention to which the utopian drive, abhorrent of
change or variations, aspired was grand indeed: no
longer that of the modest city-state of Athens, nor

even the gigantic empire of Atlantis, but the entire
planet. Henceforth, however, ideal-city planners
must operate *on a local scale.* This may be done within
a larger *structure of guiding principles* for our undoubt-
edly increasingly 'global' world. The United Nations
conference, called the Earth Summit, held in Rio
in 1992, and the United Nations City Summit,
Habitat II, held in Istanbul in 1996, led to the recommendation of a series of intentions laid out, respectively, in the Declaration of Rio and The Habitat
Agenda. These documents, prepared by the international community, are of vital importance and
provide a framework of recommendations within
which contemporary ideal cities can be projected.
Local intervention is commended and a number
of Local Agenda 21 initiatives are now working on
practical measures in cities both to improve their
immediate environment and to reduce their
negative impact on the wider environment. It has
been suggested already that one of the intentions
behind Plato's story of Atlantis was to alert attention
to the question of scale. One could argue the case
also that Thomas More appreciated this question
of global versus local intervention. The monogenitor
of the literary genre certainly appears to favour the
unlimited, uniform and universal application of the
utopian scheme, since the entirety of its imaginary
territory is subjected to the ideal isotrope. However,
the territory More projected was the size of his
homeland, whose local conditions he knew well,
not that of the entire world. The utopian ambition,
though it may function within the global guidelines
of certain principles, in today's case those necessary
for sustainable development, must acquire a new
modesty, responding specifically to local conditions, creating a heterogeneous collection of
context-sensitive projects that transcend a
multitude of realities. Without them the world
will indeed be a dull place.

APPENDICES

NOTES

Introduction

1. J. A. Murray (ed.), *A New English Dictionary on Historical Principles*, Oxford 1901.

2. R. Trousson, *Voyages aux pays de nulle part, Histoire littéraire de la pensée utopique*, Brussels 1975, p. 13. Generally, this work is a very useful source for the history of utopian literature.

3. K. Mannheim, *Ideologie und Utopie*, Bonn 1930, and Trousson, op. cit. [note 2], p. 15.

4. Quoted in *Visionary Architects*, Houston 1968, p. 109.

5. Plato, *Republic*, 501, trans. A. D. Lindsay, London 1935, p. 221.

6. Ibid., 500, p. 220.

7. 'La géométrie est la base … Toute l'époque contemporaine est donc de géométrie, éminemment.' Le Corbusier in *Urbanisme*, p. 35, quoted by F. Choay in *L'urbanisme, utopies et réalités*, 1965, p. 37 (my trans.).

8. The first uchronian work is probably the Abbé de Pure's *Epigone, histoire du siècle futur*, published in 1659.

9. Indeed, in view of the closely perceived relationship between the planning of cities and that of societies, it is not surprising that it has often been considered the duty of kings to build cities. Thomas Aquinas, who proclaimed on more than one occasion that '*Civitas communitas perfecta est*' ('The city is the ideal community'), recalled this obligation in *De regimine principum* (I, 13) in the thirteenth century, while Baldassare Castiglione, in *The Book of the Courtier*, urged his prince to follow the city-building tradition, practised so famously by Alexander the Great. Moreover, with towns considered places of virtue, a prince, given his role as intermediary between God and his people, could reconcile his subjects and the divine by building cities. See S. Lang, 'The Ideal city. From Plato to Howard', *Architectural Review*, CXII, no. 668, 1952, pp. 91–101.

10. Plato, *Republic* [note 5], p. 220.

Sources of the Ideal City
from High Antiquity to the Middle Ages

1. Ovid, *Metamorphoses*, I.

2. 4 Esdras 8:52, Luke 23:43; 2 Cor 12:4, Rev. 2:7.

3. Exodus 25:8.

4. The Temple is described in Ezekiel 40–43 and the Sanctuary in the Book of Kings 6:16–20 and the Book of Chronicles 3:8.

5. Rev. 21:1–4.

6. Rev. 21:18.

7. Herodotus, *Histories*, I, 98–99.

8. Ibid., I, 178ff.

9. N. J. Johnston, in *Cities in the Round*, Seattle and London 1983, p. 11.

10. Aristotle, *Politics*, II, 8. Trans. T. A. Sinclair, rev. ed. J. Saunders, London 1992, pp. 133–34.

11. Ibid., VII, 9, pp. 422–23.

12. Plato, *Laws*, VI, 778.

13. Ibid., V, 745.

14. Porphyry, *Life of Plotinus*, XII.

15. Herodotus, *Enquiry*, I, 98 and 179.

16. Plato, *Timaeus*, 25.

17. Preamble quoted by W. Braunfels, *Monasteries of Western Europe. The Architecture of the Orders*, London 1972, which includes a chapter on the St Gall plan. See also W. Horn and E. Born, *Plan of St. Gall: A Study of the Architecture and Economy of a Paradigmatic Carolingian Monastery*, Berkeley 1979.

18. J. Lassner, *The Topography of Baghdad in the Early Middle Ages*, Detroit 1970, p. 232, quoted by Johnston, op. cit. [note 9], p. 19.

The Idealization of the City
from the Renaissance Onwards

1. J. Burckhardt, *The Civilisation of the Renaissance in Italy*, trans. S. Middlemore, London 1960, p. 81.

2. Leonardo Bruni, *Laudatio Florentinae urbis*, trans. B. Kohl, in *The Earthly Republic: Italian Humanists on Government and Society*, ed. B. Kohl and R. G. Witt, Manchester 1978.

3. Other unillustrated editions of Vitruvius' *De Architectura* followed in Florence and Venice between 1495 and 1497. The original treatise may have included drawings and the temptation to (re)invent them resulted in illustrated editions such as that, fairly rudimentary, of Fra Giocondo of 1511. Leonardo da Vinci contributed to the more sophisticated illustrations of Cesare Cesariano's edition (Como 1521) which also had the merit of being the first Italian translation and of including a commentary. Palladio aided Daniele Barbaro for his edition published in Venice in 1556. Foreign versions were produced in French by Jean Martin in Paris and in German by Walter Ryff, known as Rivius, in Nuremberg, both in 1547, and in Spanish in Alcalá in 1582.

4. Recalled by Alberti in *Della Pittura* (1435), in Martin Kemp (ed.), *Leon Battista Alberti on Painting*, trans. C. Grayson, Harmondsworth 1991, p. 35.

5. Works dealing with these matters include *Della pittura* (1435) by Alberti, *De prospectiva pingendi* (*c.*1465) by Piero della Francesca, *Summa de arithmetica, geometria, proportioni et proportionalità* (1494) and *Divina proportione* (1509, illustrated by Leonardo da Vinci) by Luca Pacioli, and Albrecht Dürer's manual of geometry, *Underweysung der Messung, mit dem Zirkel und Richtscheyt, in Linien Ebnen und ganssen Corporen* (1525)

and his study of the proportions of the human body, *Vier bücher von menschlicher Proportion* (1528).

6. 'To conclude, such should be the Ways out of the City; short, strait and secure. When they come to the town, if the City is noble and powerful, the streets should be straight and broad, which carried an Air of Greatness and Majesty; but if it is only a small Town or a Fortification, it will be better, and as safe not for the Streets to run straight to the Gates; but to have them wind about sometimes to the Right, sometimes to the Left, near the Wall, and especially under the Towers upon the Wall; and within the Heart of the Town, it will be handsomer not to have them straight, but winding about several Ways, backwards and forwards, like the Course of a River. For thus, besides that by appearing so much the longer, they will add to the idea of the Greatness of the Town, they will likewise conduce very much to Beauty and Convenience, and be a greater Security against all Accidents and Emergencies' (Book IV).

7. L. B. Alberti, *On the Art of Building in Ten Books*, trans. J. Rykwert, N. Leach and R. Tavernor, Cambridge, Mass., 1988, p. 191.

8. L. Agostini, in *La repubblica immaginaria: 'L'aria di questi paesi suole per natura produrre uomini temperati ne' visi, docili in ogni sorti di scienza, civili nella pace, amici d'ogni uomo… ben avezzi all'obedienza'.*

9. In Manuscript B in the Bibliothèque de l'Institut de France, Paris, Leonardo's drawings for a fluvial city appear on folios 37v and 38; those for the city on several levels on fol. 15v (the entire city), 16, 36 and 37 (details). An explicative text by Leonardo regarding the latter project appears on folios 15v and 16; there we learn that 'a person who wishes to proceed through the city using only the upper roads, could do so comfortably; as is the case for someone who wants to circulate therein using only the lower ones. No chariots or other similar vehicles should pass in the high roads: these roads are reserved for persons of quality. Chariots and other forms of transport destined for the use and convenience of the people can pass in the lower roads.' The possible existence of yet another, underground, level for canals is suggested on fol. 19v, although this drawing may not relate directly to the same design for a city on several levels.

10. H. de la Croix, 'Military Architecture. The Radial City Plan in Sixteenth-Century Italy', *The Art Bulletin*, 1960, pp. 264–90.

11. Other treatises to deal with this include Francesco de Marchi's *Della architettura militare* (prepared from 1540 but published posthumously in Brescia in 1599); Pietro Cataneo's *I quattro primi libri di architettura* (1554; enlarged edition 1567), which favoured the regular polygon and may have influenced the construction of Mannheim in 1606; Jacques Androuet du Cerceau's *Livre d'Architecture* (1559); Girolamo Maggi and Iacomo F. Castriotto's *Della Fortificatione delle Città* (1564); Buonaiuto Lorini's *Delle fortificatione libri cinque* (1592); Jacques Perret's *Des Fortifications et Artifices* (1601); Vincenzo Scamozzi's *L'Idea della Architettura Universale* (1615); and Robert

Fludd's *Utriusque cosmi, majoris scilicet et minoris, metaphysica, physica atque technica historia* (1617–18).

12. F. Lestringant, 'Utopie et Réforme', in R. Schaer (ed.), *Utopie*, Paris 2000.

13. W. Morris, 'Foreword to Utopia by Thomas More', Kelmscott Press, 1893, reprinted in W. Morris, *News from Nowhere and other Writings*, Clive Wilmer (ed.), London 1998, p. 375.

14. Thomas More, *Utopia*, trans. Paul Turner, London 1961, pp. 69–74.

15. Plato tells us that upon crossing the three external bridges one encounters a circular rampart, entirely covered in numerous houses, nestled one up against another (*Critias*, 117).

16. Illustrated in the *Mondo savio e pazzo* section in the 1578 French edition.

17. T. Campanella, 'City of the Sun', in *Famous Utopias*, New York 1901, pp. 275–76.

18. Ibid., p. 279.

19. Francis Bacon, *New Atlantis*, London 1627, p. 252.

20. Ibid., p. 263.

21. Ibid., p. 249.

Exporting the Ideal to the New World

1. Vasco de Quiroga, *Información en derecho*, 1535.

2. Quoted by M. Eliade, 'Paradise and Utopia: Mythical Geography and Eschatology', in F. R. Manuel (ed.), *Utopias and Utopian Thought*, Cambridge (Mass.) 1966, p. 262.

3. G. Chinard, *L'Amérique et le Rêve exotique dans la littérature française au XVIIᵉ et au XVIIIᵉ siècle*, Paris 1934, p. 138.

4. Père Lejeune, *Relation de 1634*, VI, 228.

5. 474 towns were founded in the New World by the Spanish according to Antonio de Alcedo in his *Diccionario geográfico-histórico de las Indias Occidentales*, 1789.

6. Quoted by J. W. Reps, *Cities of the American West*, Princeton 1979.

7. From a Ms. in the National Archives in Madrid (no. 3017), published in *Hispanic American Historical Review* 4, Baltimore 1921 (pp. 745ff), translated vol. 5, 1922 (pp. 249ff).

8. Chinard, op. cit. [note 3], p. 140.

9. C. Lévi-Strauss, *Tristes Tropiques*, Paris 1955, p. 255 (my trans.).

10. E. Bacon and T. C. Bannister have detected links with Renaissance ideal-city projects in Italy: see, for example, E. Bacon, *Design of Cities*, New York 1976, and T. C. Bannister, 'Oglethorpe's Sources for the Savannah Plan', *Journal of the Society of Architectural Historians*, May 1961.

11. Jefferson note, 'Proceedings to be had under the Residence Act, 29 November 1790', quoted by J. W. Reps, *The Making of Urban America*, Princeton 1965, p. 245.

12. Letter from Washington to L'Enfant, 4 April 1791, in H. P. Caemmerer, *The Life of Pierre Charles L'Enfant,*

Planner of the City Beautiful: the City of Washington, Washington 1950, p. 144, quoted by Reps, op. cit. [note 11], p. 245.

13. Undated communication by L'Enfant entitled 'Note relative to the ground lying on the eastern branch of the river Potomac and being intended to parallel the several positions proposed within the limits between the branch and Georgetown for the seat of the Federal City'.

14. Hazard, *Annals of Pennsylvania*, 1850, quoted by A. E. J. Morris, *History of Urban Form Before the Industrial Revolutions*, Harlow (Essex) and New York 1994, p. 338.

15. Ibid., p. 339.

16. Numbers 35:1–5 and Leviticus 25.

17. Reps, op. cit. [note 11], pp. 466–72.

18. Quoted by E. Deming Andrews, *A Search for the Perfect Society*, New York 1954.

The Horizons of Knowledge

1. N. Hampson, *The Enlightenment. An Evaluation of its assumptions, attitudes and values*, London 1968, repr. 1990 (Penguin), pp. 159–61.

2. Chambers' *Encyclopedia* appeared in England in 1751, followed by the 24-volume *Dictionnaire Raisonné des Sciences, des Arts et des Métiers*, under the aegis of Denis Diderot, in France.

3. The first daily newspaper appeared in London in 1702.

4. Quoted by Hampson, op. cit. [note 1], p. 233.

5. Restif de la Bretonne envisaged village communities in the *Statuts du bourg d'Oudun* at the end of the *Paysan perverti* (1776) and the *Nouvel Emile* (1776), and those for townworkers in *Les vingt épouses des vingt associés* (1780) and *Nuits de Paris* (1794).

6. The full title in the original edition was *L'Esprit des Lois: ou du rapport que les lois doivent avoir avec la constitution de chaque gouvernement, les mœurs, le climat, la religion, le commerce, &c.*

7. Sir Joshua Reynolds, *13th Discourse*, 1786.

8. E.-L. Boullée, *Architecture, Essai sur l'Art*, Paris 1968, p. 161.

9. The plates he had not published were brought out by Daniel Ramée in 1847.

10. C.-N. Ledoux, *L'Architecture considérée sous les rapports de l'art, des mœurs et de la législation*, Paris 1804, repr. Paris 1997, p. 83.

11. Quoted in *Visionary Architects*, Houston 1968, p. 9.

12. Ledoux, op. cit. [note 10], p. 3.

13. Ibid.

14. Although there is no firm proof of this, it seems most probable that Ledoux was a freemason, a likelihood supported by the number of masonic symbols, such as the pyramid or the triangular omniscient eye, that are present in his constructions. See A. Vidler, *Ledoux*, trans. S. Grunberg, Paris 1987, pp. 56–57 and 133–41, and 'The Architecture of the Lodges' in *Oppositions*, 5, 1976.

15. Ledoux, op. cit. [note 10], pp. 184 and 182.

The Search for Order in the Age of Great Cities

1. R. Vaughan, *The Age of Great Cities*, London 1843.

2. W. Morris, *Collected Works*, XXII, pp. 352, 356; XXIII, p. 179. Quoted by N. Pevsner, *Pioneers of Modern Design. From William Morris to Walter Gropius*, revised ed. London 1975, p. 25.

3. The twelve cities with populations of over one million in 1900 were London, Paris, Berlin, Vienna, St Petersburg, Moscow and Constantinople in Europe, New York, Chicago and Philadelphia in the United States, and Tokyo and Peking in Asia.

4. For example, C. Dickens in his novels written between 1840 and 1855, *Nicholas Nickleby* and *Hard Times*, E. Sue in *Les mystères de Paris* (1842–43), V. Hugo in *Les Misérables* (1862) and E. Zola in *L'Assommoir* (1877), *Germinal* (1885) and *Travail* (1901). G. Doré's illustrations of London life were published in England in Blanchard Jerrold's *London, A Pilgrimage* (1872), and in France in Louis Enault's *Londres et les londoniens en 1875* (1876).

5. Karl Marx quoted by K. Kumar in 'Utopia and Anti-Utopia in the Twentieth Century', in *Utopia*, Paris 2000.

6. Le Grand Hornu built from *c.* 1816 to *c.* 1835 near Mons in Belgium employed between 1000 and 1500 workers in the 1830s. Now listed as a national landmark, restored and converted into an arts centre, it is composed of a massive central elliptical (and hence reminiscent of Ledoux) courtyard, flanked by a workshop for the construction of steam engines and an administrative building, the owner's residence and a workers' city, the six main streets of which form a quadrilateral pattern encompassing the industrial buildings. By 1840, this small town contained 435 houses that were rented to the employees at an average of one franc and 60 centimes per week, which represented just under a day's salary.

7. Alfred Krupp, quoted by T. Böll, 'Essen. Steel, Cannons and Workers' Houses', in *Rassegna*, XIX, 70, 1997. The town of Essen had grown, spurred by the mining of coal deposits from around 1850, from just over 6000 inhabitants in 1840 to about 40,000 by 1866, when a cholera epidemic took the lives of hundreds, for building had failed to keep pace with this expansion. The Krupp firm employed about ten per cent of the town's population in the early 1860s, when Alfred Krupp began building houses for his employees as he continued to do over the ensuing decades. Modest in appearance but achieving good standards of sanitation and furnishing, these were initially intended for the use of the specialized craftsmen (whose skills he appreciated but who, he feared, risked becoming proletarian due to the impact of heavy industry). He also constructed a 'Menage' for the migrant workforce, where the dwellings were hardly better than others in the town destined for this population.

8. K. Marx, *The Communist Manifesto Modern Edition*, London 1998, pp. 73 and 75 (containing English-language translation first published in 1888).

9. Fourier's thinking also inspired the Russian Nikolay Chernychevsky, whose novel, *What Is to Be Done?* (1863),

in which the heroine imagines a phalanstery as the ideal place for a free society, reputedly influenced Lenin. The Soviet Union later saw a rash of schemes for phalanstery-type communal buildings in the years just after the 1917 Revolution.

10. R. Owen, *The Life of Robert Owen by himself*, London 1857/58, p. 112.

11. Quoted by H. Deroche, *La société festive, du fouriérisme écrit aux fouriérismes pratiqués*, Paris 1975, p. 330.

12. T. J. Schlereth, 'Solon Spencer Beman, Pullman City et l'Europe', in J. Zukowsky (ed.), *Chicago. Naissance d'une métropole, 1872–1922*, exhibition catalogue Musée d'Orsay, Paris 1987–88.

13. See G. Darley, *Villages of Vision*, London 1975.

14. W. Morris, 'Looking Backward', review published in *The Commonweal*, 22 June 1889, repr. in W. Morris, *News from Nowhere and other writings*, C. Wilmer (ed.), London 1998, p. 354.

15. E. Howard, 'Spiritual Influences Toward Social Progress', printed in *Light*, 1910.

16. Morris, op. cit. [note 14], pp. 356–57.

17. E. Bellamy, *Equality*, New York 1897, p. 259.

18. N. Pevsner, *Pioneers of Modern Design. From William Morris to Walter Gropius*, revised ed. London 1975, p. 135.

19. Ruskin (1907), quoted by M. H. Lang, in *Designing Utopia: John Ruskin's Urban Vision for Britain and America*, Montreal, New York and London 1999, p. 9.

20. *Richard III*, II, 3.

21. E. Howard quoting Ruskin's words in a lecture of 1868 entitled 'The Mystery of Life and its Arts'. Quoted by Lang, op. cit. [note 19], pp. 40–41.

22. C. Wilmer, introduction to Morris, op. cit. [note 14], p. xxxiii.

23. Morris, op. cit. [note 14], p. 105.

24. A. López de Aberasturi, introduction to his adaptation in French of the *Teoría general de la urbanización* (1867) by the engineer Ildefonso Cerda, Paris 1979.

25. Quoted by W. L. Creese, *The Search for Environment* (1966), Baltimore 1992, p. 206.

26. Ibid., p. 148.

27. L. Mumford, 'The Fate of the Garden Cities', *Journal of the A.I.A.*, 1927.

Cities for the Machine Age

1. In, for example, Werner Hegemann's *Das steinerne Berlin*, 1930 or Catherine Bauer's *Modern Housing*, 1934.

2. Le Corbusier, *La ville radieuse*, Boulogne-sur-Seine 1935, p. 181.

3. H. Meyer, 'Die neue Welt', in *Das Werk*, no. 7, 1926, translated into English in Claude Schnaidt (ed.), *Hannes Meyer: Bauten, Projekte und Schriften/Buildings, Projects, Writings*, Teufen A.R. (Switzerland) 1965, pp. 91–95.

4. Quoted by F. Roe, *The Social Philosophy of Carlyle and Ruskin*, New York 1921, p. 184.

5. H. de Fries, *Wohnstädte der Zukunft*, Berlin 1919, quoted by W. Pehnt, *Architecture expressioniste*, Paris 1998, p. 7 (my trans.).

6. The term 'Expressionist', designating an artistic movement, which emerged around 1910–11 in opposition to Impressionism, had been applied to architecture for the first time in 1913 to the work of Bruno Taut.

7. The Deutsche Werkbund was founded in Munich in 1907 under the direction of Hermann Muthesius. As stated in article two of its constitution, its aims included ennobling the work of the craftsman in the collaboration of arts, crafts and industry.

8. W. Gropius, in *Programm des Staatlichen Bauhauses in Weimar*, 1919.

9. P. Mondrian, quoted by H.L.C. Jaffe, *Piet Mondrian*, Paris 1970, p. 53.

10. The most famous of their architectural realizations include Oud's 'De Unie' Café-restaurant in Rotterdam, Rietveld's Schröder house in Utrecht, both of 1924, and Van Doesburg's interiors, designed with Jean Arp and Sophie Taeuber-Arp, for the Café Aubette in Strasburg in 1926.

11. J. J. P. Oud, in *De Stijl*, exh. cat., Stedelijk Museum, Amsterdam, 1951, p. 80, quoted by S. Polano, 'De Stijl/Architecture = Nieuwe Beelding', in *De Stijl: 1917–1931, Visions of Utopia*, exh. cat., Walker Art Center, London, 1982, p. 4.

12. L. Mies van der Rohe, *The Art of Structure*, introduction in W. Blaser, *Mies van der Rohe*, London 1965, quoted by H.-W. Kruft, *A History of Architectural Theory: From Vitruvius to the Present*, London and New York 1994, p. 388.

13. L. Mumford, *The Highway and the City*, London 1964, p. 156.

14. In Functionalist architecture, the function, the interior, of a building determines its exterior form, and its origins, echoing as far back as Vitruvius, can be located in the nineteenth century in the writings of Viollet-le-Duc in France, Horatio Greenough (author of *Form and Function*, 1852) and Louis Sullivan (who uttered the famous aphorism, 'Form Follows Function') in America. It rejected ornament, which had already been placed under assault by architects such as Adolf Loos who wrote, in *Ornament und Verbrechen* (1908): 'Since ornament is no longer organically linked with our civilization, it is no longer an expression of our civilization. The ornament being created today is not connected … with the order of the world'; in a messianic vein, he proclaimed that, once free of ornament, 'the streets of our cities will shine like white walls, like Zion, the Holy City, the capital of Heaven. Then we shall find fulfilment.' Both quoted by Kruft, op. cit. [note 12], p. 365.

15. R. Arnheim, quoted by M. Droste, *Bauhaus, 1919–33*, Cologne 1990, p. 122.

16. Quoted by T. Böll, 'Essen. Steel, Cannons and Workers' Houses', in *Rassegna*, no. XIX, 70, 1997, pp. 39–40.

17. L. Hilberseimer, in 'Vom städtebaulichen Problem der Grossstadt', published in *Sozialistische Monatshefte*, vol. 60, no. 6, 19 June 1923, pp. 352–57.

18. L. Hilberseimer, 'Grossstadtarchitektur' (Metropolitan architecture), in *Der Sturm*, no. 4, 1924, pp. 177–89.

19. L. Hilberseimer, *Entfaltung einer Planungsidee*, Berlin 1963.

20. See Z. Sternhell, 'Fascist Ideology', in W. Laqueur (ed.), *Fascism: A Reader's Guide*, London 1979.

21. F. T. Marinetti, 'Manifesto of Futurism', published in *Le Figaro*, Paris, 20 February 1909; repr. in U. Apollonio (ed.), *Futurist Manifestos*, London 1973, pp. 21–24.

22. A. Sant'Elia, 'Manifesto of Futurist Architecture', 1914, in Apollonio, op. cit. [note 21], p. 169.

23. A. A. and V. A. Vesnin, 'Tvorcheskie otchety' [Creative accounts], *Arkhitektura SSSR*, no. 4, 1935, p. 40.

24. K. Malevich, 'O novikh sistemakh v iskusstve' [On new systems in art], Vitebsk 1920, in C. Gray, *The Russian Experiment in Art, 1863–1922*, London 1962, repr. 1976, p. 219.

25. V. E. Tatlin, quoted by Gray, op. cit. [note 24], p. 219.

26. Quoted by R. Stiltes, *Revolutionary Dreams, Utopian Vision and Experimental Life in the Russian Revolution*, New York 1991, p. 147.

27. Quoted by C. Lodder, *Russian Constructivism*, New Haven 1983, p. 277.

28. N. Punin, 'Meeting ob iskusstve', in *Iskusstvo Kommuni*, no. 1, 7 December 1918, quoted by Gray, op. cit. [note 24], p. 220.

29. See I. A. Kazous, 'L'idée d'architecture cosmique et l'avant-garde russe au début du XXᵉ siècle', in J. Clair (ed.), *Cosmos. Du Romantisme à l'Avant-garde*, Montréal 1999, pp. 194–98.

30. L. Lissitzky, '*Suprematism mirovospriiateniia*' (Le suprématisme de la perception du monde), State Tretyakov Gallery, Manuscripts Department, fonds 76, collection Unovis, 1920, quoted by Kazous, op. cit. [note 29], p. 196.

31. Quoted by V. Khazanova and O. Chvidkovski, 'L'architecture soviétique, 1900–1930', in exh. cat., *Paris-Moscou, 1900–1930*, Paris 1979, p. 302.

32. Works on Le Corbusier abound but the utopian and social aspects of his ideal cities have been discussed in R. Fishman, *Urban Utopias in the Twentieth Century*, Cambridge (Mass.) 1977.

33. Le Corbusier, *Précisions sur un état présent de l'architecture et de l'urbanisme*, Paris 1930, p. 91. Here the monks enjoyed a combination of privacy, in the cells where they meditated alone, and social life, in the communal buildings where they worked, prayed and dined in company. See P. Serenyi, 'Le Corbusier, Fourier, and the Monastery at Ema', *Art Bulletin*, 49, December 1967, pp. 277–86, which also considers his city as a modern version of the phalanstery.

34. Hénard's preoccupations with alleviating Paris traffic problems were published in instalments in *Etudes sur les transformations de Paris*, 1903–09.

35. A strong believer in the beneficial potential of technology generally and of reinforced concrete particularly, yet ideologically dominated by the Beaux-Arts tradition,

Perret had outlined a scheme in 1905 which transposed the skyscraper so dominant in Manhattan to Paris. In 1921, the magazine *L'Illustration* published an article and a drawing by Jacques Lambert of Perret's vision in which a massive, raised, 250-metre wide, 25-kilometre long avenue, regularly dotted with a series of 150–200-metre high tower blocks, each housing 3,000 people, would encircle Paris (J. Labadié, 'Les cathédrales de la vie moderne, un audacieux projet pour résoudre en hauteur la crise du logement et les problèmes de confort et d'hygiène', *L'Illustration*, 12 August 1921, p. 132). Le Corbusier objected to Perret's scheme on the basis of its location (noting that it was unnecessary to unblock the city's peripheral areas since they were not congested in the first place) in 'Le centre des grandes villes', in *Où en est l'urbanisme en France et à l'étranger*, p. 254.

36. Le Corbusier, *Towards a New Architecture*, trans. Frederick Etchells, New York 1960, p. 202.

37. Le Corbusier, *Urbanisme*, Paris 1925, p. 11 (my trans.).

38. Ibid., p. 24.

39. Ibid., p. 177.

40. Le Corbusier, *Vers le Paris de l'époque machiniste*, 15 February 1928, p. 1.

41. Le Corbusier, *La ville radieuse*, Boulogne-sur-Seine 1935, p. 340.

42. Before the Zoning Laws, the setting back of skyscrapers to ensure the street's exposure to sunlight was an idea put forth by Louis Sullivan in an article of 1891, 'The High-Building Question', and by Charles R. Lamb in one of 1898, 'Civic Architecture from its Constructive Side'. Lamb's later illustration of the principle was quick to find its way into the general press in 1908.

43. Indeed H. Ferriss had devised a visionary project – illustrated in *The Metropolis of Tomorrow* (New York 1929) – with Raymond Hood for the construction of many such inhabited bridges all around Manhattan Island in and upon which close to a million people would have been housed across the water.

44. In *The Disappearing City*, New York 1932.

45. In *The Cause of Architecture*, 1928.

46. F. L. Wright, *The Living City*, New York 1958, p. 78.

47. Wright's future America would be named Usonia, 'Samuel Butler's suggestion of a name for our nameless nation (see his *Erewhon*)', *The Living City*, p. 77.

48. F. L. Wright and B. Brownell, *Architecture and Modern Life*, New York and London 1937.

49. Wright, *The Living City*.

50. Quoted by H. A. Harrison (ed.), *The Dawn of a New Day: The New York World's Fair, 1939/40*, New York 1980, p. 4.

The Revolt of the Citizen

1. Aldo van Eyck quoted in Charles Jencks, *Modern Movements in Architecture*, London 1985, p. 311.

2. For a general survey, see R. Banham, *Megastructure.*

Urban Futures of the Recent Past, London 1976.

3. Ralph Wilcoxon, *Council of Planning Librarians Exchange Bibliography* (Monticello, Ill), 66, 1968, p. 2, quoted in Banham, op. cit. [note 2], p. 8.

4. K. Kikutake, in *Kokusai Kenchiku*, February 1959.

5. K. Kikutake, in *Kokusai Kenchiku*, January 1959.

6. *Art in America*, May–June 1979, p. 67.

7. Y. Friedman, English translation of illustrated text reproduced in *Une utopie réalisée*, exhibition catalogue Musée d'Art Moderne de la Ville de Paris, 1975.

8. Y. Friedman, in *Une utopie réalisée*, p. 25.

9. P. Restany, 'L'architecture mobile', in *Une utopie réalisée*, p. v.

10. P. Soleri, *The City in the Image of Man*, Boston 1970, p. 14.

11. A. Persitz, in *Architecture d'aujourd'hui*, Paris, June/July 1962, p. 2, quoted by Banham, op. cit. [note 2], p. 57.

12. G.-E. Debord, 'Rapport sur la construction des situations et sur les conditions de l'organisation et de l'action de la tendence situationniste internationale', reproduced in G. Berreby (ed.), *Documents relatifs à la fondation de l'Internationale Situationniste 1948–1957*, Paris 1985, pp. 607–19.

13. G.-E. Debord, 'Introduction à une critique de la géographie urbaine', in *Les lèvres nues*, 6, September 1955, reproduced in Berreby, op. cit. [note 12], p. 288.

14. P. Gallizio, 'Manifesto della pittura industriale – per un'arte unitaria applicabile', 1959, published in *Notizie Arti Figurative*, no. 9, Turin 1959.

15. Constant, 'Une autre ville pour une autre vie', *I.S.*, 3, December 1959, quoted by T. Y. Levin, 'Geopolitics of Hibernation. The Drift of Situationist Urbanism', in L. Andreotti and X. Costa (eds), *Situationists. Art, politics, urbanism*, Barcelona 1996, p. 126.

16. *Architectural Design*, June 1964, p. 304, quoted in Banham, op. cit. [note 2], p. 81.

17. L. Alloway, quoted by C. Jencks, *Modern Movements in Architecture*, London 1983, p. 272.

18. R. Banham, in *Art in America*, April 1965.

Conclusion

1. H. Girardet, *Creating Sustainable Cities*, 1999, Totnes (England), Green Books Ltd. for The Schumacher Society, p. 17. Generally speaking, this brief work gives an excellent and practical résumé of issues regarding the creation of sustainable cities.

2. Herbert Girardet (op. cit. [note 1], p. 10) has calculated that 'cities, built on only two per cent of the world's land surface, use some 75 per cent of the world's resources and discharge similar amounts of waste'.

SELECTED BIBLIOGRAPHY

ACOSTA José de, *Historia natural de las Indias*, 1590; French edition, Paris, 1598.

AGOSTINI Ludovico, *La repubblica immaginaria* (edited by L. Firpo), Turin, 1957.

AINSA Fernando, *La reconstruction de l'utopie*, Paris, 1997.

ALBERTI Leon Battista, *De re aedificatoria*, manuscript, 1485; trans. annotated by J. Rykwert, N. Leach and R. Tavernor, *On the Art of Building in Ten Books*, Cambridge (Mass.) and London, 1988.

ANDREAE Johann Valentin, *Reipublicae christianopolitanae descriptio*, Strasbourg, 1619.

ANDREOTTI Libero and COSTA Xavier (eds.), *Situationists. Art, politics, urbanism*, Barcelona, Museu d'Art Contemporani de Barcelona, 1996.

APOLLONIO Umbro, *Futurist Manifestos*, London, 1973; original edition, Cologne and London, 1970.

ARISTOTLE, *The Politics*, trans. T. A. Sinclair, revised by T.J. Saunders, London, 1992.

ATKINSON Geoffroy, *Littérature géographique française de la Renaissance* (bibliography), Paris, 1927.

BACON Francis, *New Atlantis. A Work Unfinished*, London, 1627.

BAILLIE SCOTT Hugh Mackay and others, *Garden Suburbs, Town Planning and Modern Architecture*, London, 1910 (first edition, called *Town Planning and Modern Architecture in the Hampstead Garden Suburb*, summer 1909).

BANHAM Reyner, *Megastructure: Urban Futures of the Recent Past*, London, 1976.

BAUDIN Louis, *Une théocratie socialiste: l'Etat jésuite du Paraguay*, Paris, 1962.

BAUER Hermann, *Kunst und Utopie. Studien über das Kunst- und Staatsdanken in der Renaissance*, Berlin, 1965.

BELLAMY Edward, *Looking Backward: 2000–1887*, Boston, 1888.

BELLAMY Edward, *Equality*, New York, 1897.

BELLERS John, *Proposals for Raising a College of Industry of all Useful Trades and Husbandry*, 1696.

BENTHAM Jeremy, *Panopticum*, London, 1791.

BERREBY Gérard (ed.), *Documents relatifs à la fondation de l'Internationale situationniste, 1948–1957*, Paris, 1985.

BLOCH Ernst, *Das Prinzip Hoffnung*, Frankfurt, 1957, English edition *The Principle of Hope*, Oxford, 1955–59.

BÖLL Theodor, 'Essen. Steel, cannons and workers' houses', *Rassegna*, XIX, 70, Milan, 1997.

BOLLEREY Franziska, *Architekturkonzeptionen der utopischen Sozialisten*, Berlin, 1991.

BORDONE Benedetto, *Isolario*, Venice, 1528.

BORSI Franco, *Architecture et utopie*, Paris, 1997.

BRADBURY Ray, *Fahrenheit 451*, New York, 1953.

BRAUN Georg and HOGENBERG Frans, *Civitates orbis terrarum*, 1572.

BRY Theodor de, *America*, Frankfurt, 1590.

BUCKINGHAM James Silk, *National Evils and Practical Remedies*, London, 1849.

BUDER Stanley, *Pullman. An Experiment in Industrial Order and Community Planning, 1880–1930*, New York–London–Toronto, 1967.

BULWER-LYTTON Edward George, *The Coming Race*, Edinburgh, 1871.

CABET Etienne, *Voyage et aventures de lord William Carisdall en Icarie*, Paris, 1840.

CALLENBACH Ernest, *Ecotopia, the Notebooks and Reports of William Weston*, New York, 1977; first published 1975.

CAMPANELLA Tommaso, *Politicae Civitas Solis idea reipublicae philosophicae*, appendix to part 4 of *Realis philosophicae epilogisticae*, Frankfurt, 1623.

ČAPEK Karel, *RUR (Rossum's universal robots), a fantastic melodrama*, trans. Paul Selver, Garden City, New York, 1923.

CARYL Charles W., *New Era, Presenting the Plans for the New Era Union to Help Develop and Utilize the Best Resources of this Country. Also to Employ the Best Skill there is Available to Realize the Highest Degree of Prosperity for all who will Help to Attain it. Based on Practical and Successful Business Methods*, Denver, 1897.

CASTIGLIONE Baldassare, *Il libro del cortegiano*, 1528; English trans. by sir Thomas Hoby, *The Book of the Courtier*, 1561.

CATANEO Pietro, *I quattro primi libri di architettura*, Venice, 1554.

CATANEO Pietro, *L'architettura*, Venice, 1567.

CERDÁ Ildefonso, *Teoría general de la urbanización y aplicación de sus principios y doctrinas a la Reforma y Ensanche de Barcelona*, Madrid, 1867; presented and adapted by Antonio Lopez de Aberasturi, *La théorie générale de l'urbanisation*, Paris, 1979.

CHINARD Gilbert, *L'exotisme américain dans la littérature française au XVIᵉ siècle*, Paris, 1911.

CHINARD Gilbert, *L'Amérique et le rêve exotique dans la littérature française au XVIIᵉ et au XVIIIᵉ siècle*, Paris, 1914.

CHOAY Françoise, *L'urbanisme, utopies et réalités: une anthologie*, Paris, 1965.

CHOAY Françoise, *City Planning in the 19th Century*, New York, 1970.

CHOAY Françoise, *La règle et le modèle: sur la théorie de l'architecture et de l'urbanisme*, 1980; revised edition Paris, 1996.

CIEZA DE LEÓN Pedro de, *The Incas*, Norman (Oklahoma), 1959, trans. by Harriet de Onis, edited by V.W. von Hagen.

COBO Bernabé, *History of the Inca Empire*, Austin (Texas), 1979, translated and edited by Roland Hamilton.

COHEN Jean-Louis and LORTIE André, *Des fortifs au périf: Paris, les seuils de la ville*, Paris, 1992.

COLLINS George R., *Visionary Drawings of Architecture and Planning, 20th Century through the 1960s*, Cambridge (Mass.) and London, 1979.

CREESE Walter L., *The Search for Environment. The Garden City: before and after*, Baltimore, 1992, expanded edition (first published 1966).

DAHINDEN Justus, *Structures urbaines de demain*, Paris, 1972.

DAINVILLE François de, *La géographie des humanistes*, Paris, 1940.

DARLEY Gillian, *Villages of Vision*, London, 1978.

DETHIER Jean and GUIHEUX Alain (eds.), *La Ville, art et architecture en Europe, 1870–1993*, exh. cat., Centre Georges Pompidou, Paris, 1994.

DONNELLY Ignatius, *Caesar's Column: a Story of the 20th Century*, Chicago, 1890.

DÜRER Albrecht, *Etliche Underricht zu Befestigung der Stett, Schloss und Flecker*, Nuremberg, 1527.

EMLEN Robert P., *Shaker Village Views, Illustrated Maps and Landscape Drawings by Shaker Artists of the 19th Century*, Hanover/London, 1987.

ENGELS Friedrich, *La question du logement*, Paris, 1947.

ENGELS Friedrich, *La situation de la classe laborieuse en Angleterre*, Paris, 1960.

FERRISS Hugh, *The Metropolis of Tomorrow*, New York, 1929.

FILARETE (Antonio di Petro Averlino), *Trattato di architettura*, 1460–64; English trans. with facs. of *Codex Magliabecchianus* II.I.140 (Florence, Biblioteca Nazionale), edited by John R. Spencer, *Filarete's Treatise on Architecture*, New Haven (Conn.) and London, 1965.

FIRPO Luigi, *Leonardo architetto e urbanista*, Turin, 1953.

FIRPO Luigi, 'La città ideale del Filarete', *Studi in memoria di Gioele Solari*, Turin, 1954, pp. 11–59.

FIRPO Luigi, *Lo stato ideale della Contro-Riforma*, Bari, 1957.

FISHMAN Robert, *Urban Utopias in the 20th Century, Ebenezer Howard, Frank Lloyd Wright, and Le Corbusier*, Cambridge (Mass.) and London, 1982.

FISHMAN Robert, *Bourgeois Utopias: the Rise and Fall of Suburbia*, New York, 1997.

FOURIER Charles, *Œuvres complètes*, Paris, 1966.

FRA GIOCONDO, *M. Vitruvius per Iocundum solito castigatur factus cum figuris et tabula ut iam legi et intellegi possit*, Venice, 1511.

FRIEDMAN Yona, *Utopies réalisables*, Les Coiffards, 2000.

FULLER Richard Buckminster, *Utopia or Oblivion: the Prospects for Humanity*, New York, 1969.

GARNIER Tony, *Une cité industrielle. Etude pour la construction des villes*, Paris, 1917.

GEORGE Walter Lionel, *Labour and Housing at Port Sunlight*, 1911.

GERNSBACK Hugo, *Ralph-124-C41+, a Romance of the Year 2660*, Boston, 1925 (first published in *Modern Electrics*, 1911).

GIL Juan, *Mitos y utopias del descubrimiento*, Madrid, 1989.

GINZBURG Moisey, *Stil' i epokha*, Moscow, 1924; Italian edition in GINZBURG Moisey, *Saggi sull'architettura costruttivista*, Milan, 1977.

GRESLERI Giuliano and MATTEONI Dario, *La città mondiale. Andersen, Hébrard, Otlet, Le Corbusier*, Venice, 1982.

HALL Peter, *Cities in Civilization*, New York, 1998.

HAMPSON Norman, *The Enlightenment: an Evaluation of its Assumptions, Attitudes and Values*, London, 1968; reprinted London/New York, 1990.

HARVEY Alexander, *Model Village: Bournville*, London, 1906.

HAYDEN Dolores, *The Architecture of Communitarian Socialism, 1790–1975*, Cambridge (Mass.), 1976.

HAYDEN Dolores, *Seven American Utopias*, Cambridge (Mass.) and London, 1976.

HILBERSEIMER Ludwig, *Großstadtarchitektur*, Stuttgart, 1927.

HONOUR Hugh, *The European Vision of America*, exh. cat., Cleveland Museum of Art, 1975.

HOWARD Ebenezer, *To-Morrow: a Peaceful Path to Real Reform*, London, 1898; and second edition under the title *Garden Cities of To-Morrow*, 1902.

HUXLEY Aldous, *Brave New World*, London, 1932.

HUXLEY Aldous, *Ape and Essence*, New York, 1948.

HUXLEY Aldous, *Island, a Novel*, New York, 1962.

JACOBS Jane, *The Death and Life of Great American Cities*, New York, 1961.

JEAN Georges, *Voyages en Utopie*, Paris, 1994.

JENCKS Charles, *Modern Movements in Architecture*, 2nd revised edition, London, 1985.

JOHNSTON Norman J., *Cities in the Round*, Seattle and London, 1983.

KAUFMANN Emil, *Trois architectes révolutionnaires*, Paris, 1978.

KLEIN Robert, 'L'urbanisme utopique de Filarete à Andreae', in *Les utopies à la Renaissance*, 1961 colloquium, Brussels and Paris, 1963.

KOSTOF Spiro, *The City Shaped: Urban Patterns and Meanings through History*, London, 1991.

KOSTOF Spiro, *The City Assembled: the Elements of Urban Form through History*, London, 1992.

KRUFT Hanno-Walter, *Städte in Utopia, die Idealstadt vom 15. bis zum 18. Jahrhundert*, Munich, 1989.

KRUFT Hanno-Walter, *A History of Architectural Theory: from Vitruvius to the Present*, London and New York, 1994.

LABORDE Alexandre de, *Les manuscrits à peintures de la cité de Dieu de saint Augustin*, Paris, 1909.

LAFITAU Joseph-François, *Mœurs des sauvages américains comparées aux mœurs des premiers temps*, Paris, 1724.

LAMBERT Jean-Clarence (ed.), *New Babylon, Constant, art et utopie, textes situationnistes*, Paris, 1997.

LANG Michael H., *Designing Utopia, John Ruskin's Urban Vision for Britain and America*, Montreal–New York–London, 1999.

LANG S., 'The ideal city: from Plato to Howard', *Architectural Review*, London, CXII, no. 668, 1952.

LAPOUGE Gilles, *Utopie and civilisations*, 1973; new edition Paris, 1990.

LAS CASAS Bartolomé de, *Historia de las Indias*, Madrid, 1542.

LAUGIER Marc-Antoine, *Essai sur l'architecture*, Paris, 1753.

LAVEDAN Pierre, *Histoire de l'urbanisme, Renaissance et Temps modernes*, Paris, 1941.

LEBESQUE Sabine and FENTENER VAN VLISSINGEN Hélène, *Yona Friedman. Structures Serving the Unpredictable*, Rotterdam, 1999.

LE CORBUSIER, *Urbanisme*, Paris, 1942; trans. by John Rodker, *The City of To-morrow and its planning*, London, reprinted 1987.

LE CORBUSIER, *La Ville radieuse*, Boulogne-sur-Seine, 1935.

LE CORBUSIER, *La charte d'Athènes*, Paris, 1943.

LEDOUX Claude-Nicolas, *L'architecture considérée sous le rapport de l'art, des mœurs et de la législation*, Paris, 1804; reprinted Paris, 1997.

LEGUIN Ursula K., *The Dispossessed, an Ambiguous Utopia*, New York, 1974.

LEHOUCK Emile, *Vie de Charles Fourier: l'homme dans sa vérité*, Paris, 1978.

PÈRE LE JEUNE, *Relation de ce qui s'est passé en la Nouvelle France en l'année 1634, envoyée au père provincial de la Compagnie de Jésus en la Province de France*, Paris, 1635.

LÉVI-STRAUSS Claude, *Tristes tropiques*, Paris, 1955.

LEWIS Arthur O., *Utopian Literature in the Pennsylvanian State University Libraries: a Selected Bibliography*, University Park (Penn.), 1984.

LORINI Buonaiuto, *Delle fortificationi libri cinque*, Venice, 1592.

MACK Charles, *Pienza, the Creation of a Renaissance City*, Ithaca (New York), 1987.

MAGGI Girolamo and CASTRIOTTO Iacomo, *Della fortificatione della città*, Venice, 1564.

MANNHEIM Karl, *Ideology and Utopia*, London, 1936.

MARCHI Francesco de, *Della architettura militare*, Brescia, 1599.

MASLEN T. J., *Suggestions for the Improvement of our Towns and Houses*, London, 1843.

MERCIER Louis Sébastien, *L'an 2440. Rêve s'il en fut jamais*, London, 1772.

MÉTRAUX Alfred, *La civilisation matérielle des tribus Tupi-Guarani*, Paris, 1928.

MIDANT Jean-Paul (ed.), *Dictionnaire de l'architecture du XXᵉ siècle*, Paris, 1996.

MONTGOMERY Robert, *A Discourse Concerning the Design'd Establishment of a New Colony to the South of Carolina*, London, 1717.

MORE Thomas, *De optimo reipublicae statu deque nova insula Utopia*, Louvain, 1516.

MORELLY, *Code de la nature, ou le véritable esprit de ses lois*, 1755; edited by Gilbert Chinard, Paris, 1950.

MORGAN John Minter, *Revolt of the Bees*, London, 1826.

MORLEY Henry, *Ideal Commonwealth*, London, 1885.

MORRIS William, *News from Nowhere; or, an Epoch of Rest. Being Some Chapters from a Utopian Romance*; first published in *The Commonweal*, 6, nos. 209–247, January 11–October 1, 1890; unauthorized first book edition, Boston (Mass.), 1890; first authorized book edition, London, 1891.

MORRIS William, *The Earthly Paradise: a Poem*, New York, 1905.

MUCCHIELLI Roger, *Le mythe de la cité idéale*, Paris, 1960.

MUMFORD Lewis, *The Story of Utopia*, New York, 1922.

OECHSLIN Werner, 'J.J. Moll's Napoléonville as a "Terrestrial Paradise"', *Daidalos, Berlin Architectural Journal*, no. 7, March 1983.

ORWELL George, *Animal Farm: a Fairy Story*, London, 1945.

ORWELL George, *Nineteen Eighty-Four, a Novel*, London, 1949.

OWEN Robert, *A New View of Society; or, Essays on the Principle of the Formation of the Human Character, and the Application of the Principle to Practice. By One of His Majesty's Justices of Peace for the Country of Lanark (pseud.)*, London, 1813.

PACIOLI Luca, *Divina proportione, opera a tutti glingegni perspicaci e curiosi necessaria que ciascun studioso di philosophia, prospectiva, pictura, sculptura, architectura, musica e altre mathematici suavissima, sottile e admirabile doctrina conseguira [...] de secretissima scientia*, Venice, 1509.

PAQUOT Thierry, *L'utopie ou l'idéal piégé*, Paris, 1996.

PATRIZZI Francesco, *La città felice*, Venice, 1553.

PATTE Pierre, *Monumens érigés en France à la gloire de Louis XV*, Paris, 1765.

PATTE Pierre, *Mémoires sur les objets les plus importants de l'architecture*, Paris, 1769.

PEMBERTON Robert, *The Happy Colony. Dedicated to the Workmen of Great Britain*, London, 1854; reprinted New York, 1985.

PETITFILS Jean-Christian, *La vie quotidienne des communautés utopistes au XIXᵉ siècle*, Paris, 1982.

PEVSNER Nikolaus, *Pioneers of Modern Design: from William Morris to Walter Gropius*, London, 1936, and New York, 1991.

PLATO, *Critias*; trans. and introd. by Jean-François Pradeau, Paris, 1997.

PLATO, *The Republic*, trans. A. D. Lindsay M. A., London, 1935.
PUGIN Augustus Welby Northmore, *Contrasts; or a Parallel between the Architecture of the 15th and 19th Centuries*, 1836; reprinted New York, 1969.

RABELAIS François, *L'abbaye de Thélème*, 1531.
RALEIGH sir Walter, *The Discoverie of the Large, Rich, and Bewtiful Empyre of Guiana, with a Relation of the Great and Golden City of Manoa (which the Spanyards Call El Dorado)*, etc. *Performed in the Yeare 1595*, London, 1596.
RAMUSIO Giovanni Battista, *Terzio volume delle navigationi e viaggi*, Venice, 1556.
REPS John W., *The Making of Urban America: a History of City Planning in the United States*, Princeton (N.J.), 1965.
RICHARDSON Benjamin Ward, *Hygeia, a City of Health*, London, 1876.
ROSENAU Helen, *The Ideal City: its Architectural Evolution*, London, 1974.
ROUDANT Jean, *Les villes imaginaires dans la littérature française*, Paris, 1990.
ROUSSEAU Jean-Jacques, *Du contrat social*, 1762; edited by Ronald Grimsley, Oxford, 1972.
ROWE Colin and KOETTER Fred, *Collage City*, Cambridge (Mass.) and London, 1978.
RUSKIN John, *Crown of Wild Olive*, 1866; reprinted London, 1907.
RUSKIN John, *Sesame and Lilies*, 1864; reprinted London, 1908.

SCAMOZZI Vincenzo, *L'idea della architettura universale*, Venice, 1615.
SCHEERBART Paul, *Glasarchitektur*, Berlin, 1914.
SERVIER Jean, *L'utopie*, Paris, 1979.
SERVIER Jean, *Histoire de l'utopie*, revised ed., Paris, 1991.
SHARP Thomas, *Town and Countryside: Some Aspects of Urban and Rural Development*, London, 1932.
SOLERI Paolo, *Arcology: the City in the Image of Man*, Cambridge (Mass.), 1969.
SORIA Y MATA Arturo, *La ciudad lineal*, Madrid, 1894.
SORIA Y MATA Arturo, *La Cité linéaire. Conception nouvelle pour l'aménagement des villes*, translated and introduced by Georges Benoît-Levy, Paris, 1979.
SOUSTELLE Jacques, *Daily Life of the Aztecs*, London, 1961.
STITES Richard, *Revolutionary Dreams: Utopian Vision and Experimental Life in the Russian Revolution*, New York and Oxford, 1989.

TAFURI Manfredo, *Architecture and Utopia: Design and Capitalist Development*, 1973; trans. by Barbara Luigia La Penta, Cambridge (Mass.) and London, 1976.
TAUT Bruno, *Alpine Architektur*, Hagen, 1919.
TAUT Bruno, *Die Stadtkrone*, Jena, 1919.
TAUT Bruno, *Die Auflösung der Städte*, Hagen, 1920.

TAUT Bruno, *Characteristics of German Town Planning Up to Date*, Letchworth, n.d.
TROUSSON Raymond, *Voyages aux pays de nulle part: histoire littéraire de la pensée utopique*, Brussels, 1975.

UNWIN Raymond, *Town Planning in Practice*, London, 1909.
UNWIN Raymond, 'The city beautiful from converging views of social reform', *Lectures on Land and Labour*, Swanwick, Interdenominational Summer School, June 20–29 1914, London, 1914.
UNWIN Raymond, *Columbia University Lectures*, 1936–37.

VERCELLONI Virgilio, *Atlante storico dell'idea europea della città ideale*, Milan, 1994.
VERHAEREN Emile, *Les campagnes hallucinées*, 1893; *Les villes tentaculaires*, 1895, edited by Maurice Piron, Paris, 1982.
VERNE Jules, *Une Ville idéale*, 1875, edited by Daniel Compère, Amiens, 1999.
VIDLER Anthony, *Claude Nicolas Ledoux, Architecture and Social Reform at the End of the Ancien Regime*, Cambridge (Mass.), 1990.
VITRUVIUS, *De architectura libri decem*. Latin-English edition, translated by Frank Granger, London–Cambridge, 1931 (see also Fra Giocondo).

WALDSEEMÜLLER Martin, *Cosmographiae introductio cum quibusdam geometriae ac astronomiae principiis as eam rem necessariis. Insuper quator Americi Vespucii navigationes*, St. Dié, 1507 (Introduction to cosmography ... with four Voyages of Amerigo Vespucci; this has Vespucci's map with America not attached to Asia).
WEISS Robert, *The Renaissance Discovery of Classical Antiquity*, Oxford, 1969.
WELLS Herbert George, *The Time Machine: an Invention*, London, 1895.
WELLS Herbert George, *When the Sleeper Wakes*, New York, 1899.
WELLS Herbert George, *The Shape of Things to Come: the Ultimate Revolution*, London, 1933.
WRIGHT Frank Lloyd, *The Disappearing City*, New York, 1932; new edition entitled *The Industrial Revolution Runs Away*, New York, 1969.
WRIGHT Frank Lloyd, *The Living City*, New York, 1958.

ZAMIATIN Ievgueni, *We*, authorized translation from the Russian by Gregory Zilboorg, New York, 1924.

Collective works/Miscellaneous

Les années 1920: l'âge des métropoles, exh. cat., The Montreal Museum of Fine Arts, 1991.
Archigram, Centre Georges Pompidou, Paris, 1994.
Art Into Life, Russian Constructivism, 1914–1932, exh. cat., Henry Art Gallery of the University of Washington, Seattle, New York, 1990.
De Stijl: 1917–1931, Visions of Utopia, exh. cat., Walker Art Center, Oxford, 1982.
Film Architecture, Set Designs from Metropolis to Blade Runner, edited by Dietrich Neumann, Munich and New York, 1996.
Futurisme and Futurismes, exh. cat., Palazzo Grassi, Venice; French edition Paris, 1986.
The Garden City Conference at Bournville: Report of Proceedings, London, 1901.
The Guise Familistère or the Equivalents of Wealth, Brussels, 1976.
Léonard da Vinci, ingénieur et architecte, exh. cat., The Montreal Museum of Fine Arts, 1987.
Paris–Moscou, exh. cat., Centre Georges Pompidou, Paris, 1979.
Philip II's Royal Ordinances concerning the laying out of the New Towns, issue from the Escorial in 1573, from ms. 3.017 in the National Archives in Madrid, published in *Hispanic American Historical Review*, vol. 4, Baltimore, 1921, pp. 745ff.; trans. vol. 5, Baltimore, 1922, pp. 249ff.
Theatre in Revolution, Russian Avant-Garde Stage Design, 1913–1935, exh. cat., The Fine Arts Museums of San Francisco, New York, 1991.
SARGENT Lyman Tower and SCHAER Roland (eds.), *Utopia. The Search for the Ideal Society in the Western World*, exh. cat., Bibliothèque Nationale de France, Paris, and New York Public Library, New York and London, 2000.
'Planning with people advocacy in East Harlem', *Forum*, XXIII, 4, 1972.

Ideal Cities

Utopianism and the (Un)Built Environment

by Ruth Eaton
was published in the year two thousand and two.

Cover design and layout by Stéphan Alberty.

Typeset by Anagram, Ghent, in Fred Smeijers' Quadraat.

Colour separations by P.A.G. Power Flash, Brussels.
Printed and bound by Editoriale Lloyd, Trieste.

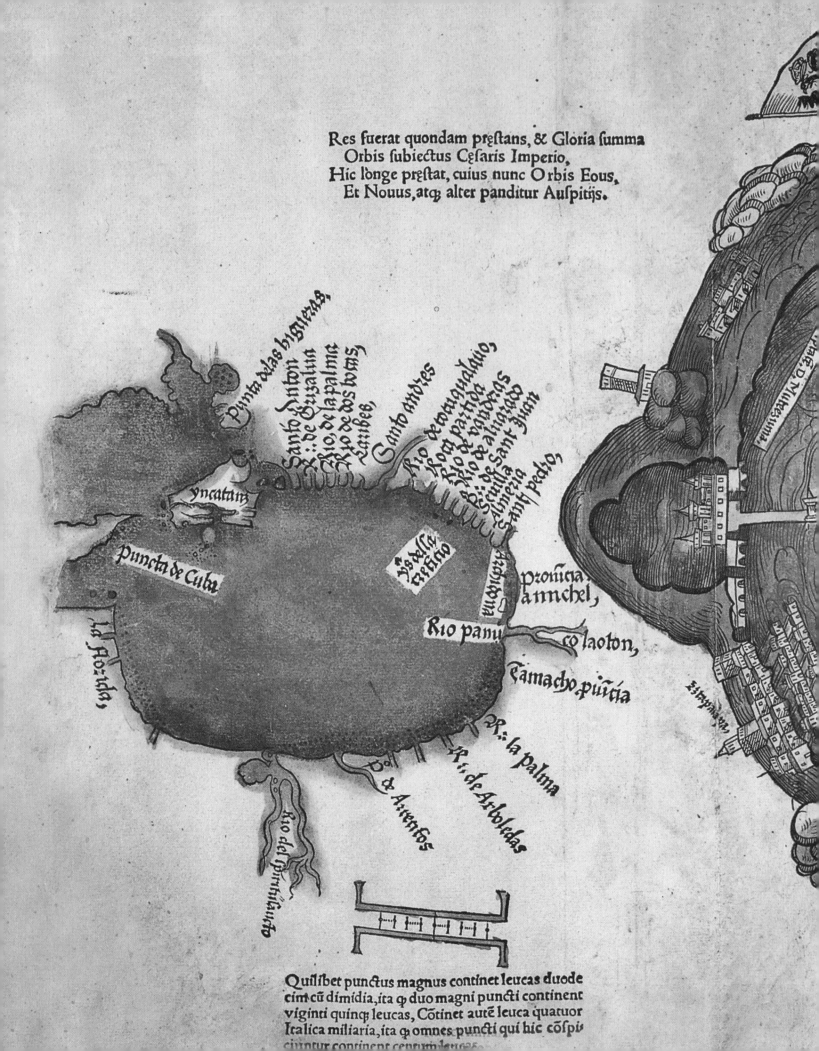

Res fuerat quondam prestans, & Gloria summa
Orbis subiectus Cesaris Imperio,
Hic longe prestat, cuius nunc Orbis Eous,
Et Nouus, atq; alter panditur Auspitijs.

Punta delas biguieras
Santo julian
Rio: de Gruzalim
Rio: dela palma
Rio de dos bocas
Escribes
Ganto andres
Rio de soguadaluio
Rota partida
Rio de vaporda
Rio de alngrads
Escutla de Sant juan
Almezia
Santo pedro

yncatam

Puncta de Cuba

ys della
cueficio

Archidona
prouincia
annchel,

la florida

Rio panu

co laoton,

Camacho piutia

R.: la palma

R.: de Arboledas

R. de Azentos

Rio del spirith sancto